Postmodernism for Historians

Callum G. Brown

PEARSON
Longman

Harlow, England • London • New York • Boston • San Francisco • Toronto • Sydney • Singapore • Hong Kong
Tokyo • Seoul • Taipei • New Delhi • Cape Town • Madrid • Mexico City • Amsterdam • Munich • Paris • Milan

Contents

Box inserts

Acknowledgements

This book arose out of team-teaching two historical theory classes at Strathclyde University. The first was an undergraduate class, and I learned much from B.R. (Tom) Tomlinson (now of SOAS) and Ronnie Johnston (now of Glasgow Caledonian University) as we tried out new methods of delivery. I am grateful to Tom for allowing me to use the scheme of his lectures in parts of Chapter 1. On the M.Phil. Social History taught jointly with Glasgow University, I learned much from Eileen Yeo, Arthur McIvor and from the students. I am grateful to Hilary Young for guiding me to some sources on Marxism and the self and to Karen Macdonald for introducing me to the postmodern history of flea markets. I am especially grateful to those who read an earlier draft, and made suggestions for improvement: Lynn Abrams, Richard J. Evans, Gordon Martel, James Mills, Alun Munslow, Mark Nixon and Nathalie Rosset. Each of these spent considerable time reading and giving me advice, and I really appreciate it (even when not everyone endorsed my views). Lynn, as always, is my succour and my strength. I finished the book four days before our nuptials – the same day she finished hers. Since we lead such parallel lives, it is high time that she had a book dedicated to her, so here it is.

Introduction

This book promotes the use of postmodern theory in History (the subject with a capital 'H') in the study of history (the past with a small 'h'). It argues that being a student of History in the early twenty-first century requires an informed knowledge of the postmodernist position. Postmodernism is now to be found across many subjects in Arts, Humanities and Social Sciences. But in History, postmodernism needs to be laid out in the special circumstances of studying the past. This book aims to do that. It is not a *defence* of postmodernism in History, nor does it engage with the debates between historians about whether postmodernism is a good or bad thing. Instead, it provides an account of the theory, the theorists and the applications in historical study. Only the last chapter presents some brief consideration of the criticism directed at postmodernist History.

Postmodernism is something more than a high-brow theory of knowledge. It is also one of the most mystically 'cool' words of our contemporary society. It seems to crop up everywhere – on television features and on radio arts programmes, in newspapers, where it adorns architecture columns, book reviews and art criticism, and can be found used by sketch-writing columnists musing on politics, society and the modern condition. The word graces glossy magazines – picture-pieces on furniture, interior design and cookery articles. It has even been used in gardening and fashion magazines. Postmodern is a fashionable, 'now' word of the wine bar and salon. Journalists like it. It is contemporary and hip. But what does it mean? The connection between postmodernism and popular culture is an important one. As we shall see, the theory feeds off the connection. For critics of postmodernism, this merely serves to increase irritation and controversy. But just because postmodernism is fashionable, that is no reason to avoid it or fail to explore it seriously. Indeed, it is imperative to understand a term that is in use so widely in popular culture, and in scholarship in History and other disciplines.

Many books describe postmodernism as 'a danger to History'. The History profession and the History student are deemed to be in serious need of fighting off the postmodern 'threat'. Since 1990 the scaremongering has led to great debates in journals and at online History websites. Debates have been fierce, complicated and have sometimes involved personal attacks. However, this is usually unhelpful to the student. Reading debate does not make it easy to learn theories and the links between them. Nor does it readily show how historians have been influenced by theory in their research and books. Nor does it give the student some ideas about how to use postmodern theory to assess History books and articles critically, and to construct personal essay, dissertation or thesis topics.

Character

The character of the book is intended as distinctive. Firstly, it is written by an historian who teaches and researches History for a living. I am not a theorist, nor a philosopher, and the theory I offer will be distilled and presented on a need-to-know basis. Second, I write as an enthusiast for postmodernist History. My own research and writing in History topics have been transformed in the last decade by my new awareness of the perspectives, agendas and methods of postmodernist History. I believe that I am an immensely better historian for having taken the time to learn and apply postmodern theory. Third, the book gives priority to demonstrating postmodernism as theory and as applied method in History. It sidesteps debate and controversy in favour of laying out postmodernism as a connected series of theories and methods. I want to show how postmodernism works for the historian, how the theory can be infused into what we all do. Fourth and last, I want to convince the reader of the merits of postmodernism for studies in History. There ought to be *something* of use here to each student of the subject, even if it is not the whole package.

Aims

The aims of the book are, first, to leave the reader enabled and confident to move on afterwards to read more theory, if desired. Second, I want to enable the reader to see postmodernist techniques in operation in History books and journal articles. And third, I want to enable the inclusion of some postmodernist perspective in the student's 'reading' of History books, and in research in History (for essays or a dissertation, for instance).

Structure

The structure of the book is designed to achieve these aims. It distils post-modernist theory down to an essence of seven main themes. Following the first of these, the empiricist inheritance, the remaining six are sign, discourse, poststructuralism, text, self and morality. These are arranged in the rough order of the development of the theory, most of it emerging during the course of the twentieth century. Each of these chapters has sections on theory and on application in History. In the section on application, I show how the theory has been used by historians, and give ideas about how to select topics and methods to construct personal work at undergraduate or even graduate level. As the book proceeds, the theory and application build up, layer upon layer, showing the development of what postmodernist historians do in their work. For every student of History in search of a project to do, there should be at least one interesting research method described in this book. At the end, a chapter on criticism of postmodernism in History briefly lays out how the theory has been attacked

Each chapter contains box inserts providing brief biographies of leading theorists and quick definitions of key postmodern terms, and a guide to further reading. Other more general terms used in the History profession appear in bold text and are defined in the glossary. The further reading at the end of the chapter guides the reader to key texts.

To use this book, it is probably best to start at the beginning and work through. However, it is possible to start at Chapter 2 on the sign, as that is where the distinctively *postmodern* theory kicks in. It is also possible to start at the chapter that most interests the reader, and to go back to previous chapters only when something needs explanation. But remember that the elements of postmodern theory in the six chapters link together. There is an overall philosophy to postmodernism, and the core of it comes at the beginning on sign and discourse. Whatever you choose, dive in and discover the enrichment that so many historians have found in postmodern theory and method.

The origins of postmodernism

Postmodernism has caused a massive shake-up in the subject of History. The impact has been tectonic, shifting all sorts of presumptions about the subject and the nature of the craft of being an historian. And yet, postmodernism started well outside the History profession.

It started in the late nineteenth century in a number of spheres. One was amongst a small number of philosophers who we can now see were very influential. One was Friedrich Nietzsche, who said: 'There are no facts in themselves. It is always necessary to begin by introducing a meaning in order that there can be a fact.'[1] This brief phrase condenses so much of what was to be elaborated after his death into an entire philosophical tradition. It galvanises postmodernist theorists.

Box 0.1   *Friedrich Nietzsche (1844–1900)*

Nietzsche was a German philosopher, most famous for proclaiming that God is dead. He became notorious for undermining traditional philosophy. His writings contemplate the difficulties of language in the act of comprehending the world. He subverted the certainty of knowing how knowledge itself was produced by asserting that every fact is filtered through human perception. He argued that man should concentrate on the production of strength and energy instead of the timidity of reason, domesticity and democracy. He urged adulation for 'superman' – the human will or power to create new thought and humanity. His seemingly anti-Christian sentiment was widely interpreted as meaning that 'might is right', and that anti-democratic government was legitimate. But he was a key figure in the twentieth-century search for alternatives to Christian, western and Enlightenment notions of progress. As such, he generated some key philosophical positions that are now celebrated in postmodernism.

Initially, more influential in many ways was the sphere of the painter and sculptor. Until the late nineteenth century, most of art rested on a 'realist' presumption – that the purpose of drawing, painting and sculpture was to render physical objects and scenes in a literal representation. But from the 1880s until the 1930s, trends emerged in the art world that questioned the ability of humans to make a 'true' representation of the world. Questions were raised about the language of representation in art – of paint and sculpturing material – and the ability of the human eye to see, and then the human mind to translate into artistic form, in a way that accurately reflected the world. Ironically, this happened at the same time as the birth of photography gave an apparent ability to produce infallible representation of the seen world. For artists, photographs that apparently 'could not lie' raised the question of whether paintings and sculpture must aspire to present deeper meanings of the world than any literal or 'real' method could. The English landscape artist John Constable had already played with impressionist painting and drawing in the 1810s (making *impressions* of the world, not attempting realist copies of it). But it was really in the late nineteenth and early twentieth centuries that a succession of artistic movements was born in Europe to challenge conventional skills, ways of seeing, and ways of understanding the world. These movements included impressionism, cubism, and surrealism. Such non-realistic representations were initially highly controversial, but by the later twentieth century the leading exponents had become famous – Magritte, Pablo Picasso, Salvador Dali and Henry Moore. The challenge to the 'real' in the creative professions became a movement of artistic revolt and moved into other areas, including architecture, design (of furniture and products) and advertising. In each of these, the bold, ordered and often straight lines of the nineteenth century were challenged by irregular shapes, curves and more disordered spaces. New media were adopted in art – installation art works, film and video art, and multi-media work. In this way, central concepts of a knowable and representational 'reality' were de-centred, explored, questioned, subverted and played with through art, while at the same time the very language of art and the means of expression of human emotion were expanded.

In the literary world, there were also movements from the end of the nineteenth century to subvert traditional forms of narration and meaning. The novel had developed as the most popular and developed art form, but it had been used in highly regimented ways of narration (notably heroic adventure and romance). These forms were challenged by the work of novelists like Joseph Conrad, whose *Heart of Darkness* (1902) became an enormously influential inversion of the traditional novel form, turning upside down the notion of superior white, Christian European civilised culture and its exportation to the 'uncivilised' 'pagans' of 'darkest Africa'. In the process, such works subverted the traditional **whig** notion of Euro-centric progress in history, the notion of an ever-improving movement of the human condition, the idea that democracy and civilisation were always growing, and that civilisation grew by the spread of the European imperial order and its legal systems.

The period from the 1880s to the 1930s also witnessed challenges to the traditional sexual and social class order. Revolution of all sorts was in the air, including first-wave feminism, the gay challenge to the criminalisation of homosexuality, and the emergence of jazz and blues music. These defied many norms of western society – marriage, chastity before marriage, the monopoly of heterosexual relations, and the existence of the divide between 'serious' and popular culture. The European world of the late nineteenth century witnessed the height of its imperial expansion, religious puritanism and social repression. But it became very quickly denigrated and lampooned. 'Victorianism' expressed the most repressed of societies, one that polarised 'rough' and 'respectable', in which art became one of the few media that at the time could challenge conformist lifestyle and ideas. Artists and a small number of intellectuals challenged the existing order, conflating sexual, political and artistic rebellion – a classic example being the English gay socialist poet Oscar Wilde who in 1895 was imprisoned in Reading gaol for homosexual offences.

These trends in art and literature in the late nineteenth and early twentieth centuries did not at the time bear a clear-cut term. They have tended ever since to be referred to by specialists in art and literature as 'modernism'.

Box 0.2   *Modernism/modernity*

In art, literature, design and architecture, this refers to the movement that started in the late nineteenth/early twentieth centuries for post-realist representation. This recognised the absence of a core 'reality' or 'truth' that can be represented by creative artists. Confusingly, this movement equates to the same anti-realist tradition called 'postmodernism' in philosophy, History and cultural studies. This confusion (that modernism in art subjects = postmodernism in philosophical subjects) just needs to be accepted. There seems to be no way of getting around it.

Postmodernists and others in cultural history will refer to modernism as the system of knowledge that preceded postmodernism. Modernism is taken to be broadly the ideas produced by the eighteenth-century Enlightenment and which dominated western thought c.1800–c. 1960. This period is referred to as **modernity**. We study this in Chapter 1.

From the 1910s this kind of critical questioning expanded to the academic world of language, philosophy, literature studies, and the study of popular culture. But it did not enter the world of the historian until the 1960s, and, in the case of most British historians, not until the 1980s and 1990s. By then, 'postmodernism' had become the term of choice for describing all those fields of endeavour in which there was a turning against 'realism', received wisdom, hierarchy, imperialism and convention. Thus, postmodernism has a quality of challenge to it.

The two core principles of postmodernism

We can start to see that there are two opening and fundamental principles of postmodernism. The first is that reality is unrepresentable in human forms of culture (whether written, spoken, visual or dramatic). Postmodernism holds 'reality' to be unrepresentable. (Note that, because of the problem of showing it, I put the word 'reality' in inverted commas in most places.).

Box 0.3   *Reality*

For traditional scholars, trained in empiricist philosophy, events happened and can be discovered, recorded, and represented by the expertise of the professional social scientist or historian in a textual narrative. For postmodernists, events happened, processes occurred, reality exists, but none of these can be accurately represented as those things in any way, in any form, then or later. Postmodernism denies that it is possible to show reality – only versions of it. There are three essential reasons for this failure. First, reality is huge and unrepresentable. Second, this process involves subjective choice, destroying neutrality and introducing subjectivity. Third, reality cannot be conveyed (repeated, transmitted or displayed) in its own format (however you describe that) but only in human-constructed words, sounds, pictures and images. What you get from this process is not reality, but a **text**. Therefore, when a postmodernist speaks of 'reality', it is often in inverted commas because of the impossibility for humans to show it. We shall explore the reasons in more detail in Chapter 2.

The second fundamental principle of postmodernism follows from this: with an inability to represent reality, no authoritative account can exist of anything. Nobody can know everything about a subject, and there is *never* only one authority on a given subject. This means that the definition I (or anybody else) provide of postmodernism will never be complete or authoritative. My account is personal, contingent (upon new knowledge) and temporary. It will be offered incomplete and without closure, as I, like anybody else, am quite properly constantly revising my understanding. I expect my exposition here to leave questions and doubts in the reader's mind, leaving the opportunity for further exploration. Just as there is no central manifesto or plan or theory of postmodernism, equally there is no one definition of what constitutes postmodernist History. So, what I am going to provide in this book is *my understanding of postmodernism*. The choice of theories to include, and the examples from History writings, are my own. They might not be everybody's final selection, but they are the ones I believe best exemplify the subject.

Having established those two foundation principles, it is important to state what postmodernism is not. Postmodernism is not an ideology. It is not like Marxism, or liberalism, or conservatism, or fascism. Nor is it a state of government or economy, like feudalism, capitalism or communism. It is not a policy for government, like *laissez-faire* or welfarism, nor is it a set of coherent beliefs (like a religion). So, postmodernism does not replace any of these. However, postmodernism does have ideological implications. It *enables* a whole host of ideologies to exist. These include feminism, postcolonialism, gay liberation and queer theory. It will philosophically allow other ideologies, like Marxism, to exist, without logically overturning them as programmes of social action. So, for instance, it is entirely possible for a postmodernist to believe him/herself to be a postmodernist, a feminist and a Marxist at the same time.

Because it is not an ideology, postmodernism also allows moral and ideological connections to be drawn *between* different ideologies. In today's world, those who are anti-racist also tend to be anti-sexist, anti-homophobic, anti-religious bigotry, anti-globalisation and so on. There tends to be an association between these positions, and we usually encounter them bundled together in one overlapping moral position. How has this occurred? An argument of the postmodernist is that since the mid-twentieth century, we have been living in a period known as postmodernity, or sometimes the postmodern condition.

Box 0.4   *Postmodernity/the postmodern condition*

This is the intellectual, social and moral condition that superseded modernity at some point in the twentieth century (probably in the 1960s). It is characterised by a rejection and subversion of some of the key intellectual, social and moral principles of Enlightenment modernity. The key intellectual principle to be rejected is the notion of 'truth' that can be verified through empirical research. In relation to social principles, postmodernity proposes the abolition of social class, rank, racial, religious or equivalent vestiges of a modernist society (the abolition being known as 'poststructuralism', to which we return later). The rejection of Enlightenment moral principles rests upon the absence of empirical foundations to morality, and instead the need for moral decision by the individual and society based on the desirability of social, gender, racial, and religious equality. Taken together, the postmodern condition is one in which old-fashioned certainty over knowledge and morality has been undermined. But it is replaced by a new moral framework characterised by opposition to authoritative voices and a vibrant questioning intellect that have led to new moral concerns – including environmentalism, anti-globalisation, and equality.

Postmodernist theory argues that the postmodern condition emerged as new ways of intellectual thought and new moral thinking which matured in the mid-twentieth century. In Europe, much of North America and many parts of the developing world, the postmodern condition deeply affected the way in which individuals assessed their own identities and responded to peoples of different background. It also affected the way in which people looked upon humankind's place on the planet. These two focuses – respect for the body and for the planet – are often summarised as anti-essentialism and environmentalism. They have been linked to older ideologies (such as Marxism) and political movements (such as liberation movements in the developing world and anti-capitalist movements). In this way, postmodernity is seen to permit the alliance of older and newer forms of radicalism.

Postmodernism is something that allows these connections to exist. By not being an ideology, postmodernism is a way of understanding **knowledge**. It is a way of understanding how humans gain knowledge from the world. Postmodernism as a knowledge theory is concerned with (1) how we order, configure, assemble and display knowledge (in verbal, written or image form); (2) how that knowledge is experienced by every individual (involving negotiation between acceptance and repudiation of knowledge) as s/he constructs and develops his/her personal identity; (3) how each individual reflects his or her identity (based on that knowledge) back into society. Those three things describe what postmodernism does. It has other applications. One is as a way of understanding previous knowledges in the past. Past and present knowledge can be very different. Postmodernism therefore focuses on the *mechanics* of knowledge and identity, how these are constructed and circulated, and how they differ from century to century and place to place. So, postmodernism is an intellectual foundation for understanding society, history, culture and psychology. It is thus a very big and woolly 'thing'. It is not limited to one creed or people, position or standpoint. It is so big, it claims to be the successor to the Enlightenment. This is a very large claim.

But, what has this to do with History (the academic subject)? A very great deal. Many historians would argue that eighteenth- and nineteenth-century western societies looked to History to guide the construction of their civilisation, including their morality. The lessons of the past became used as a guide to developing a sense of right and wrong. This was especially the case in relation to nation-state building and the construction of Empire, in both of which History-writing tended to become based on patriotism and a patriotic sense of moral worth. The old-fashioned History

book was often deeply patriotic, xenophobic (hating foreigners) and sometimes racist. The past was used to support these positions. Postmodern
historians take issue with this use of the past. They would tend to agree
that History (the subject) is closely connected with moral issues, and that
our own moral concerns as human beings often provide the motivation for
historical research and writing. But postmodernists would deny that
history (i.e. the past) *teaches* us morality, that a knowledge of the past provides an irrefutable base for morality in the present day. In one very
important sense, the postmodern condition has seen a lessening of the
sense of morality being hitched to patriotism – revealed as a growing dis-
comfiture with ardent nationalist claims and an opposition to imperialism.
Such tendencies have not disappeared from our society, but have lost intellectual justification and support. What this has done is show up the
absence of a core set of moral issues upon which all societies and peoples
can agree as knowledge and as morality.

From these starting points, postmodern History develops in all sorts of
directions. There is a vast array of History books and research projects
based on elements from postmodern History method. The elements are
diverse, and they are used in different combinations by historians. There is
no entire postmodern method that is used by a single historian. There is a
kind of 'cherry picking' of theory and method from the postmodern canon.
People can pick the bits of postmodernist theory desired and the methods
that might fit immediate study or research needs. Many of the methods are
not necessarily always seen as postmodern. There are many scholars who
wish to have no association, even tangentially, with any part of postmodernism, but who use elements of its method. In following chapters, we shall
come across research techniques called *semiology, discourse analysis,* and
poststructuralism which are used by some historians who would deny
being postmodernist. And so be it. Nevertheless, the argument of this book
is that there is an underlying chain of thinking linking all of these methods
in History study, and that it is called 'postmodernism'.

Any postmodernist historian is not being a postmodernist all of the
time. Like every historian, the postmodernist must conduct empirical
research, establishing that events occurred and the order of them, checking
sources that verify the facts of the case, and making decisions of judgement
(balance of probabilities may be the best term) where absolute certainty is
not possible.

But an historian needs to be conscious of certain perspectives cham-
pioned by (though not the sole preserve of) postmodernism. These include
the subjectivity in selecting historical events and sources to study, how

these are pre-figured by the historian when approaching the topic and then given in narratives used to write up research results, and the personal and political hypotheses that are brought by the historian to the field of study. The process of researching and writing History is one of moving upward from judgements over the small constitutive events of history (the past), through interpretation of documents, the bundling of events into historical processes, and then on to judgement of larger issues concerning those events (a judgement given by the historian in books and articles circulating the results). The further the historian is removed from consideration of the constitutive events of the past towards the narration of the past, the more the historian needs to think about how s/he has brought biases of one kind or another into study. Neutrality is impossible in this process. Enter the practice of thinking postmodern.

There are two final things to bear in mind when reading this book. First, most practising academic historians do not learn theory from theorists, and then deploy it in their studies. Rather, they tend to see how other scholars (including anthropologists, sociologists and literary specialists) have absorbed and used theory, and then copy the techniques into their own domain. Historians are probably the least likely academics to preface their books with theoretical explanation. I point to this not by way of criticising my profession (though I might), but rather to highlight the obvious, and to calm the nerves of any reader trembling at the prospect of prefacing every History essay and dissertation with long passages of theory.

Second, I do not argue that all the theory and techniques that follow need to be applied by every historian all the time. I do not argue that every section is relevant to every historical topic, theme or approach of a reading or researching historian. But I would argue that an awareness of postmodernist theory as a whole is important for all historians, and that all should be thinking about the applicability of some of the issues most of the time.

Notes

1   Quoted in R. Barthes, 'The Discourse of History', *Comparative Criticism*, 3 (1981), pp. 7–20.

CHAPTER 1

Empiricism

Empiricism of the late seventeenth, eighteenth, nineteenth and early twentieth centuries is the root of postmodernism. Out of the various phases of the Enlightenment came a philosophy of knowledge that is still extremely influential today. It defined our modern form of education and learning, created modern science and social science, and forged the academic discipline of History. This chapter explores it briefly, and how it has become the root of postmodernism.

Theory

Postmodernism is a critique of modernism. It is a reaction to the modernism of intellectual thought that dominated from around 1800 to 1960 – a period of dominance known as modernity. As major philosophical positions, modernism and postmodernism are opposites as ying and yang. There is much in modernism that postmodernism denies, subverts and inverts (as we shall see). Equally, though, there is much from modernism that is adopted by postmodernism. Most of what postmodernism takes from modernism can be described as the empiricist skill-base. Equally, most of what postmodernism criticises in modernism may be described as empiricist philosophy. This seems at first to be confusing, but it is readily explained.

The Enlightenment

The pre-modern world before c.1600 had been composed of ranks and orders, of feudal and Christian hierarchies that defined God and Christ above kings and queens, who in turn ruled over the people. All of society was arranged in layers in which each person owed allegiance to those above. Pre-modern knowledge itself had been perceived in the same way – in layers of authority. Information was understood in terms of layers in which access to knowledge was privileged, with the top privilege belonging to God and to monarchs. Knowledge was divine, God-given, as was the right to govern. Knowledge reflected society by being understood in terms of layers.

This system of knowledge started to break down in the early Enlightenment (c.1650 – 1770), known to some scholars as the Classical period of thought. This redefined European civilisation by a new intellectual, social and moral movement. Its very name, 'Enlightenment', describes a coming out of darkness into light, a movement from ignorance and superstition to the light of knowledge and benevolence. The revolution in knowledge accelerated during the *later* Enlightenment (c.1770 – c.1830). It is the impact of this later Enlightenment that is critical to understanding the heritage of the Enlightenment, and the eventual emergence of postmodernism. After the Enlightenment came a period referred to by postmodernists (and many others) as 'modernity'. It lasted from about 1800 to about 1960. Modernity was a period in which the system of knowledge promoted by the Enlightenment came to dominate, though filtered through political and religious movements and ideals which adapted to its modes of thinking. In total, the history of the West was dominated for over 200 years by the Enlightenment and its heritage. We must spend a few moments considering what postmodernists identify as the key characteristics of the Enlightenment.

The Enlightenment created a new centre of intellectual life erected upon a concern for rationality. Rationality was a system of thinking based on empiricism – discovering reality (or the truth) – then applying reason to derive conclusions and further new thoughts from that knowledge.

Box 1.1   *Rationality/empiricism*

Rationality is the system of reasoning by logic, usually induction (from example to generalisation). The system attained an iconic status within the Enlightenment as embodying the basis of scientific method in all forms of human inquiry (including History), banishing myth and superstition, and having moral attributes in defining the functionalist tolerance of the modern democratic state.

Within rationality, empiricism is the system of acquiring knowledge in cognitive terms, checking sources and preparing them for study (with which postmodernists agree). Separately, it is a philosophy of knowledge that posits that cognitive empirical method gains access to a reality and to incontrovertible truth at the level of interpretation (with which postmodernists do not agree).

Where previously intellectual life had presented knowledge as a revelation emanating from religion (the Christian religion, to whose God knowledge was submissive), the Enlightenment emphasised that science had an empirical independence from religious ideas. From seventeenth-century pioneers of new science like Galileo and Newton can be traced early beginnings of modern notions of God-free science based on observation, experimentation and inductive reasoning – a formula for defining science that reached a high standing in the eighteenth and nineteenth centuries. This extended well beyond science to apply reason in philosophy (as represented by men like Voltaire, Rousseau and Hume), political science (as represented by Locke) and in History (by Vico). New notions of constitutional government, of human rights (including toleration of difference) and of democracy were to grow from the same intellectual roots. More broadly, a new humanist morality was to emerge from Enlightenment thought, and to keep developing. This was a morality that emphasised the educative power of reason (rather than the shackling power of a vengeful state) to transform the individual (especially the young, the deviant, the criminal, the insane and the disabled). This was achieved by means of the state's corrective power in the form of its new medical and intellectual apparatuses. The individual citizen was called upon in this system of knowledge to adopt an internal rationality to guide behaviour and morality – a rationality that could be discerned from history (the past) as much as from God.

So, justification by historical knowledge became a substitute for justification by divine knowledge. This was a two-stage process. The early Enlightenment eroded hierarchies of knowledge by its characteristic classification and ordering of knowledge in alphabetical encyclopaedias. The later Enlightenment after c.1770 moved on to arranging knowledge in narratives, and especially in the form of historical narratives. This was pioneered especially by Giambattista Vico (1688–1744) who argued for a universal history that every nation passed through (sometimes repeatedly), composed of three periods of human development (the ages of gods, heroes and men) – a theory of historical rather than eternal human nature, separating the historical from the physical sciences. This was a major intellectual breach with the pre-modern world of ranks and orders, and a breach from the early Enlightenment's obsession with encyclopaedic ordering.

This signalled the arrival of History (the subject) on the scene as central to the intellectual system of modernity. This happened for two main reasons. Firstly, History provided the empirical evidence from the past for the origins of things under investigation. Instead of understanding things according to their place within rank orders, we could understand all manner of scientific or governmental issues by knowing what had gone before. A history of something, be it science or humanity, conferred authority, substance and a justification. This is still a powerful notion in our contemporary world. But secondly, History underlay the Enlightenment because of the centrality of the notion of progress – of the upward movement of mankind from primitive states to civilised states, and the belief that the present state was the best that there had ever been. This optimistic certainty in the upward trajectory of history is known as whig History.

Underlying the History that was promoted by Enlightenment thought in modernity from 1800 to 1960 was the idea of reality. The Enlightenment promoted the idea that all of science and learning was devoted to the discovery of reality. Man might not know the whole of this reality, but he knew some of it, and he could (and probably would) discover the rest of it in time. This reality ranged widely and was the object of research in many fields. It was to be found in astronomy, science and medicine (in all of which Enlightenment scientists were busy at work) and in economics (where the laws of economics were discerned by people like Adam Smith and David Ricardo). In demography Thomas Malthus contributed to discerning laws of population growth and the factors that retarded it. In what became known as sociology, human society started to be understood in terms of structures (like social class and gender) by which the impact of economic and demographic change might account for how society was evolving. In psychology, doctors started to claim province over not just the body but also the mind, where they discerned a 'normal' mind to be admired and an 'abnormal' mind that could be cured.

From this discoverable reality, social science and modern government emerged. Civil servants started to apply the best of this new knowledge to the problems of good management of state institutions and social conditions (especially in industrial cities). Social scientists developed new professions (like that of social worker) and techniques, with which to apply the new knowledge in the solution of practical problems. Society started to be managed by a rationality based on knowledge. In this way, knowledge became 'useful', or what is known as 'applied' – meaning that it had application to real problems. Our modern world became based on professions and institutions founded on the expansion of knowledge, the circulation of applied skills, and the dissemination of belief in the rational solution of all human problems.

Rationality implied an 'empiricist method'. This was the collection of evidence by meticulous research, good recording, and minute concern for the origins and authenticity of every item of information. The good researcher took notes of where information came from, and wrote this up in reports with footnotes and bibliographies. One consequence of this was the temptation to prioritise empiricism – the collection and ordering of 'facts' – above all other activities in rational reasoning. Facts could become an obsession of the observer. In this way, there was a strong sense in which modernism characterised the search for knowledge as a virtuous exercise, and objectivity and neutrality became seen as the virtuous characteristics of the inquirer. Moral certainty became attached to 'facts', and reference to 'facts' became a clincher in argument and debate. (One that is heard today is the notion of 'good science' as an irrefutable basis for decision-making in government.) In the Enlightenment system, 'knowledge' became envisioned as practical, purposeful and virtuous, contributing to a knowable and discoverable central reality. Ironically, many Christian clergy became the most fierce advocates and practitioners of 'knowledge' collection in the eighteenth century. They joined scientists, doctors and social scientists in promoting local history, archaeology, vaccination against illness, and modern learning. In this way, most Christian churches sought to reposition and modernise themselves in the age of the Enlightenment.

The Enlightenment privileged scientific method in all branches of human endeavour. It set in train the development of modern universities, education, government, discovery (of this world and the cosmos) and the modern tolerant Christian religion. The Enlightenment shaped key western concepts of democracy, tolerance, liberal values, freedom of conscience, and free-market economics. The law, justice and punishment became judged by new 'rational' measures that abhorred absolutist monarchy (because of its inefficiency, absurdity and lack of reasoned justification) and pre-modern Christian religion (because of its irrationality, intolerance and barbarity). In this sense, the Enlightenment made modern Europe. It was decent, logical and reasonable. It made much of the modern world in its own image.

However, the Enlightenment is not a blame-free territory. Later in this chapter we shall approach the postmodernist criticisms of it.

Empiricism and history

At the root of the modernist system of knowledge lies empiricism. Empiricism is seen to be a simple, common-sense method of objectivity and fact-collection in which all knowledge has to be proven before it can be accepted. It rejects *a priori* knowledge (that is, knowledge that is assumed to exist without any proof being required). It relies solely on experience (or observation or reading) of knowledge. When combined with inductive reasoning, it allows the scholar to move from particular bits of knowledge (cases) to generalisations (conclusions). This process involves an awareness of the past. Everything in science, nature and human experience is to be understood by discovering and appreciating the history of everything – of words, things, the planet, the animals, the history of human societies and individuals. As the later Enlightenment overtook the earlier, it allowed History (the subject) to replace the divine order of things, and allowed the historical narrative to replace the encyclopaedia.

An immediate consequence was the raised status of the narrative. Until the eighteenth century, the writing of History had been taken to be akin to the writing of novels or poetry. Indeed, much of the History written in the mediaeval and early-modern periods was written either in the form of a novel, or in poetic form. History was seen in many ways as a creative and an artistic exercise using oral tradition and folk tales. Indeed, in **pre-modernity** many felt that there had been no essential difference drawn between recounting History and recounting fiction. This changed, however. For the new breed of Enlightenment empiricists, pre-modern History-writing had been fictive rather than, as it was to become prized in modernity, 'factual'. So, History was changed by the Enlightenment into the task of observation (through reading documents and interpreting arte-facts), and constructing logical and consistent general conclusions about what happened in the past. Being an historian came to be seen as being a scientist of the past. As J.B. Bury, Regius Professor of Modern History at the University of Cambridge, declared in his inaugural lecture in 1903: 'History is a science, no less and no more.'[1]

To meet this requirement in the new History discipline, the historical narrative had to meet exacting standards. An historian's writing-up leads from the state of existing knowledge through the new facts to a new con-clusion. If passed by the acceptance of other historians through a process known as **peer review**, the new conclusion enters the body of known knowledge to form, in turn, the starting point for the next historian. Differences of interpretation arise and are resolved by judgement of the most relevant facts and the most plausible explanation of them. The pro-fessionalism of the historian is judged on these abilities. Their earliest exponent, Leopold von Ranke, regarded the historian as being in 'a struggle with documents'. He summed up the task of the historian in the preface of his first book. This has been translated as: 'To history has been assigned the office of judging the past, of instructing the present for the benefit of future ages. To such high offices this work does not aspire: it wants only to show what actually happened.' A second version of the translation is that the History book 'merely wants to show how, essentially, things happened'.[2] What became seen as an empiricist historical method emerged from the example he set, emphasising the testing of primary sources for forgery and internal consistency, comparing accounts, and challenging older histories based on memory, folk-wisdom or literary tradition without records written by reliable (usually upper-class or government) people. The more primary sources used, the more reliable the History, leading to what one postmodernist historian, Alun Munslow, has termed the reconstructionist approach to the past – the use of sources to reconstruct the past as near as possible to its 'real' condition.

With empiricist method placed central to historical skills, the historian was raised to the status of a trained professional, free as far as possible of bias, prejudice and ideology, aiming to understand the past in its own terms. The History-writings produced in this tradition tended to focus on power – meaning political, administrative, military and diplomatic history. History became about great men, few women, and was limited as a subject to areas which mattered and which had significant 'reliable' written records (from elite sources, generally). The past was conceived by most practitioners as an upward movement of mankind (and I mean mankind) to reach a present that was close to perfect. This made the History subject parallel with evolutionary sciences like geology and Darwinian biology. Man was evolving to a better, finer state, and that state was to be measured in terms of governments, constitutions, means of administration, and moral, high cultural and educational development. The History produced emphasised its own neutrality, chronology and ordering of facts in a supposedly objective historical narrative, constructed by the historian's skills honed in training with older historians. History could join the rest of the science-dominated Academy.

Social-science History

The social sciences have long been seen as being hostile to empiricism. For a long time, from around 1900 to 1980, empiricists saw themselves as 'defending History' from sociologists, economists and political scientists who seemed to believe that sociological theories could produce rules or paradigms by which models of the past could be set up. In reality, though, the traditional empiricist historian often feared the social science historian for political reasons. The empiricist tended to a right-wing, free-market conservatism that placed the elites and government as both the driving force of history and at the centre of historical interest. By contrast, the social science historian tended to a left-wing radicalism (often Marxism) that placed historical materialism and class struggle as the driving force and focus of history.

But this face-off between empiricist History and social science History was both an intellectual illusion and deeply ironic. It was an illusion because their systems of knowledge were really pretty similar. Since c.1980 general appreciation of this similarity has grown as empiricist and social science historians have been driven together in a mutual admiration of the Enlightenment and a mutual loathing of postmodernism. Empiricist History of the old school, it must be said, to a great extent withered in the late twentieth century. This has left social science historians as often the most vociferous critics of postmodern History. The baton of 'defending History' from postmodernism has passed from empiricist to social scientist.

Social science had at its core the theories of sociology. These originated in the eighteenth and early nineteenth centuries with Adam Smith, David Ricardo and Thomas Malthus. In the later nineteenth and twentieth centuries they developed further, with key theorists including Karl Marx, Friedrich Engels, Max Weber, Sigmund Freud and Emile Durkheim. Unlike historians of the empirical tradition, social science historians set out to *explain* the past, not just to describe it or narrate it. They asked 'Why?' questions much more than the 'What?' questions of the empiricist tradition: Why did the British Empire develop? Why was slavery economic? For British Marxist historians, for example, a key question in studying the period since 1780 was: 'Why was there no working-class revolution in Britain?' At the same time, the method came to be deployed for predictive and prophetic purposes. Marxism understood History and predicted the future using historical materialism. This was the notion that the clash of competing economic interests of different social classes (in every period of the past) has driven history forward in an inevitable movement of human societies from primitivism to an ideal state of communism. General laws or principles of society and model-building became the order of the day in historical research, applying rule-based structures upon the past, leading to an emphasis on social structures (such as social ranks, classes or orders) in study.

Social-science history was not confined by sociological ideas. It included great diversity of approach, employing different **categories of analysis** as the organising system of History-writing. Whilst Marxist historians used class struggle in the economic sphere as their dominant category, conservative economic historians understood historical change in terms of rational economic choice – the principle that people make economic choices with a logic for self-enhancement. *Annalist* historians looked for continuities across history defined by climate and geography. Weberians and Gramscist Marxists put emphasis on cultural change rather than the economic in history. Yet all of these groups shared a search for rules. They often shared a use of statistical method in a general belief in the power of empirical historical scholarship to reveal the 'truth' of the past. (The depth of this belief varied, and was weakened amongst historicist Marxists, like Gramsci, who regarded truth as historically variable.) They also shared a belief in the progress of human civilisation towards a better condition. They held a joint conviction that History as a subject could assist in understanding the contemporary human condition by its ability to inform applied subjects (such as town planning, business studies, political science and industrial relations). And they believed that History was more empirical (like a science) than aesthetic (like Literature Studies).

Box 1.2   *Antonio Gramsci (1891–1937)*

Gramsci was an Italian Marxist who was imprisoned during 1929–33 under Mussolini's Fascist government. During this period he wrote *Prison Notebooks*, a work that redefined Marxist thought. Troubled at the failure of the Left to win the support of the Italian working classes, he queried the dominance of the economic base–superstructure division (in which, in conventional Marxist theory, the economic base of production determined class relations in the social superstructure). Put crudely, Gramsci felt workers were radical at work, but conservative at home. So, Gramsci shifted emphasis to cultural production as the way in which the forces of reaction sustained loyalty to the economic status quo – in institutions such as churches, schools, and so on. Through this, a 'cultural hegemony' was imposed as a social control upon the people. This led to a new social history that examined mechanisms of control and imposed quiescence through social institutions. This approach became very influential in History-writing, especially amongst a new cultural Marxist group in Britain in the 1960s and 1970s, but also amongst Indian subaltern historians in the 1980s and 1990s. Though this approach is still important, postmodernist ideas have attracted many former Gramscist historians who found, in the end, that cultural hegemony and social control were crude and inaccurate concepts that diverted attention from people to systems.

By the late twentieth century, the History profession was a vital part of worldwide social science, shadowing virtually every other academic discipline to claim a special place as a service subject to other academics. (For example, there came into being a History of Science, History of Medicine, History of Education, History of Social Policy and so on.) It also claimed that it trained History students in a unique breadth of skills – in archives-searching, document-handling and analysis, mapping, computing and statistics, to name but some. These skills together made the historian especially capable in the 'real world' of decision-making in the civil service, in finance and modern management. The historian was not only the one who understood society and how it came to be now, but s/he was the one able to make balanced judgements in the face of competing sources and different types of information.

By this means, the History profession staked a claim to be based on an empiricism derived from Enlightenment example, modernised through social science, and erected as an academic subject on rationality. The outcomes the History profession could produce – the knowledge of the past – were reliable, constantly updated by new knowledge, 'practical' and 'useful' in applied social science, and entirely consonant with the emerging worlds of science, engineering and medicine. History took its place at the top table of the new secular academies.

Application in history

To be a good historian, it is thought you have to be good in empiricist method, and be seen to have a full grasp of facts. This involves the application of scholarship skills to a series of questions. These occur on different levels. On the upper level are the big questions of: What happened, when did it happen, and why did it happen? At the second level of scholarship, the historian answers these questions by asking: What is the existing state of historical knowledge? And what hypotheses best fit the known facts? At the third level, the historian tests the existing state of knowledge by locating new documents and other sources, or re-evaluating already known ones, checking their date and place of origin, their authorship, their destiny and circulation, and how these discoveries alter the existing state of understanding. Next and last, the historian writes a report or a narrative of the issue, replete with edited evidence and how to interpret it, properly sourced with footnotes, and publishes this in book or article form to be checked by **peer review** by other historians. If after being read by other historians the published account alters in some degree the existing state of knowledge, it acquires a degree of acceptance that other scholars then come along to challenge and re-assess, in turn to repeat the process of investigation in an endless cycle of moving knowledge forward.

This method of doing History is broadly what all academic and professional historians aspire to the world over. But empiricism is often accused of having affected not just *how* history is studied, but *what* is studied. Until the middle of the twentieth century, historians of the Rankean school tended to be concerned with political, constitutional and imperial power – with history 'from the top down'. The history of wars and 'big' people, of the elites, was usually placed centre-stage. But with the development of social science history – especially left-wing and Marxist – in the middle decades of the twentieth century, there was an attempt to invert this priority. History 'from the bottom up' focused on the common people, their experiences in life as recounted often in their own words, and assessed the state of society from the point of view of the weakest members not merely through the policies and agencies of the powerful.

Yet, for all that the shift from top-down to bottom-up History represented a major political shift from right to left politically, there was a sustained attachment to whig History. Pretty constant improvement in the human condition remained an assumption. And there was a continued underlying reliance on top-down agency – meaning that an elite changed the course of history, not the weak. The elite might be the bourgeois revolutionary vanguard, the intellectual, the politician, the military general or the capitalist. In any case, this History tended to emphasise implicitly the powerlessness of 'ordinary' people in the face of the ebbs and flows of more commanding forces. One consequence was that some historians continued to use words which implied the docility of the people in history, their intellectual inferiority, and sometimes their uncivilised state – words like 'the masses', 'the intellectuals' (and thus their implied less well-educated opposites), 'the deluded' and 'the heathens'. The common people seemed to be denied **agency** – or the power to change History. This power lay elsewhere. The written History tended generally to privilege the agency and activities of white, Christian, European men, and rather rarely the non-Christian, non-European, the black and women.

In one particular field of study, empiricism not only changes what is studied but *is* what is studied. This is the history of ideas. When this area of historical research turns its attention to the history of empiricism, then empiricism is not merely the *method* of study but is also the *object* of study. To look at the influence of empiricism since the seventeenth and eighteenth centuries, the historian employs an empiricist method to gather evidence in order to construct the story. But it is also of necessity studying the *history of the method*. This is a unique situation. The temptation is, of course, to praise empiricism as a development of the Enlightenment for originating the system of historical knowledge that the historian is using. Indeed, it seems difficult to do otherwise. For this reason, the Enlightenment has remained largely above criticism for professional historians. Until recently.

The period from the eighteenth to the mid-twentieth centuries is taken as the time when the Enlightenment fostered a world increasingly dominated by empiricism. Postmodernism arose in the late twentieth century to criticise it.

Postmodernist attitudes to empiricism

Postmodernism is founded on a critique of empiricism. This section summarises this.

The three natures of empiricism

The postmodernist critic distinguishes three different aspects of empiricism. These are empiricism as *an event*, empiricism as *a method*, and empiricism as *a philosophy of knowledge*. To each of these, the postmodernist has different attitudes.

Empiricism as *an event* is the Enlightenment. The Enlightenment is an event in the History of ideas within which empiricist method and empiricism as a philosophy of knowledge originated. Before postmodernism, judging the Enlightenment as an historical event used to be mostly unproblematic. The professional historian came into being as a result of its heritage. The History profession owed its existence to empiricist method, and belonged to the broad academic world of science, medicine and social science. History as a subject would not be studied, nor this book read, without its long shadow. In response, the History profession has been traditionally extremely generous in its judgement of the Enlightenment. It has been especially kind in describing the decay of the *ancien régime* and barbarity, and the promotion of human rights and democratic ideals. Most nations are especially proud of their own eighteenth-century philosophers who contributed to Enlightenment thought, and they are often national heroes. And aside from philosophy, the Enlightenment is widely taken to represent a general movement of modernisation, technical and educational advance, and liberalisation of many aspects of autocratic (often religious) culture. So, the Enlightenment has long been regarded as 'a good thing' with high motives and some pretty neat ideas that only fell short (if at all) in not succeeding in persuading governments to implement fully Enlightenment principles of democracy and social fairness.

Postmodernists have tended to judge the Enlightenment rather differently, however. Almost entirely since 1960, they have reassessed the Enlightenment as having an impact that confounded the ideals of some of its own leading lights by being neither benign nor benevolent. Instead, the Enlightenment stands accused of *intellectualising* (not necessarily originating) some of the key problems of the world from the mid-eighteenth to the mid-twentieth centuries. Postmodernists and some others will point to how the men (and a few women), working in the shadow of and in the name of the Enlightenment, developed intellectual, scientific and medical justifications, positions and prejudices that we today abhor. These positions include:

a. social elitism (justified by Enlightenment thought as necessary for a well-functioning society),

b. gender division of labour and education, thus marginalising women (justified on biological grounds),

c. racial prejudice (that justified whites as superior to other races on medical and religious grounds),

d. religious prejudice (that set Christianity, or a branch of it, as superior to all other religions),

e. acceptance of capitalism, and especially its free-market variety, as the best economic system (justified by regarding economics as a social science with its own laws),

f. free possession of the world's environment (that accepted the resources of the world as broadly at humankind's free disposal),

g. European imperialism (justified for its benevolence, supposed liberalism, and its creation of order and prosperity in the non-European world).

Postmodernists would highlight how each of these positions emerged in a strong intellectual form from the Enlightenment, became government policy in European nations, and acted to the detriment of the world and its societies. The detrimental consequences include: the modern class system; women's confinement to home and 'women's menial work'; European empires that exploited peoples of colour by trying to convert them to Christianity, and industrialism and despoliation of the planet.

In this sense, postmodernism is the critique of the Enlightenment. Postmodernism wants to destabilise the intellectual acceptance of the Enlightenment and the philosophical justifications it makes for the prejudicial positions listed above. Many postmodernist historians focus their research on the history of Europe from c.1650 to c.1960, re-evaluating the Enlightenment and modernity as the source of the contemporary world's massive problems. Postmodernists argue that many previous historians were too much *inside* the Enlightenment, too immersed in its values and presumptions, to write its history with the 'objectivity' so prized by them. This is an irony – that an 'objective' history of the Enlightenment must be self-reverential (revering and praising its own methods) as well as self-referential (supposedly proving its case by referring, or footnoting, to itself). Postmodernism reveals a contradictory position. As a result, some postmodernists might argue that such a History is intellectually untenable.

Empiricism as *a method* is the second aspect distinguished by the postmodernist. This is the method by which empiricism defines knowledge. Empiricism argues that knowledge is acquired through an apparatus of human observation, experience, testing of authenticity, verification, corroboration and presentation for judgement (or **peer review**) by others in a value-free form. Even if the *consequences* of empiricism are challenged, postmodernists most certainly do not reject empiricist methods. Like all historians, the postmodernist needs empiricist method for the essential skills, and any student of History *must* learn and deploy them.

The postmodernist distinguishes a third aspect of empiricism, however – empiricism as *a philosophy of knowledge*. And this is seen as being full of problems. In the work of many academics across science and non-science disciplines, there is an implicit notion that empiricism constitutes all that is necessary to knowledge – that it is a complete system of knowledge with no other connections. This notion is that human knowledge acquisition is *nothing more* than empiricism, and *needs* nothing more than this for the advancement of each discipline. In the case of History, the writing of the past has been seen by some empiricists as being satisfactorily embraced by empiricist method.

One such empiricist historian was Geoffrey Elton, a leading right-wing historian, who regarded empiricism as the only worthwhile basis of professional training in the History discipline. The training, he stated, should be composed of what he called 'essentials', or basic skills, that allow History to speak for itself through the facts contained in historical sources. There are probably few professional historians who would now share Elton's outlook on History being allowed to speak for itself. His purist empiricist position brought him to dispute with other historians over decades – including non-postmodernists. Elton criticised E. H. Carr, a left-wing historian, who ostensibly tried to distance himself from empirical method by arguing that History is made by historians, with historical 'facts' only having significance once an historian makes use of them. On the basis of this, Elton described Carr (probably unfairly) as a 'sceptical relativist' who seemed to doubt the certainty of the facts about the past. More recently, Arthur Marwick has been the most strident defender of traditional empirical method and the privileged skills used by elite and skilled historians. He wrote that 'history is an autonomous discipline with its own specialised methods'.[3] Richard Evans is widely regarded as a key defender of the cognitive significance of empiricism in the History profession. But even he rejected Elton's empiricism as a stand-alone philosophy of knowledge in the History profession, and has criticised Marwick's case in support of empiricism. So, there is no clear-cut, universal empiricist position in the History subject today – much as is the case with postmodernism.

But postmodernism attacks more than the question of whether History is a stand-alone profession based on empiricist method. The postmodernist will argue that many empiricists are confusing two things. The accusation is that they confuse *method* with *philosophy*. An acceptance of empiricist *method* is actually being turned by some empiricists into a justification for the *whole nature* of study. We need to explore this.

The event, the fact and the narrative

The postmodernist argues that empiricism as a philosophy of knowledge is deeply flawed. A good way in which these flaws are revealed is in the relationship between *events* and *facts*. These are two of the most frequently used words in History books in discussing the nature and use of History as a discipline. They are words that seem to encapsulate the essence of the historian's work, calling up the essential material upon which the historian is working to craft the subject. We teach and learn in History using events and facts. So central are they to what we do as historians that the words act as a prism for debate between empiricism and postmodernism. They focus the problem.

Events and *facts* seem at first glance to be the same thing in History. If we take an event to cover any occurrence (whether a short event or a longer process), then it is the constituent upon which the History book is written. On the face of it, it might seem that the fact is the same thing as the event. Indeed, in a purist empiricism, there might not be any distinction drawn between these two. A *fact* of history relates directly to an *event*, to a reality that occurred and that has been recorded for posterity, and that is

now being described by the historian. However, historian Richard Evans
makes some distinction. He writes, 'An event is a fact, but a fact is not
necessarily an event.' Here, he suggests that 'history is not just about
events, it is about many other aspects of the past as well'.[4] This is undoubt-
edly the case. He speaks of buildings from the past as being one element of
the 'many other aspects'. But this is not a major distinction at all. The past
is actually composed *only* of events, including the moments of design and
construction of a building. The materiality of the past is a product of
events just as much as other incidents. Events come in all different lengths
of duration. And superficially, the fact and the event seem to have a close
affinity.

But a postmodernist theorist of History regards 'the fact' and 'the
event' as entirely different. The event is something that happened in the
past, the fact is a human construction (or representation or statement) of
it. The event occurred, the fact is a record and expression of it. The event
is neutral. But the fact is built upon documents or records of the event,
making it laden with problems of accuracy, bias, editing, significance, and
the sheer restrictions of human description. This is the shift from that
which can be ascertained to have happened to that which is being packaged for representation in successive historical statements. There is a
movement here. When events become packaged by an historian in statements, they lose their neutrality. This is the historian imposing a shape on
the past. The historian is not merely holding up a mirror to past events.
The package s/he constructs cannot be complete in the same way as the
past is, and nor can the package ever reflect the chaos of the past.

Truth may be ably represented when an event becomes the basis of a
simple statement. The event may be plucked on its own from the chaos of
past events and made into a fact-statement like: 'The Bastille was overrun
by people on 14 July 1789.' But this statement on its own does not constitute the History discipline doing its work. History as an academic subject
is not merely about plucking events from chaos. The statement has to be
transformed into something else. History requires the placing of every fact-
statement against the backdrop of other fact-statements to make an
interpretation in a narrative-statement. A narrative-statement would be:
'The overrunning of the Bastille marked the commencement of the French
Revolution.' Here, there is a statement involving a judgement of significance and a comparison of many facts which puts the Bastille event above
the others. The 'French Revolution' is promulgated as a term that collects
many events together in one concept, the term having been created after
the Bastille event itself. Whoever originated it, the term has become in itself

an analytical concept. The historian has accepted it and is using it in a judgement that puts a medley of events together under the one name. This is historical analysis. This is the historian at work.

In this way, the fact-statement quickly loses its neutrality as it is drawn away from the event (in its context of the chaos of the past) and becomes a narrative-statement. Order and interpretation are imposed upon the *fact*, thereby changing its linkage with the event which induced it. There is a slippage of the linkage between the event, fact-statement and narrative-statement. These three are moving apart. They are not the same things. However, many historians overlook this slippage, and often tend to attribute to the narrative-statement the status of a 'fact'. The more an historian states: 'That is a fact' about a past event, the more we should be alert to the slippage going on between event and fact. We should also be alerted by excessive statements of 'That is a fact' to a possible dispute going on about whether the 'fact' is 'true'. The historian is pleading a case, we might suspect. If there were no dispute, there would be less likelihood of needing to shout about it.

So, once an event of the past is described, it becomes something else – it becomes a narrative. On its own, it will be a small narrative, short on words and perhaps reasonably uncomplicated. However, the historian's job is to combine small narratives about small events into significant bigger narratives about larger events and processes. The bigger the narrative, the more valuable is the work of the historian. The writing of History concerns generalisation, summation, hypothesising and proof, and none of that is achievable with the singular fact-statement. So, the transition from fact to narrative is necessary. But this transition disrupts the linkage between fact and the original event, and cannot allow the retention of an undisturbed neutral 'truth' within the fact-statement. The transformation from event to fact-statement to narrative-statement cannot retain objectivity and neutrality. To claim that the narrative-statement is in the same category as the event or the fact-statement is a conflation of empirical *method* with the empiricist *philosophy*.

What was at the outset merely a simple empiricist method of discovering and checking historical events has turned into something much bigger, more complex, open to dispute and potentially controversial.

The postmodernist historian starts from the position that empiricism as a philosophy of knowledge is a problem. At its core, it claims to deliver a certainty about the single event in the past, and thus about the past in general. The postmodernist does not believe this. S/he does not believe this because (1) certainty is undermined by the need to judge which events are important and which are not important. Significance is always a judgement of the historian, and that can only be made after the event. The historian is making judgements all the time about significance on the basis of long-term knowledge. If s/he is not, there is little point to the academic subject. S/he does not believe in delivery of a certainty about the past because (2) the research agenda is never neutral. The historian has made a decision to study a topic for any number of personal or political reasons. The agenda of historical study is always being set by where we are now – by our current ideological, political, social or other concerns. For example, until the 1990s, the notion of environmental history was practically unknown. But now with concerns about global warming, melting ice-caps, industrial pollution and so on, there are large numbers of historians working on the environmental history of different countries, funded by large government research awards. The last 30 years has seen the agenda of history constantly expanded by contemporary politics: the history of women, gender, race, religious bigotry, drugs usage and laws, how wars end (as well as begin) and so on. Every age writes its own historical agenda. But most important of all, the postmodernist does not believe that a certainty about the past can be delivered by History because of (3) narrative. As we shall see in later chapters, it is completely impossible for the historical narrative – a History book or article – to be written using only empiricism. There is never any neutrality in a story. History is concerned with narrative – with fitting one small piece of the past into a broad story. Narratives are necessary means for making sense of data. Information on its own, recalled in seemingly haphazard or unsystematised ways, fails to convey much meaning or sense. Random facts from the past tell us nothing and, more importantly, explain nothing. There are all sorts of transformations, edits, and judgements going on that vary meanings and certainly undermine the concept of one authoritative account of everything in the past.

So, the postmodernist identifies an intellectual problem lying in those who express a certainty about the historical *fact*. S/he then identifies a second problem that follows on – a political and moral problem. If anybody claims to be able to deliver a certainty that cannot be challenged, written History becomes undemocratic and dangerous. It suggests an ability to reconstruct the past with fixity, in a format that allows complete absence of doubt. What tends to happen is that the notion of an authoritative understanding of the facts of the past becomes transformed into a notion of an authoritative understanding of morality in all of history. Morality tends to become seen as fact-based and history-based. What is morally right is conjoined in the imagination with what is thought to be factually right and, moreover, unchanging. This becomes a power wielded by elites, by one generation over the next, and by custodians of heritage who brandish their patriotic stewardship of nation, race or religion. This makes for an inclination to use the past as the foundation for seeing moral correctness as unchanging. Authority over the one becomes an authority over the other.

The postmodernist does not like this. The postmodernist is suspicious of 'authority' and of the hierarchy that lies behind it. Hierarchies may be unavoidable, but they need to be treated with constant scepticism and challenge. Behind every hierarchy lies the exertion of intellectual power, and with that exertion there are those who feel empowered by this History. The empowered have often been the white, male, middle- and upper-class, Christian, Euro-centric, heterosexual, political establishment. Those who are being disempowered have tended to be the black, female, working class and poor, non-Christian and the politically unrepresented. Authority fostered in the written History that the Enlightenment encouraged in the nineteenth and twentieth centuries tended to use 'reason' to promulgate historical rules, creeds, credos and models. The world and its past became reducible to knowable facts and an inescapable and universal morality. Postmodernists want to upset all of this.

Conclusion

Empiricism is the basic method in all scholarship. It bears endless repetition that the empiricist skills of verification, close textual attention, proper and rational sourcing, referencing and so on, remain absolutely central to all that historical scholarship does, whether postmodernist or not. In this regard, the Enlightenment created the method of the modern historian.

But empirical *method* is one thing. The other is the empiricist *philosophy of knowledge*, or modernism, and that most certainly is challenged. Empiricism gives the illusion of delivering fact, truth and reality, by slipping from the event to a human narrative that describes the event. This slippage is from empiricism as method, to empiricism as a philosophy of knowledge. In the process of slippage, the fact becomes coloured by all sorts of influences and biases, becomes an interpretation, but masquerades as truth. It is a verbal fabrication of the past. Friedrich Nietzsche wrote in 1873 of truth as a linguistic illusion:

What, then, is truth? A mobile army of metaphors, metonymies, anthropomorphisms, in short a sum of human relations which have been subjected to poetic and rhetorical intensification, translation, and decoration, and which, after they have been in use for a long time, strike a people as firmly established, canonical, and binding: truths are illusions of which we have forgotten that they are illusions, metaphors which have become worn by frequent use and have lost all sensuous vigour, coins which, having lost their stamp, are now regarded as metal and no longer as coins.[5]

The key verbal devices of this 'mobile army' we shall explain later in the book. Certainty emerges as a linguistic construction which, Nietzsche went on, 'prompts a moral impulse' to doubt the denier of certainty, to see in doubt the very basis of immorality. This is a massive irony. Nietzsche says doubt itself becomes superior to fact and moral certainty. This seems like craziness. It seems to be completely absurd and inverted in logic. It overturns everything we are trained to believe as students at school and in college. It may be difficult to grasp that doubt is superior to certainty. This is why postmodernism is truly revolutionary as a philosophical system of thought.

The remainder of the book will try to explain this. We proceed to look at how the Enlightenment's empiricist philosophy of knowledge is being overturned by postmodernism. This has a certain difficulty to it. We are proposing to attack the Enlightenment as a philosophy of knowledge, despite the fact that it forms the very basis of the method of the scholar. As the French postmodern philosopher Jacques Derrida wrote in 1967, 'the revolution against reason can be made only within it'.[6] So, we use reason as a method to undermine reason as a philosophy.

Guide to further reading

For fine introductions to the Enlightenment, see Roy Porter, *The Enlightenment* (London, Macmillan, 1990) and Thomas Munck, *The Enlightenment: A Comparative Social History 1721–1794* (London, Arnold, 2000). To explore a range of historians' attitudes to empiricist method and philosophy, see the readings in John Tosh (ed.), *Historians on History* (Harlow, Pearson Education, 2000) and Anna Green and Kathleen Troup (eds), *The Houses of History: A Critical Reader in Twentieth-century History and Theory* (Manchester, Manchester University Press, 1999).

The book that is widely regarded as the most influential defence of empiricist values in the History subject is R. Evans, *In Defence of History*

(London, Granta, 1997 and later revisions). A strong argument in favour of empiricism as both method and as a philosophy of knowledge is in Arthur Marwick, *The New Nature of History; Knowledge, Evidence, Language* (Basingstoke, Palgrave, 2001). For a postmodern critique of the empiricist philosophy of knowledge as used in History, see Alun Munslow, *Deconstructing History* (London, Routledge, 1997). For a specific postmodern critique of Geoffrey Elton and E.H. Carr, see Keith Jenkins, *On 'What is History?'* (London and New York, Routledge, 1995), especially pp. 43–63.

To look at the role of Vico, see V.B. Leitch (gen. ed.) *The Norton Anthology of Theory and Criticism* (New York, Norton, 2001), pp. 399–400; G. Vico, *The First New Science* (orig. 1725, Cambridge, Cambridge University Press, 2002) and H. White, *Tropics of Discourse: Essays in Cultural Criticism* (Baltimore, Johns Hopkins University Press, 1978), pp. 197–217.

Notes

1 J.B. Bury, cited in C. Parker, The *English Historical Tradition since 1850* (Edinburgh, John Donald, 1990), p. 83.

2 In order, L. von Ranke as translated by Fritz Stern, quoted in R. Evans, *In Defence of History* (London, Granta, 1997), p. 17, and in M. Hughes-Warrington, *Fifty Key Thinkers on History* (London, Routledge, 2000), p. 257.

3 A. Marwick, *The New Nature of History: Knowledge, Evidence, Language* (Basingstoke, Palgrave, 2001) p. 17.

4 Evans, *Defence*, pp. 78–9.

5 Quoted in V.B.Leitch (gen. ed.) *The Norton Anthology of Theory and Criticism* (New York, Norton, 1990), p. 880.

6 J. Derrida, *Writing and Difference* (orig. 1967, London, Routledge, 2001), p. 42.

CHAPTER 2

Sign

Postmodernism is a philosophy of knowledge. It constructs an understanding of what knowledge is that contrasts to that of the Enlightenment. It dismantles the entire system of knowledge that was created by empiricism and, starting from scratch, it constructs a new knowledge system. To do this, it starts at the very beginnings of what knowledge is – with *the sign*. The theory and study of the sign developed between the 1910s and the 1960s into an academic sub-discipline known as **semiology** (alternatively known as semiotics).

Theory

The intellectual origins of postmodernism lie in language studies. Three leading figures dominate this field – Saussure, Barthes and Foucault.

Elementary semiotics

At the heart of all postmodernist theory is semiotics. This section is the core of postmodernist theory, containing the big conceptual leap. The theory is not easy for everyone, but if you grasp it, then the rest of postmodern theory should fall into place with less difficulty.

Postmodern theory started in the early twentieth century. The key figure at its beginning was Ferdinand de Saussure.

Until Saussure in the early twentieth century, languages were studied in terms of the evolution of words. Linguists took a word to be a denoter of a thing. In English, the word 'mouse' denoted a small rodent: the relationship between word and object (or **referent**) was simple, exclusive and unequivocal. Saussure found this a limited conception.

Firstly, he was unhappy with the definition of 'a word'. A word is not the only way in which humans may convey to each other the notion of a

---

Box 2.1   *Ferdinand de Saussure (1857–1913)*

A Swiss academic educated at Berlin, Leipzig and Paris, Saussure learned
many languages, including Gothic and old German, Sanskrit, Latin and
Lithuanian. From 1891 until his death he was a professor at the
University of Geneva. From 1906 he taught a course on General
Linguistics; he conceived the problems in the subject as it then was, and
started to construct an alternative system. However, he never wrote up
his work. Indeed, his ideas came to be spread after his death only because
his students wrote up their lecture notes into book form. His principal
idea came from his unhappiness with the state of linguistics – the study of
language – which until then had been little more than a history of languages, and not a theory of them. He focused scholarly attention on *the
sign* as the basic unit of knowledge. By looking at means of communication that were constructed not only of words but of gestures, drawings
and other human communications, Saussure showed that language was
constructed of signs which bore no relationship to the things being
signed. He broke the conceptual link between a word and an object. This
revolutionised intellectual history. Saussure is widely regarded as the
founder of structuralism, the inspirer of poststructuralism, and the cause
of the '**linguistic turn**' of the late twentieth century.

---

thing such as a mouse. For instance, a drawing of a (rodent) mouse acts in
the same way, being another form of language that could hold the same
meaning as the word 'mouse'. Thus, Saussure urged us to think not in
terms of words but of **signs**, and not of languages but of sign systems.
Saussure gave as examples of sign systems: the deaf-and-dumb alphabet,
religious rites, and nautical flags. We can also add many other sign systems
– road signs, diagrammatical signs (on lavatory doors, in airport termi-
nals), human gestures, body posture, photographs. Anything which tells
another person something, gives them a message, is a sign. A sign may be
defined as anything that stands for (or signifies) something other than
itself. So, Saussure's first big message was that language was not restricted
to words.

Secondly, Saussure criticised the assumption that language was nothing
more than a system of nomenclature (a naming system) that corresponded
words to things. It assumed that humans had ideas and then created words
for those ideas. He argued that signs and ideas must come into existence
through interaction. He said that signs relate to two different areas: language and speech. In the French, these were *langue* and *parole, langue*

being a mental entity shared by those communicating with each other, while *parole* is the vocal entity, a sound or series of sounds, or the concrete usage. (Theorists since Saussure have expanded the scope of *parole* to include written and other sign-systems.) Saussure said that every sign has two parts – a **signifier** and a **signified**. The signified is the *langue* (the mental conception of the object), and the signifier is the *parole* (the sound of a word, or the drawing of an object). Academics now usually speak of 'signified' and 'signifier'. The signified is not the object itself, but the pre-existing (or learned) mental conception of that object. The object (the referent) is not part of the sign system, but is exterior to it. So, 'mouse' (the word) refers to a concept of the animal, and not the animal itself.

Now, Saussure prioritised the signified over the signifier (the concept over the word), meaning that mental concepts give structure and under-standing to the way we speak. This made Saussure the founder of **structuralism**, which in the 1950s, four decades after his death, developed as the leading approach to culture and society. From structuralism devel-oped poststructuralism and the **linguistic turn**. Saussure was the inspirer of each. Structuralism emphasised the structure of social class as the thing that made the signified (the concept of class) more important than the sig-nifier (the word 'class'). But poststructuralists from the late 1960s reversed this prioritisation, emphasising the *impermanence* of structures. They pri-oritised signifiers over structures (word over the concept, or language over structure). This is why the term 'linguistic turn' developed. Poststructuralism gave birth in the 1970s to what we now call postmod-ernism. We tackle these issues in Chapter 4.

The last three paragraphs are probably the single most important bit of theory in the book. Go back over them if you need to.

The third thing that Saussure criticised was the notion of the certainty of the link between a sign and its object – the certainty and permanence that the word 'mouse' meant a rodent. Saussure denied this. He said that the linguistic sign is arbitrary and randomly chosen. Any word might be selected to denote mouse – such as 'elephant'. There was no pre-ordained rule that said it had to be 'mouse'. Further, the whole sign-system was arbi-trary in that there is nothing in the word 'mouse' that can be said to *resemble* the animal. By the same token, similar signifiers to 'mouse' have nothing to do with the animal – 'house', 'louse', 'douse', 'mouth'. Inversely, similar signifieds to a mouse have signifiers without any resem-blance – hamster, shrew, rat bear no resemblance to the word 'mouse'. In this way, in Saussurean thinking, a language is characterised by an arbi-trary link between signifier and signified, and an arbitrary link of signified to its object. However, he pointed out that the signified – the *concept* of the mouse (the animal) – is just one concept, and it cannot be confused with another concept. By contrast, the signifier can be confused. The signifier can change its signified. The signifier 'mouse' (the word) has since 1985 developed a new meaning – the small table-top device with a ball and buttons for moving the cursor on a computer screen. This is the result of a comical association of the computer mouse (its outline shape and a wire resembling a tail) with an animal mouse. Here a linkage is drawn between two concepts to foster an identical signifier. Thus, one signifier ('mouse') has acquired two signifieds (the animal and the computer device).

Fourthly, Saussure said a language system works on the basis of dualities or oppositions. Signs have meaning because they have linear relationships with some different signs, and non-linear relationships with others. For instance, the word 'mouse' as a sign derives meaning only when it is linked with other signs in a linear relationship – as in 'mousetrap' or 'mouse button', each of which have different signifieds. This is how we know what object we are referring to. At the same time, the sign 'mouse' derives meaning because we mentally put it in opposition (or duality) with other signs: mouse–rat, mouse–cat, mouse–screen, mouse–keyboard. Translating this, we understand the meaning of the single sign 'mouse' because of a hidden instant process of recognition we go through which says something like: 'Yes, the mouse, from the mouse-hole, but no, not the rat.' So each sign has an on/off function, indicating 'this' but 'not that'. According to Saussure, a sign system only operates because it makes linear and oppositional connections with different signs. No sign stands on its own. It only works as part of a complex system.

From these four points was to emerge the whole of the intellectual system known as postmodernism. It is worth ensuring that you have grasped them before proceeding. Here they are in summary:

1 Languages are not confined to words, but include any system of communication that uses signs.

2 A sign is composed of a signifier (vocal sound) and a signified (the mental concept or structure that speaker and listener share). The structure precedes the signifier in existence (said Saussure). Prioritising the structure pre-casts knowledge amongst hearers, creating a structuralist understanding of knowledge. The referent (the thing) to which the sign points is not part of the sign.

3 A signified is established quite arbitrarily and bears no resemblance to its referent. Each signified (the mental concept) has only one signifier, but a signifier can have more than one signified.

4 Every sign acquires meaning by belonging to a network of other signs
   – some similar signs, and some dissimilar signs. There is in every sign
   a suggestion of another, oppositional sign, giving an on/off quality to
   all signs.

So, what is the significance of this? Saussure's four major points made uncertain our attitude to knowledge. From the 1920s, other linguists were
de-coupling signs from the objects they referred to (the referents), transforming many academic disciplines. At the very root of all knowledge, all
learning, all academic subjects and all education, is language. Words are our
very trade. You listen to language in lectures, you read it in books, and you
write it in words and signs in emails, text-messages, letters, essays and
exams. Saussure's work undermined the certainty of a connection between a
word and a thing, making the link conditional and equivocal. Meaning and
the sign separated, leaving many academics with no absolute, scientific certainty that a signifier related to a specific signified through an agreed sign.

   The work of Saussure was continued by Roland Barthes in the 1950s, 1960s
and 1970s, shifting it out from a pure study of language to a study of culture.

Box 2.2   *Roland Barthes (1915–80)*

Barthes was a French theorist, theatre and literature critic, and popu-
lariser of cultural studies. His most famous work was in the 1950s when
he published magazine articles deconstructing icons of popular culture.
These ranged from activities like wrestling and the preaching of Billy
Graham to things like soap powder, cars and the Eiffel Tower. His work
has made him immensely popular as it is relatively easy, and fascinating,
to understand. He undertook many studies, including ones of clothes and
of the sign-based Japanese language. His articles were republished in two
books *Mythologies* and the follow-up, *The Eiffel Tower*, and these
remain models of how to investigate the language in popular culture, the
messages that are shared by people within a culture, and how these are
normalised into a dominant and unquestioned system of knowledge.
Drawing on a French Marxist tradition, Barthes used his theory to
explain how the forces of conservativism could effortlessly restrain revolution through popular culture. Initially a structuralist, he is credited with
developing poststructuralism in the late 1960s by his awareness that in
knowledge the signified precedes the structure. He therefore reversed
Saussure's understanding. His work was seminal in creating semiology
(the science of signs) and cultural studies. Elected in 1976 to the chair of
Literary Semiology at the Collège de France, he died after being tragically
run over by a Parisian lorry.

In France in the 1940s and 1950s, Barthes used semiological theory to explain the dominance and durability of bourgeois imperialist-capitalist culture. Like many left-wing and Marxist intellectuals (such as Antonio Gramsci in Italy), Barthes believed that the class struggle was being won by the elites not only because of economic or political oppression, but also by cultural power. Whilst Gramsci explained this through concepts of 'social control' and 'cultural hegemony' (through control of the churches, leisure and education), Barthes argued that an oppressive ideology was normalised in society by *silent sign systems* in everyday popular **culture**. He approached his studies through literary and theatre criticism, arguing against the French literary tradition of clarity in language – a natural or realistic style of writing, a normative style. Barthes said that this tradition was spurious, that realistic writing was impossible, and that the attempt created an artificiality of style in which **ideological** presumptions were silently reinforced between reader and writer. Instead, he aspired initially to a writing style completely free of bourgeois presumptions and ideology, a 'writing with degree zero', but later abandoned this as impossible. But from this, he turned to show how to analyse popular culture for embedded silent signs and their meanings. This made Barthes an originator of the study of popular culture.

One of the best examples of his work is an analysis of a popular wrestling match – the professional version, which many people see as 'staged', fixed and a sham. He points out that the function of the wrestler, unlike that of a boxer or judo contestant, is not to win. His function is to go exactly through the motions that are expected of him, as in the grand gestures of ancient Greek tragedy. Barthes says: 'In wrestling, as on the stage of antiquity, one is not ashamed of one's suffering, one knows how to cry, one has a liking for tears.' The arm-lock and the forearm smash produce exaggerated displays of suffering. 'Each sign in wrestling is therefore endowed with an absolute clarity, since one must always understand everything on the spot. As soon as the adversaries are in the ring, the public is overwhelmed with the obviousness of the roles.' Wrestling is like algebra: we know how the equation will move along and work out. It is a grand tragi-comedy on life: 'What is thus displayed for the public is the great spectacle of Suffering, Defeat and Justice.' So, the wrestling match is a planned metaphor for our moral lives, each action 'a pure and full signification' which is nothing but 'an ideal understanding of things'. Good and evil emerge in exaggerated form, uninterrupted by any 'real' contest. Wrestling is a performance with an elaborate set of codes. It is a language with its own meanings.[1]

Barthes' revelation that wrestling has its own language opened the doors to cultural studies – to the study of hidden languages in everyday life that have political meanings. The language is understood instantly by producer and consumer of signs. A sign like an illegal wrestling hold relates to a signified (or concept) – injustice – which in itself is a signifier of a larger signified, what Barthes called a 'myth', of wrestling as a moral language. Only within this larger myth system is each sign understood. This is a two-stage process. The first he called primary signification (or denotation), where a signifier denotes a signified to create a sign. This is only possible because that sign instantly belongs as *a signified* in a secondary signification (the connotation) of a large myth system.

So, Barthes said that every sign belongs within a myth. The myth is not necessarily untrue, but is an accepted part of culture. This makes language work. Everybody in a culture understands not just the sign but also the myth to which it belongs. The sign already exists – it is not new – in a pre-existing sign system. Barthes showed that signs and sign systems were embedded codes with normative meanings. Barthes called all of this 'the semiological system', and the study of the hidden meanings he called '**semiology**'.

One important change to theory was floated by Barthes. He asserted that signs are not arbitrary. Unlike Saussure, Barthes was a politically motivated left-winger living in right-wing France in the 1950s, and he observed that sign systems are highly motivated and deeply structured by political power. Understanding each sign meant placing it in its political context – within its structure. Initially, Barthes followed Saussure in seeing the structure as preceding the signifier, but in later life he came to reverse this, giving birth to poststructuralism (which we return to in Chapter 4).

Written/spoken signs

Saussure privileged the spoken word over the written word. He argued that the spoken word is anterior, immediate and essential, whilst the written word is inferior, fixed in time, and no more than an imprecise surrogate. So, the suggestion is that the spoken word was understood historically before the written word.

Roland Barthes and other French theorists reversed this privileging. The empiricist presumption of 'realist' writing and knowledge assumed that the signified came before the signifier, but these new theorists suggested the reverse – that written formats (such as pre-historic drawings on cave walls) preceded the verbal, putting the signifier before the signified. One theorist, Michel Foucault, wrote that 'it is the primal nature of language to be written',[2] that humankind has always sought to communicate in written (including graphic) formats, and that in recent history the Renaissance gave absolute privilege to writing. Another theorist, Jacques Derrida, argued that the immediacy of the speaker and the urgency of the audience make verbal speech difficult to interpret, whilst the written is the natural form for interrogation and the deepest understanding. He said that: '... what opens meaning and language is writing as the disappearance of natural presence'.[3] The spoken word, he noted, lacks what the written word allows – 'deferred, reserved, enveloped, rolled up' words that can be properly analysed in reflective comfort. He showed that there is a false presumption in western philosophical thought (from the Greek philosopher Plato onwards) that the speaker has a privileged understanding of meaning, above any that is written down by a scribe. This error is linked, he suggests, to the more dangerous fallacy of a central reality – derived from the notion that something exists to be discovered if only the scholar can access it by finding the 'authentic' voice, more especially evident in a live speech. This is a presumption of 'reality' and authenticity in a speaker, attacked especially by Derrida. He derided the traditional view that the signifier (such as a word) becomes transparent and dissolves into invisibility in its act of suggesting a signified (the referent or object) – the notion that a signifier fades into the background as the viewer understands the thing being signified. (An example of this notion is that if someone says to you, 'There is a mouse in the room', you firstly hear the word 'mouse', then it disappears as you replace it with the *concept* of the mouse you retrieve from memory.) Derrida proclaimed this a false presumption since it tends to suggest a presence of the referent, and privileges senses of 'reality' and 'certainty' in human understanding of things. From his criticism, he developed the practice of **deconstruction** of **texts** – an academic technique that emphasises and privileges the study of the written (signifier) over the verbal (signified). We come to this in Chapter 5.

Sign modes and forms/mediums

Since the time of Saussure and Barthes, semioticians have come to acknowledge the existence of different modes (or types) of sign. The first mode is the symbolic, in which the signifier does not resemble the signified, and is entirely arbitrary: the word 'mouse' bears no resemblance to the animal. The second is the iconic sign, in which the sign takes on a cartoon-like resemblance to the signified by indicating or lampooning some essence – its metaphorical shape (the cartoon of a man on a Gents toilet door), or its representation in gesture (such as a two-fingered 'V' sign and its rude meaning in much of western culture). The third is the indexical mode in which the signifier is not arbitrary (as Saussure suggested) but is directly connected to the signified – in a recording (a photograph or video), signatures (including trademarks), and measurements (by a clock and a barometer). In each of these three modes – symbolic, iconic and indexical – signs work in different ways. (However, in a photograph all three systems may work at once. Barthes postulated that the still photograph has unique semiotic quality, possibly of a captured 'reality' devoid of a signed meaning.)

The signified also became the object of study in the late twentieth century. Some scholars, notably in cultural and media studies, often call it 'the form' or 'the medium', and suggest that it has the capacity *on its own* for meaning. Barthes regarded this as fundamental: 'Semiology is a science of forms, since it studies signification apart from their content.'[4] The form or medium may be a book, a newspaper, a theatre play, a song, or vinyl or CD recording, and in given contexts each may contain meanings. The theorist Marshall McLuhan wrote in 1964 that literacy (writing, speeches, books, newspapers) was typographic technology that had imposed over four centuries 'principles of continuity, uniformity and repeatability' as a medium in which the message was of rationality in western society. But radio, he said, was a contrary electric medium. Its content can only play other media (music, plays, speech), transmitted with an immediacy that gave it 'its power to turn the psyche and society into a single echo chamber'. Moreover, the meaning in radio could be transformed, even unintentionally. In 1938, a New York radio station broadcast a dramatised version of H.G. Wells's novel *Invasion from Mars* in the **form** (or medium) of a radio station interrupting normal music programming to make news reports about an alien invasion by Martians. Thousands of listeners *believed* the form to be a 'news-reality' broadcast, not a radio-play, and a mass panic ensued as thousands fled the city, causing road traffic accidents and some deaths. From this, McLuhan suggested that 'the medium was the message'. He said, 'In the electric age man seems to the conventional West to become irrational.'[5] Since then, some cultural theorists argue that the print medium was the medium that gave vent to modernity, and that electric media (and especially the web on the internet) now enable postmodernity.

Literalness of the sign

Signs are further categorised into analogical (where signs adopt metaphorical qualities, like a clock face showing the hour of the day) and digital (as in a digital watch showing a precise numbering of hours, minutes and seconds in what purports to be a literal representation of time – which has no material form). Some semiology notes the stronger attachment of humans to analogical signs – perhaps because they seem to romanticise the signified, and defy the over-rationalisation and over-structuring of our world through digital representation. This makes analogue equipment seem more stylish – more 'postmodern'. It suggests a retreat in popular culture from literalness.

Signs can thus range in their *distance* from their referent (the object they point to). Their form may seem close or distant in appropriateness. This can be deliberate distancing so as to make signs only understood by certain groups in a society, or to cause deliberate confusion. For instance, satirical comedy uses signs to which there is more than one meaning, and play on the distance between literal and inverted meanings. To say 'Do you get the joke?' in satire is to ask if you read the sign correctly. Analogical signs thus develop an important function, especially historically. The historian who approaches past societies expecting rational, straightforward digital signs (i.e. clear and unequivocal signposting from the signifier to the signified) for things (referents) may be confronted with signs whose meaning is extremely hard to discern. Moreover, because a given signifier may signify more than one signified (and thus generate two or more signs), it is entirely possible – even culturally very common – for one analogue sign to be hidden in another digital or analogue one. An example of this issue will be given in the section on Application in History.

How signs relate to 'reality'

How signs relate to the objects to which they are pointing – to 'reality' – is an area of great importance in postmodernism. It introduces the notion of different constructions of **knowledge** – suggesting, as many current theoreticians suggest, the existence over time of multiple knowledges.

Saussure argued that the sign bears no direct relationship to anything outside the sign. As a linguist, he argued that humans only construct reality within a closed sign system. This was not a denial of the existence of reality – only that reality cannot be perceived by humans outside of the sign system. So, the signified is not the object itself, only a mental construction that mimics it. Consequently, the signified is socially constructed by its circulation between a user and consumer of the sign in a given society.

The implication of this is very significant: instead of the world determining the order of our language, our language determines the order of the world. Since the 1960s, this notion has set in train some of the key advances in postmodernism. Michel Foucault was the great theorist of this.

Box 2.3   *Michel Foucault (1926–84)*

Many regard Foucault as the most influential writer and thinker of the second half of the twentieth century. His influence endures. He is certainly the most important figure of postmodernism. As a philosopher, theorist and historian, he argued that knowledge is socially constructed by different ages (what he called 'epistemes'), and that the age of modernity from the eighteenth to the mid-twentieth centuries created a knowledge system that postmodernists must dismantle. This included undermining modernist essentialist discourses on gender, homo- and heterosexuality, race and mental health (which caused sexism, homophobia, racism and prejudice towards the learning disabled). More widely, it included displacing the age of reason with an age in which truth was recognised as unstable, and in which the uncertainty of science and medical science was revealed. His work transformed structuralism into poststructuralism, giving birth to the challenge to the social sciences and their constant state of self-scrutiny ever since. Put crudely, Foucault argued that if structures are socially constructed items of knowledge, then there can be no *science* (which implies certainty over rules or laws) in the study of society at all. Through books on the history of discourses (notably *Madness and Civilisation* (1961)) and books on knowledge (especially *The Order of Things* (1966) and *The Archaeology of Knowledge* (1969)), he provided the central texts of postmodernist scholarship. He was the first postmodernist to deeply influence the academic world (ranging from literature studies, through sociology, History and geography, and on to cultural studies). He was the first to stimulate both left-wing radicals and new radicals (notably feminist scholars). He transformed the method of scholarship, first, by prioritising the study of discourses (giving rise to a system of inquiry we explore in Chapter 3), and second, by urging scholars to ignore the author (of literature and historical sources) in favour of the reader (who must already understand the knowledge of signs and myths in the author's writing, as Barthes had argued). This transformed academic study in much of the arts, humanities and social sciences in the late twentieth century.

Foucault wrote extensively on how the European mind has under-stood the world by creating rank orders. In his book *The Order of Things* (1966), Foucault argued that in Europe between 1000 and 1960 there were three major epochs of knowledge which he termed 'epis-temes'. 'In any given culture and at any given moment', Foucault wrote, 'there is always only one *episteme* that defines the conditions of possibility of all knowledge, whether expressed in theory or silently invested in a practice.' The western episteme he sub-divided into the Renaissance episteme (approximately 1450–1650), the classical epis-teme (1650–1800), and the modern episteme (1800–1966). (There is also the suggestion that at his time of writing, in 1966, he sensed that the modern episteme was crumbling, giving rise to the postmodern episteme.)

Box 2.4 *Episteme*

An epoch of knowledge, of which three are often studied, following the lead of Michel Foucault. The episteme of pre-modernity (pre-1800) was characterised by the *ordering* of signs, modernity (1800–1960) by the *history* of signs, and postmodernity (c.1960–) is consumed by the *inten-sity* of signs in 'hyper-reality' (which we explore below on pages 82–3). Epistemes may overlap and be at different stages in different places. Thus, it might be argued that the United States since the 1960s has had an overlap of modernity and postmodernity in the struggle between conser-vatism and (post)modern liberalism, between religious fundamentalism and secularism.

Foucault said that sign systems worked differently in each episteme.

In the Renaissance, he argued, a sign (most often a word) was intended to bear the qualities of the thing it was signifying. The signifier and signified were, in this form of knowledge, taken to be tied together. The sign was an *essence* of the thing. 'In its original form', Foucault wrote, 'when it was given to men by God himself, language was an absol-utely certain and transparent sign for things, because it resembled them. The names of things were lodged in the things they designated.' To understand the world of things, therefore, Renaissance knowledge sought to represent the words – the signs – as ciphers to be understood. Signs were likenesses, what Foucault termed the 'similitudes', of the things they represented, and were there for man to decipher. So, the study of language in the sixteenth century was organised beside the study of science, with the knowledge of things linked by their names.

Encyclopaedias coupled words to things by means of adjacency, kinship, analogy and subordination found in the natural world itself. The printed lists of names of things indicated how the names and the things were both ranked by the list itself. Hierarchies of words corresponded to hierarchies of things, leading to interpretation being circular – commenting in signs (words) that engrossed the things, by trying to approximate *to* the thing, by language trying to *be* the thing. Learning was trapped in an endless circular pursuit of better understanding the very words that signified their properties.

In the following Classical period of 1650–1800, Foucault argued, there was a revolution in knowledge, with language breaking off its affinity with things. Signs or words as *essences* of things changed into signs as *markers* of things. There was a linguistic turn by philosophers of the late seventeenth and eighteenth centuries, a sort of pre-Enlightenment, in which the sign became an *analogy* of the thing. This opened up intellectual analysis to genuine commentary. Reason now dictated that the signified (the thing) must pre-date the sign and the signifier, and that things were no longer ordered by affinity (in lists) but by opposition (in pairs of opposites). So, analysis of the world became dominated by opposites: man/woman, Christian/heathen, sane/mad, respectable/rough, science/superstition, and so on. Where previously there had been close affinities – in the wise fool, for instance, who could see things 'normal people' could not – after c.1650 good and bad became assigned to these pairs. This led to studying the history of language as a way of understanding civilisation. Foucault quotes Diderot in the 1750s: 'The language of a people gives us its vocabulary, and its vocabulary is a sufficiently faithful and authoritative record of all the knowledge of the people; simply by comparing the different states of a nation's vocabulary at different times one could form an idea of its progress.'[6] From an awareness of language as bearing the history of our world in words, what we now call 'analysis' arose in the commentaries of early Enlightenment scholarship.

Then, episteme change came again, according to Foucault, in the late eighteenth century, in the late Enlightenment. Here, the system of knowledge evolved as the trilogy of *signifier—signified—sign*. This made reason, as built on empirical evidence, the route to a knowable 'truth' and a 'reality' that could be represented in scientific words. Science and scientific method came to rule in all human sciences, society and government. This system of science-based knowledge monopolised the West until the mid-twentieth century, being the basis for modern higher education and thus the basis for promoting History as a subject. It could deliver an understanding of the roots of everything, a system for showing origins, for accounting by a story of progression for the advancement of civilisation from a primitive state to its increasingly perfected state in modern Europe.

The mid-twentieth century was the jumping-off point for Foucault's intellectual challenge. He challenged the presumption of Enlightenment science, its belief in truth and reality. He doubted the ability of observation in a state of 'neutrality' using scientific method, to deliver a single, unchallengeable description and analysis of the world. The scientists of the Enlightenment had in 1800–1900 overturned the work of the Classical theoreticians of 1650–1800, who in their turn had undone the Renaissance concept that the sign engrossed 'reality' in a divinely inspired union of words and things. Now, Foucault urged a new 'linguistic turn' in the late twentieth century to reveal the social construction of the sign and the meaning of language.

This is where Foucault's work drives the historian (and other scholars) towards revolutionising how to study. If accepted, the implication of semiology – the study of signs – is that the sign has the ability to convey meanings. Within the culture in which they circulate, those meanings take five characteristics. These are (1) apparently normative (that is, they appear normal, correct and indisputable); (2) *apparently* universal in time and place; (3) in a sense overlooked and unremarked in their own time and place because they are normative and thus without contradiction; and (4) part of wider myth systems. Those complex and hidden meanings of the sign (5) do *not* include 'reality'.

In the postmodernist position, the implication of this semiotic logic is that signs are the building blocks in the *construction* (approximation or modelling, if you like) of what we humans think 'reality' is. But signs do not enable the *reconstruction* (or imitation) of reality. The postmodernist argument is that because the world is made up of an infinity of events, big and small, and history was similarly composed of an infinity of events, the human encompassing of 'reality' has limitations. These are:

● First, a human representation of 'reality' can never be complete (the mind, the books the libraries, the computers are all way too small to engross something so huge).

● Second, it can never replicate the complexity of relations between things.

- Third, such a representation can only be attempted by giving signs (names) to everything, and these are culturally determined.

- Fourth, the representation can only be attempted by ordering those signs – that is, putting the structured signs of a given culture into culturally influenced lists, or stories, or narratives which did not exist in 'reality' and which bear no resemblance to it .

- And fifth, the representation of reality will change from period to period, and culture to culture, and from the perspective of the constructor, and is thus impermanent – thereby denying its own possibility.

For each of these reasons, 'reality' is demonstrably unreconstructable. No historian can do this. This is a fundamental and non-negotiable conclusion of the postmodernist, the litmus test that separates the postmodernist from the non-postmodernist.

Theory summary

This chapter has discussed the theory behind what is known as 'the linguistic turn' – the turning upon language as the primary problem of academic research and debate. The concept of the sign as the way to understand knowledge was the big breakthrough towards postmodernism. It did not, on its own, cause postmodernism, but it presaged it. Use of sign-analysis, or semiology, is not limited to postmodernists. If modern theories of the sign are understood, the rest of postmodernist theory starts to fall into place with a compelling logic. But many scholars (including many historians) deploy semiology without being postmodernists because sign-analysis is a basic method of historical analysis.

The theory discussed here is that 'reality' is something made *in culture* with the signs, myths, discourses and texts created by that culture. It has no 'existence' beyond those signs, myths and so on. This is not a denial that history is composed of events, the small and verifiable constituents of the past. It is just a denial that those events can be pieced together to make some neutrally observed, complete and verifiable whole in History the subject. As a discipline, History cannot reconstruct the past nor portray reality.

Application in History

Semiology is very powerful as an applied method in History when it is combined with other techniques (which we shall encounter in the next four

chapters). But, there are two major research areas which are purely semiological in focus. The first is the historian's use of language. The second is
decoding signs.

Historians' words

Semiotics has compelled all academics, including historians, to look very
closely at the words they use. This is especially important when we use
words in narratives – like History books and essays. This looking closely
is called **reflexivity**, or **problematising** the words we use, and sometimes
de-centring the words we use. Together, these mean we *turn upon* language. We give our attention to words, as the very heart of interpreting
things we read and write in History. We think about language in historical
sources and in History books.

For the good student sitting down to write an essay, the first thing to
do is to 'turn' on the words, the terms, the presumptions in an essay question. Discuss, turn over, and explore the possible ambiguities, dubiety of
meaning, the multiplicity of presumptions in the question. In studying
social history, for instance, we should think about the meaning of terms
like 'social class', 'plebeian', 'proletariat' and so on. We should consider
why we are using those terms (and how we understand them), and how the
meanings we have relate or fail to relate to the meanings used by contemporaries in the period being studied. Does the term 'working class' mean
the same in 2005 as it did in 1805? Is it possible and legitimate to use it in
relation to 1705 or 1605 when not all the terms were in use? What are we
trying to infer by using terms as analytical tools that were not used at the
time?

This kind of reflexive concern is now meat and drink to the historian,
and the postmodernist would argue that reflexive concern with the signifiers and what signifieds we are intending must be explored and made
plain. This is not an act in disabling language, but in showing a complete
awareness that words are conveying hidden meanings before we even get
into the first footnote. It is the foundation for the wider practice of reflexivity to which we return in Chapter 6 on Self.

Decoding (1): Cats and Witches

In History, the sign can be studied at the macro or the micro level – signs
that define entire cultures, and small signs that provide a way into understanding larger issues in cultural history.

A classic micro-study of signs was that of the 'Cat Massacre' in eighteenth-century Paris. In 1985, the historical anthropologist Robert Darnton published an essay-length study of a document that purported to describe a single event in a Paris print works in 1735 – the execution and mock trial of cats by print workers, while their master and his wife were away from home. The district of Paris had been plagued for days by cats' howls at night, and the workers were annoyed. Darnton applied principles of sign-study, coupled with great knowledge of the historical context of Paris, the print industry, labour and social relations, to deconstruct a 990-word account by one worker who was present. Darnton focused on the worker's concept of the joke and our inability to 'get it'. 'Where is the humour in a group of grown men bleating like goats and banging with their tools while an adolescent re-enacts the ritual slaughter of a defense-less animal? Our own inability to get the joke is an indication of the distance that separates us from the workers of pre-industrial Europe.'[7] Darnton dwelt on the medium (the mock trial) and the key sign (the cat). As medium, he argued that the 'trial' was composed of the overlapping of common media in early-modern society – burlesque, carnival, rough music and mock trials. These were united in a single ceremony expressing worker-power.

This power inverted the social order by turning the world upside down, equating the cat with the master's wife and the master's wife with being a witch. He showed how cats were central to the carnival, being used con-stantly in ritual enactment of human executions, and mock trials in artisan trades. As a sign, Darnton said that the cat had specific denotations in Parisian society – as a sexual and especially female sign, as a sign of the bourgeoisie, and as a metaphor for witchcraft. As sexual metaphor, the French terms *'le chat, la chaste, le minet'* meant the same thing in French as 'pussy' in English, and Darnton showed how French culture associated a man's ability to woo cats with wooing women. The cat was also a symbol of the female bourgeois (whilst male artisans tended to see them as a nuisance to be chased out and exterminated). The cat suggested witch-craft, and the linking of cats to ill fortune was (and remains) widespread in European culture. So, motivated by a dispute with the master over wages, the workers adopted the joke 'worker rebellion' of a mock trial, killing the beloved cat of the master's wife and then 'trying' it *as if* they were trying the bourgeois *in absentia*. Labour protest used humour by pointing to the wife's extra-marital affair, her likeness to a witch, and to the master's cuckolding. On discovering the execution of her cat, she, being more aware than her husband, told him that the workers had attacked her sexual honour and that they wanted to murder him – whilst the master, being oblivious to his wife's infidelity, apparently failed to get the point. The insult was so carefully constructed from the cultural media and signs of the period, Darnton argues, that it masked the workers from retribution, leaving them free to re-enact it several times in a revelry of carnival.

Darnton is a famous critic of postmodernism, yet his exceptional scholarship is widely considered to be postmodernist in method. His study of the cat massacre is certainly grounded on the perspectives and sensitivity of the semiotician. His work is not without controversy, and we shall return to his study of the cat in Chapter 5 when we look at the theory of the text. But on its own, Darnton's article-length study is a classic study of signs in History.

A second well-known study of signs is Diane Purkiss's analysis of the witch in early-modern England. The significance of 'witch' as a sign has been studied directly (as well as indirectly by many scholars like Darnton, above), and it has taken on new levels of interest from the work of Purkiss in treating it as a sign needing to be read in both its sixteenth- and seventeenth-century context and in the twentieth-century context in which the historian operates. She used a very close reading of accounts of witches in the twentieth century and at the time of the witch-hunt to show 'how the witch acts as a carrier for the fears, desires, and fantasies of women and men both now and in the early modern period'. She showed how the one sign 'witch' has had various signifieds and different myth systems that need careful understanding of their immense symbolism.

Purkiss found significant sign-features in the narratives of depositions written down from witch accounts and witnesses. She identifies food as a constant theme of witchcraft, not just as a context but as a target of witch powers. Witches were seen as targeting food for demonic transformation. Food would be transformed by witches into other commodities, implying (says Purkiss) subversion of the natural female good order of the larder and the kitchen. Purkiss reveals the witch, too often regarded solely as the church's or man's 'other', being imagined by the female accusers and witnesses of the sixteenth century as the antihousewife, antimother, antiwetnurse, and antihousekeeper. This made a female witch something for other women to fear in their own selves about house and maternity. The witch became a demon to remind women of their shortcomings. She shows that in both processes of being bewitched and being unwitched, the body of the early-modern English witch was perceived as characterised as being literally fluid, composed of liquid rather than solid flesh. Purkiss interprets one case, where a woman seems to choose to behave as a witch was expected to behave, as an act of resistance to male puritan divines. With church vilification of the feminine, women turned more to magic and fairy tales to fill the gap left by a hostile reformed church trying to erase and abandon control of popular memory of 'popish' ritual. This was a process in which women had agency. Witch trial deposition became a process of rewriting existing cultural materiel and women, in part at least, 'scripted their own story'.

Taking the story forward, Purkiss shows how the witch was transferred from trial deposition to the Elizabethan stage, appearing in nearly every one of Shakespeare's plays – whether as metaphor, joke, story or piece of the plot. Purkiss suggests this may have represented a growing urban–rural, bourgeois–plebeian division in which the witch was idealised by urban ruling orders. Rather than increasingly *fearing* witches, the middle orders by 1600 were having their growing scepticism of magic nourished by dramatists mining popular beliefs for fantastical plots to be used in subversive or satirical ways. The witch becomes 'a muddled signifier' in the early seventeenth century as scepticism grew, and drama reflected this – to the extent, Purkiss says, that London theatres were closed when puritans banned sceptical portrayal of demonic subjects on the stage during witch trials of the 1640s.

Purkiss's work is controversial, in part because, as a literature specialist, she is seen by a few historians as displaying an absence of sufficient concern with verifying the actual experience of the witch-hunt and witchcraft of the period. But that is another and quite legitimate story to arise out of the witch issue. For feminist scholarship, the numerical dominance of women amongst those accused of witchcraft (and of adjacent, female-dominated 'crimes' like evil-speaking) makes her study of the witch as a sign a very fruitful combination of postmodern literary and historical skills.

Decoding (2): Carnival

The birth of modern cultural history in the 1960s and 1970s rested on study of carnival and the world turned upside down, and used study of signs and the media in which they are located. The carnival in mediaeval and early-modern Europe emerged as a prime medium of popular culture in which structure, order and change in society could be discerned. Historian Bob Scribner placed carnival central to the Reformation in Germany as a medium within which the Catholic order was pilloried in humour, thereby turning the world upside down in ritualised, temporary displays involving masks, elaborate floats and the election of temporary alternative elites to the priests. In another study, Scribner applied Barthes' theories in an interpretation of popular woodcuts during the German Reformation. Scribner revealed a world of thought (not found in written or printed documents) in which traditional cultural signs with old meanings were *re-coded* with new, Protestant meanings.

Historians came to interpret the signs within carnival as a temporary inversion of the power order of society: a common man being elected Lord of Misrule, a young lad being made Boy Bishop, a leading harvester being made Lord of the Harvest. While the Lord of the Harvest performed an economic as well as symbolic and judicial function, the Boy Bishop represented a sign of temporary social inversion, another world of carnivalesque to which the people resorted in a strong tradition from the late mediaeval to the nineteenth centuries. Yet, historians have seen the burlesque located within carnival not merely as a temporary inversion of the social order, able to remind authority of the power that still resides with the people (often in purely physical terms), but as a language available for peasant revolt and even for revolution – as in Emmanuel Le Roy Ladurie's study of carnival at the town of Romans in France. Even into the nineteenth century, carnival represented a medium profuse with signs usable as a force for social commentary and change. Obversely, societies where carnival and indeed all non-word signs *disappear* are also of interest. Anthropologist Jack Goody has pioneered study of the disappearance of images (mimesis) in favour of the Word (Scripture) amongst the Calvinist and puritan Reformers of the sixteenth and seventeenth centuries (in Scotland especially), when all the media of mimicry (from paintings to drama) were banned for undermining the desired unknowability of the Divine.

Awareness of the digital versus analogue nature of signs is a common feature of the historian's job, especially in relation to the study of popular culture. One example occurred in a carnival context – on Tuesday 22 January 1443 in Norwich when a merchant, John Gladman, rode on horseback 'like a crowned king' through the streets. He was then in the midst of a high-profile dispute over rights to some grain mills. He was prosecuted for attempting to set up as a new king and start an insurrection in the city. However, the defence was that the riding had involved 'makyng myrth, disportes and pleyes' – in other words, a merry drama involving disguise. Where before interpretations had revolved around one account or the other, historian Chris Humphrey's analysis was that both were 'true'. He concluded that the riding was a deliberate copy of the customary annual Shrovetide parade in which someone would guise as the king, permitting ritualised fun-poking and complaint at a mock monarch. But the event had proceeded *deliberately* on a different day a month earlier to give it an edge of heightened criticism. So, it was a pursuit of a well-established and legally accepted right (and rite) to mimic the monarch, but by doing so on a date not authorised for such mimicry, real criticism was thereby suggested. The signifier was constituted not just of the act of mimicry but also of the date; the one without the other was open to different interpretation, and made a different sign. Such mock king and mock mayor celebrations were to remain a feature of European life until the nineteenth century, involving days of ostensible exclamations of loyalty to royalty, but which turned, often without any real change in the behaviour of the crowd, into ritualised attack on monarchy and authority. So, mock kings and such like could be both acts of loyalty (in a digital or 'straight' sign) and acts of treason or republicanism (in a mimicry that was analogical, including irony and satire). So, careful reading of a sign as analogue or digital, or possibly both, is of some moment to the historian.

In this work, social historians draw closer to the theories and agendas of anthropologists, especially symbolic anthropology. They argue that ritual behaviour should be interpreted as signs that act to define and affirm boundary groups ranging through kinship families, communities and nations. Rituals became signs to be decoded. For historians of popular culture, calendar customs have become extremely important for examining the nature and meaning of identity, social organisation and power: mumming plays, guising in masks, riding or beating the bounds on foot or horseback, sword-dances, funeral rituals and so on. Signs in ritual are important, not just for the passive circulation of ideas, but as media in whose ritual production the individual participates – including rituals of monarchy, the state and religion. Historians are thereby drawn further away from established theories that view the common people as pawns of powerful people and ideologies, and increasingly see them as agents of history – whether for change or tradition.

Decoding (3): Food, old age, death

Piero Camporesi produced revealing studies which decoded the rituals of food and drink consumption in seventeenth- and eighteenth-century Italy, and showed how such protocols could reveal detailed aspects of the social and gender order. On a similar tack, the history of the family is understood increasingly through the rituals and symbols in the home – what John

Gillis calls 'the symbolic universes', e.g. of meals, of ageing – the changing rites being seen as marker posts for the changing nature of the family. Getting old was seen in the nineteenth and early twentieth centuries as a linear journey through life, but in what has been called 'the postmodern era of aging' it has been replaced since the late twentieth century by the notion of 'a perpetual state of becoming' – retraining, re-educating, recycling. The study of war memorials, and of the rituals of war remembrance and the representations of bodies in art and prose, has developed into a major field of inquiry into the changing nature of masculinity and of the impact of war, especially in the early twentieth century. Indeed, the crisis of masculinity of the 1910s and 1920s has been discerned by historians very much in the form of materialised signs – monuments of men injured, dying or defeated in spirit, and of rituals remembering loss, not celebrating victory.

Semiotic analysis has increased the perceived importance of understanding culture to the work of the historian. A given ritual might be found in the twelfth and twentieth centuries in almost identical form, but did it mean the same 800 years later? Empiricist historians have in the past tended to answer this 'yes', assessing ritual on the criterion of 'tradition': a ritual is 'genuine' (or real) if it is authentically old, but 'invented' and thus not 'real' if it is new (however that newness was measured). But cultural historians of the semiotic age turned this on its head. They argued that the survival of *form* did not imply the survival of *meaning*, and indeed it was entirely possible for the meaning to have changed very dramatically whilst the form stood more or less still. In other words, the form was a vehicle in which the signifier and signified had very loose connections. The instability of meaning in sign systems became translated to historical contexts – the changing meaning of the English Guy Fawkes bonfire and fireworks ritual between the 1660s and the present day being an obvious example, when the form remained little changed. In my own study of the Shetland winter fire festival of Up-helly-aa, I found at different times a ritual form (guising, or mumming, in masks to the accompaniment of fire and gunpowder charges) that changed meaning *and* a meaning (celebrating community freedom from civil and church control) that changed form. The sign could survive but the referent could change. So, diachronic study (of changing sign-meaning over time) and synchronic study (meaning changes between different contexts or places) both developed within History.

Semiotics provided cultural history with the theory-shift from empirical certainty to cultural instability as far as the meaning within cultural activity was concerned. Cultural history emerged with a system of thought that saw in the symbolic and ritual activity keys for understanding societies and power systems in the past. By undermining the certainty of empirical significance to events in the past being the same as in our place and time, the study of signs also undermined traditional certainties of value judgement placed by historians in rituals. Speaking of eighteenth-century plebeian protest, the cultural Marxist historian Edward Thompson said that the historian's task was 'decoding the evidence of behaviour'.[8] Where once the division between high and low culture in rituals was understood as a calibration of social advance and civilisation, social and cultural historians have now overturned hierarchies of culture and their certainties of meaning in favour of exploiting ritual to understand the hidden languages within cultures.

For the student to do

Decoding the past is not an invention of the postmodernists, but it is has been especially well theorised by them and made commonplace in branches of History where it was previously absent. For the student in search of a dissertation topic, there are many application opportunities.

One of the best sorts of historical feature to approach is that of ritual. Rituals come in very many forms – from official religious rites (christenings, marriages, funerals) to the semi-official (the churching of 'unclean' women after childbirth), to the rituals of the seasons (sowing, harvesting, May Day, New Year and Christmas), to annual festivals of local identity, many of which still survive in some form or other today. There were often common features to rites and rituals: guising (or mumming), offerings, short dramas, inversions of roles (boys dressing as adults, men as women, servants as lords), music with songs, and sometimes lampooning and satirical attacks upon key figures in the community, using music, song and posters. These events offer opportunities for gathering empirical information on how rituals were observed in different periods, contrasting differences, and then decoding what meanings may lie behind the various elements. Rituals can be more fascinating when they need to be 'rediscovered' – within riots, street-fights, trades union marches, church communions, political demonstrations, or temperance parades. This can be enormously enriching and entertaining, yet theoretically challenging.

Roland Barthes offers an example of what a student could do in relation to politics and race. He was concerned with the survival and dominance of capitalist-bourgeois-imperialist culture in France in the 1950s. He came to understand that this dominance relied on the way that a culture of racist imperialism (which promoted the superiority of the white over the black, and the affection of the African black for French imperialism) was made normal in French society. He studied this through images found in a magazine – in particular, an image of a black African soldier saluting the French flag. This sign denoted superiority and affection which everyone in France was encouraged to believe was true. This *making normal* in culture, making a universal and incontestable proposition of life, is something the student can study. How were images of black people in Britain in the 1880s or the 1950s normalising messages about British colonial superiority? What language was used to describe black people? How far, and when, did these signs diminish?

The student may wish to spend time studying the twentieth century, when, many scholars argue, signs became more important. There was an increased intensity of signs in popular culture, a heightened changeability to signs, more diversity to them, and a much greater significance for the sign as a marker of social change. Signs in advertising, comic-strip stories, non-verbal images in our daily lives (including in film and television) have become more common since the 1960s and the electric revolution in media. The student has great opportunity for study here.

Many signs are most often located in rituals. The American historical anthropologist Clifford Geertz stated: 'Practically, two approaches, two sets of understanding, must converge if one is to interpret a culture: a description of particular symbolic forms (a ritual gesture, an hieratic statue) as defined expressions: and a contextualization of such forms within the whole structure of meaning of which they are a part and in terms of which they get their definition.'[9] This is describing the sign–myth link marked out by Barthes. Decoding of signs has developed as a major concern of historians. It is not limited to postmodernists, and has been used for decades. But it is now a much more common device of the historian and offers great opportunities for the student in History.

Guide to further reading

Theory

For a modern comprehensive guide to the theory of signs, see the excellent D. Chandler, *Semiotics: The Basics* (London, Routledge, 2002). On theory of the sign, start with R. Barthes, *Mythologies* (orig. 1957, English edition, London, Vintage, 1993), reading its examples of how to study popular culture, and then conclude with the last chapter on theory in 'Myth today'.

More difficult but extremely rewarding is M. Foucault, *The Order of Things* (orig. 1966, reprinted English edition, London, Routledge 2002). On the theory of the medium is the message, see M. McLuhan, *Understanding Media: The Extensions of Man* (orig. 1964, Cambridge, Mass., MIT Press, 1994). For a useful introduction to symbolic anthropology, see A.P. Cohen, *The Symbolic Construction of Community* (Chichester, Ellis Horwood, 1985).

History

The classic study of the cat as a sign is R. Darnton, *The Great Cat Massacre and Other Episodes in French Cultural History* (orig. 1985, New York, Basic Books, 1999), pp. 75–104. Deconstructing the sign of the witch over 400 years is undertaken in D. Purkiss, *The Witch in History: Early-modern and Twentieth-century Representations* (London, Routledge, 1996). For signs in the German Reformation, see R.W. Scribner, *Popular Culture and Popular Movements in Reformation Germany* (London, Hambledon Press, 1987), especially pp. 70–101, and R.W. Scribner, *For the Sake of Simple Folk: Popular Propaganda for the German Reformation* (Cambridge, Cambridge University Press, 1980). One of the best and most concise examples of decoding signs in historical anthropology is the history of peasant struggle for rights in the forest, recounted in P. Sahlins, *Forest Rites: The War of the Demoiselles in Nineteenth-Century France* (Cambridge, Mass., Harvard University Press, 1994). A challenging study of signs and theatre is J. Goody, *Representations and Contradictions: Ambivalence towards Images, Theatre, Fiction, Relics and Sexuality* (Oxford, Blackwell, 1997).

On decoding signs in carnival, see N.Z. Davis, *Society and Culture in Early Modern France* (London, Duckworth, 1975), especially pp. 97–151; P. Burke, *The Historical Anthropology of Early Modern Italy* (Cambridge, Cambridge University Press, 1987); B. Bushaway, *By Rite: Custom, Ceremony and Community in England 1700–1880* (London, Junction, 1982); E. Le Roy Ladurie, *Carnival in Romans: A People's Uprising 1579–1580* (Harmondsworth, Penguin, 1981); E. Le Roy Ladurie, *Montaillou: Cathars and Catholics in a French Village 1294–1324* (London, Scolar, 1978); and C. Humphrey, *The Politics of Carnival: Festive Misrule in Medieval England* (Manchester, Manchester University Press, 2001). For my own decoding of signs and forms in a fire festival in the nineteenth and twentieth centuries, see C.G. Brown, *Up-helly-aa:*

Custom, Culture and Community in Shetland (Manchester, Manchester University Press, 1998).

On decoding eating and drinking customs, try P. Camporesi, *The Magic Harvest: Food, Folklore and Society* (Cambridge, Polity, 1989) and P. Camporesi, *Exotic Brew: The Art of Living in the Age of Enlightenment* (Cambridge, Polity, 1994). Signs in family life are scrutinised in J.R. Gillis, *A World of Their Own Making: A History of Myth and Ritual in Family Life* (Oxford, Oxford University Press, 1997) and signs concerning injured bodies in the twentieth century are studied in J. Bourke, *Dismembering the Male: Men's Bodies, Britain and the Great War* (London, Reaktion Books, 1996).

Notes

1 R. Barthes, *Mythologies* (orig. 1957, English edition, London, Vintage, 1993).

2 M. Foucault, *The Order of Things* (orig. 1966, reprinted English edn, London, Routledge 2002), p. 42.

3 J. Derrida, *Of Grammatology* (1967) quoted in V.B. Leitch (gen. ed.) *The Norton Anthology of Theory and Criticism* (New York, Norton, 2001), p. 1826.

4 Barthes, *Mythologies*, p. 111.

5 M. McLuhan, *Understanding Media: The Extensions of Man,* (orig. 1964, Cambridge, Mass., MIT Press, 1994) pp. 10, 15, 299–300.

6 Foucault, *The Order*, pp. 39, 40, 42, 97, 183.

7 R. Darnton, *The Great Cat Massacre and Other Episodes in French Cultural History* (orig. 1985, New York, Basic Books, 1999), pp. 77–8.

8 E.P. Thompson, *Customs in Common* (London, Merlin, 1991), p. 73.

9 C. Geertz, *Negara: The Theatre State in Nineteenth-Century Bali* (Princeton, Princeton University Press, 1980), p. 103.

CHAPTER 3

Discourse

The sign is the basic unit of the postmodernist conception of the system of knowledge. Signs come lumped together to make up the *discourse*, which was theorised in the 1960s and 1970s. This is the major vehicle within knowledge for conveying meaning. The **discourse** is what historians and other academics most talk about in their study of culture and society, whether in the past or now, and you will see the word frequently in History books, especially in social and cultural history. This chapter explains the theory and the application of this central postmodern concept.

Theory

Defining discourse

The discourse has become so much used in the academy that there may not be a central agreed definition. Even Foucault, its greatest theorist, spoke in 1969 of 'discourse' as something 'which I have used and abused in many different senses.'[1] The recognition of its centrality is not confined by any means to postmodernists. As early as 1929, the Russian Marxist Voloshinov was concerned with the social power within language, and he was approvingly described by the modern Marxist theorist Terry Eagleton as 'the father of what has since come to be called "discourse analysis"'.[2] The discourse has become widely recognised as a focus for investigation by historians of different topics, periods and countries, and by historians who deploy differing **categories of analysis**, differing methods, and differing ideological starting points.

Michel Foucault envisaged the discourse as the pivotal link in a chain of links by which a '**knowledge**' could exist within a given cultural condition (or episteme). The discourse is the *location* of this knowledge (and is also the one most accessible for study). The discourse is the most noticeable cultural entity in the whole chain of links. We can recognise discourse quite easily in culture. This is how I understand the chain that he proposed:

sign–statement–positivity–discourse (and its sites of exteriority)
–discursive formation–episteme

This needs explanation. Starting at the left, the chain moves towards the right. We have already met the **sign** (composed of the signifier–signified–sign). It is individual, small and possibly fleeting and impermanent. At the other extreme, we have encountered the **episteme** – a vast system of knowledge of a whole historical epoch (like modernity from c.1800 to 1960). It will govern ways of thinking and understanding the world for millions of people over generations. The sign and the episteme are the two extremes of knowledge – one small, the other vast. In between are links that enable the system of knowledge of the episteme to exist. These links allow each sign to come into being.

Foucault's explanation is as follows. The sign is a meaning that can only exist at the same time and at the same place as other signs with similar or supportive meanings. Together, these signs require a statement. The statement is not a grammatical or linguistic formation, but is a set of (unwritten) rules of existence for the signs. The statement defines the possibilities of appearance for each sign. It has no single author, but rather the authors (such as writers or scientists or clergy) are assigned by the statement. In other words, the statement grants authority to the authors, and determines what each can say. Similarly, the statement cannot exist on its own. Foucault said '... [A] statement always belongs to a series or a whole, always plays a role among other statements, deriving support from them and distinguishing itself from them: it is always part of a network of statements, in which it has a role, however minimal it may be, to play.'[3] This mutual existence is based on each statement having an 'enunciative function' in which each and every statement in that co-existence is constantly circulated and affirmed in the culture. The original statement exists as an act of memory in society, endowed with the ability to be modified but to retain a weightiness and constancy of use. So, the effect of a statement is not transitory but enduring.

'Positivity' is perhaps the most obscure of Foucault's terms in this chain. By it he means the putting into practice of statements and the discourses that they constitute. This practical application may be done by professional bodies and societies that provide a quasi-official imprimatur or authority. More loosely, 'positivity' is a description of enactment (by, for example, a professional body of a science discipline that publishes a journal) that turns statements into **discourses** and more than mere expressions of opinion. Positivity is the thing that makes them statements that matter in a society, whilst Foucault additionally suggests *interpositivity* as the interaction between them (between different science societies, such as geology and geography societies) to create mutual respect and recognition for their common interests and discursive formation.

A discourse, unlike a sign or a statement, is not a material thing. It is a message which is embedded in the signs, and which arises from them as a group of statements. Foucault wrote that 'the term discourse can be defined as the group of statements that belong to a single system of formation'[4] – a discursive formation within which many statements and a very large number of signs co-exist in mutual support. Barthes described the nature of the discourse. First, it is immediately obvious to its target audience. It requires no study for the intended reader to understand it. A discourse is plainly obvious. Indeed, it is so obvious as to be the norm. Second, a discourse is encountered innocently in everyday life and causes no shock, no surprise, as it is already naturalised in every reader (Barthes: it 'transforms history into nature'). It has a history, a past, which makes it suitable for historical (or diachronic) study. Third, the reader does not see the discourse as a semiological system purveying a value or a command, but as a fact. The semiology is hidden by the discourse; to be a semiologist is to stand outside the discourse and be able to disbelieve its 'fact'.[5] Foucault puts this another way by saying that a discourse creates a truth-effect. The reader always thinks a discourse is true. The discourse is like a sign in its qualities. It sits in opposition to another discourse. Just as the sign 'mouse' relates positively (vertically) to 'hole', so the discourse on the good 'housewife' relates to 'respectable'. Equally, just as 'mouse' relates oppositionally (horizontally) to 'rat', so 'housewife' relates oppositionally to 'harlot'. In a simplistic way, a discourse is conceived as an injunction that something is good, its opposite is bad. There is thus a *this/that*, or *on/off* quality to discourses. This means that embedded in every discourse is a sense of 'the other', even when it is not specifically mentioned.

The individual discourse may be a large or small injunction, but works with other discourses in a discursive formation of mutually supporting messages. Each discourse gains an acceptance outside of its own positivity (or specialist field) in what Foucault terms 'sites of exteriority'. These sites are places like newspapers, the academic press, government reports, the churches and other professions where the discourse gains acceptance. This acceptance often takes the form of a policy of the civil state. It is a site exterior to the originating positivity or profession.

Lastly, these sites of exteriority allow discourses to unite in a discursive formation. This is a unity of mutually supporting messages that grow into a huge body of knowledge and understanding that becomes the *knowledge system* of an episteme. The system of knowledge of an epoch is thus supported by a complex network of elites and agencies of the state, science, the churches and other bodies which each have specialist discourses that they circulate to each other, mutually supporting those of other elite groups and agencies. They create a massive system of political power and authority, wedded to a system of knowledge which they affirm and protect. This is well rooted, deeply embedded in the official and popular culture of the episteme, and difficult to dislodge or challenge. Knowledge is power. But power is not the *acquisition* of knowledge; it is not the elites collecting items of data. Rather, power is the *practice* of knowledge as a socially constructed system, within which the elites spread their messages or discourses.

These six layers, taken together, are put forward by Foucault as ways of understanding 'the archaeology of knowledge'. In order to understand how it works, here is a brief example of how the chain of knowledge might operate in practice.

The word 'witch' was a powerful sign of early-modern Europe. Popular culture was dominated by the notion of the witch, and the use of the term as a device of community policing, especially against women. Official church and state witch-hunts in the sixteenth and seventeenth centuries brought thousands to trial accused of witchcraft, with women making up as much as 80 per cent of the total. Here is a brief and schematic way in which we might understand how the scholar might interpret the impact of 'the witch' as a sign by progressing through the six layers of knowledge.

- *sign* – The female 'witch', composed of the word 'witch' as the signifier and the concept of the woman possessed by the devil as the signified. In the early-modern period, this sign existed side by side with another sign – that of the 'disorderly woman', who must be controlled, and her piety ensured by discipline. This was to be imposed by an idealised strong family man who, if he failed in this task, was to be considered weak and ineffectual. In this context, the witch was a sign that invariably reflected badly upon men and their masculinity.

- *statement* – The statement accompanying this sign originated in the late mediaeval period, when official and popular concern with superstition and women in particular acquired a new resonance that increased at the Reformation. From c.1350–c.1730 (depending on country), state and church instituted commissions and laws that encouraged the demonisation of female witches in European society. These laws provided the statement – the official blessing – to the circulation of the sign of 'the witch'.

- *positivity* – The state and the churches (both Catholic and Protestant, though especially the latter in northern European countries), sanctioned legislation, commissions and procedures in civil and religious courts that encouraged evidence from informers that resulted in thousands of trials and executions, predominantly of women. This positivity put the sign of 'the witch' into a practice of the society.

- *discourse* – The discourse, or message, of the sign is that Christian society is riddled with an anti-Christian conspiracy, organised in covens around a male devil, in which women predominate, and which makes women the principal cause of impiety in communities.

- *discursive formation* – The discourse on the witch sat beside other discourses on women that characterised them as unruly, potentially dangerous to the Christian family, and to Christian society at large, and that conversely (as every discourse has an 'other') depicted piety as mostly masculine in construction. Many other discourses joined that on 'the witch' – discourses concerning the church, superstitious practices and the witch's use of demonic powers to undermine the economic livelihood of neighbours.

- *episteme* – This is the time in the pre-modern and Classical epistemes (c.1350–c.1730) when 'the witch' sign had this meaning. This is when the 'knowledge' that women were susceptible to being witches found authentication in a wider gender construction of society, and in the absolutist notion of the monarchy and the divine origin of knowledge. The 'witch' was only one element of the wider system of pre-modern knowledge.

In this way, the discourse sits in the middle of any system of knowledge. It is the place, as Foucault suggests, where knowledge resides. But it depends on the one side on the existence of supportive signs which generate signifiers embedded in culture, and on the other side on the larger knowledge system – the episteme – providing context and support for each sign. But it is the discourse that the individual knows and confronts. It is not a thing, in Foucault's view, but a *practice* – a doing, an activity and a normalised thing in society, one enjoining activity and conformity. To transgress the injunction of a discourse is to become deviant. The discourse is thus about **power** to which elites will commend each member of society to adhere.

Postmodernism suggests that the way to understand society is by the connections *language–knowledge–power*. The ultimate power in a society is not the physical control of the army or police. Nor is it the collection of knowledge. It is power vested in language that demands that every individual internalises it and by which s/he becomes self-disciplined. The citizen becomes his/her own policeman through a language of discourses dominating their thoughts and activities. This internalised power became more powerful in Foucault's estimation in modernity, following the Enlightenment from around 1800 to 1960, when 'reason' became a device to encourage self-discipline in the individual. The dominant words used and circulated in daily life encouraged individuals to enforce social norms upon themselves, their family and community. Before 1800, said Foucault, the *ancien régime* was based strongly on overt physical control of the individual – through the regal state, feudal relationships and the church, backed up by fierce punishments for transgressors. By contrast, urban and industrial Europe after 1800 saw most manorial, state and church power dissolve in favour of a bourgeois puritanical code of behaviour enforced mainly by family and community. Foucault believed this made discourses more important after 1800 because it shifted power from the state to the individual, from external to internal. This proposition attracts many historians to discourse analysis – looking at what discourses were circulating in society.

Historians are also attracted to the relationship of the individual to the discourse. Though Foucault's work exaggerated the power of the discourse over the individual, other scholars have since argued for the power of the individual to negotiate their attitude to the discourse. This means that there was no blanket acceptance of discourse. Far from it. Every individual is drawn into a critical awareness of a range of options – from accepting a discourse, to rejecting it, and positions of semi-acceptance that might conceal a deeper rejection. An individual might recognise the 'official' discourse that a man and woman should be virgins on marriage. But each individual decides on their attitude to this idea whilst by no means broadcasting an outright opposition to it. This is the type of negotiation we make in daily life – whether to obey a social norm, or just to appear to accept it, or to reject it. The variations could be endless and subtle. This topic of the relationship of the discourse to the self, to the individual, generates a great deal of research in postmodernist History, and we return to it in Chapter 6.

Discourses are not limited by period or place. They are everywhere in human experience. The postmodernist argues that the scholar needs to be very conscious of where discourse may be lurking – in almost every human form of communication, including clothes, grimaces, and ritual. We today as a multi-cultural society note the tolerance of difference in our moral regime. We recognise that discourse is a vessel for prejudice – including racial prejudice, xenophobia, sexism, religious bigotry, and homophobia. We instinctively understand these as linked **essentialisms**, with a common origin. Postmodernism explains this common origin as the system of knowledge of modernity. Today, we are much more sensitive and reflexive to language-use than was the case in the past, and this sensitivity should make us better historians.

The discourse of History

Roland Barthes argued that the historian is never neutral. The writing of History, he said, projects its own discourse – the discourse of History.

Barthes says that this has a distinguishing feature. All discourses work because they seem to be true. Most discourses claim that their truth is contained within, by being *a priori* obvious and eternal. Two sexist men exchanging the sexist discourse 'Men are superior to women' contain 'the truth' within their exchange, with no need for further referents to support it. But the discourse of written History, spoken between a History lecturer and a student, for instance, seems true for a different reason. Written History relates to an external fact that cannot be contained in the discourse. The referent is external to the discourse. In other words, uniquely for a discourse, there is no attempt by an historian to pretend that the past (which is the signified/referent) is contained in the discourse. It is gone and unrepeatable. The historian uniquely claims a circulating discourse to be true by arguing that it is not *a priori* true, but has been accepted in the profession as a result of rational thought, empirical endeavour and research. It is the claim that the historian is a professional who must be trusted, on the basis of **peer** support, in his/her judgement. This is unique. The signified or referent seems to disappear in the historical discourse. The historian justifies his/her 'fact' by making the signified dissolve, in favour of the absorption of 'the real' into the sign. This happens in the historian's narration which, because of his/her professional and tested ability to narrate the past, makes the fact 'real' within the narrative. The 'fact' is the historian's substitute for the past, and is drawn into the historical narrative. As Barthes said, the History narrative 'draws its "truth" from the careful attention to narration, the architecture of articulations and the abundance of expanded elements (known, in this case, as "concrete details")'. The result is that historical narrative becomes both the sign and the proof of reality.[6]

This is a controversial postmodernist proposition. Empiricism argued that History could be neutral, scientific, rational, empirical and judgement-free. Many historians resist Barthes' suggestion that the History narrative consists of discourses. Barthes says that every word used in a History book is a sign, every sentence has a discourse, and often more than one. The historian is being judgemental at every turn. Postmodernism argues that all of History-writing is discourse.

Authorship

Who is the author of a discourse? This is an important issue for the postmodernist. The short answer is that there is none. This is because, with a discourse conveying a major meaning, the discourse exists prior to any author who circulates it. To be understood, the author must be writing a message already known by the reader.

In a famous essay in 1968 called *The Death of the Author*, Roland Barthes argued that in the act of writing, the author 'dies'. The text that is left exists free from the author, and becomes a work of the reader. A novel only exists in the reader (and in the act of reading), because every reader 'reads' the novel differently, according to their understandings of myth and language, and their own experiences. A text is separated from the author. What he or she writes depends on mythological languages that pre-existed the act of the author writing.

Barthes attributed little room for the creativity of the author in narrative. Freedom is greatest at the level of the sentence, where the author's creativity may be little more than embellishment. The freedom diminishes at the higher levels of narrative structure, such as writing the plot (known as *emplotment*), where the choices are all pre-known to reader and author alike (and are clichés). A book or a film or an article only manages to achieve a communication between author and a reader because the reader already knows the myth system to which it adheres. Otherwise, it would fail to communicate. Barthes went further and argued that there is no real distinction between biography and autobiography – that in autobiography an author is writing a biography of the person he/she imagines him/herself to be, and has no claim to privilege over 'the truth' of his/her own past. There is no 'reality' to the autobiographical 'I' which is any more authentic, privileged or authoritative than that of an outside biographer. This reinforces the notion that there is no authoritative interpretation of any text, even that of one's own life.

Foucault affirmed Barthes' points on the author. It was not the author who wrote, but society itself, or the dominant classes within it. Foucault argued that historians spent too much time studying the author of a document, when its importance was in circulating discourses that were understood by all those who read it. That understanding came from the work (i.e. the discourses) having been in existence *before the author wrote*. Thus, Foucault wrote: 'the author does not precede the works', meaning that, on the contrary, the works (the discourses and sign-system) precede the author setting about authorship of a text.

This means changing the tasks of the historian – from merely reflecting on who wrote a document and what facts can be learned from it, to also considering what discourses it contains, and who gains power from their circulation. As Foucault pointed out:

All discourses, whatever their status, form, value, and whatever the treatment to which they will be subjected, develop in the anonymity of a murmur. [In being aware of this,] We would no longer hear the questions that have been rehashed for so long: Who really spoke? Is it really he and not someone else? With what authenticity or originality? And what part of his deepest self did he express in his discourse? Instead, there would be other questions, like these: What are the modes of existence of this discourse? Where has it been used, how can it circulate, and who can appropriate it for himself? What are the places in it where there is room, for possible subjects? Who can assume these various subject functions? And behind all these questions, we would hear hardly anything but the stirring of an indifference: What difference does it make who is speaking?[7]

This should not be accepted as a call by postmodernist historians to abandon empirical verification of historical sources. Rather, it indicates that the real power in a document, its discursive power, existed before the author wrote. To the historian, this should mean that the culture that generates the discursive formation is far more potent than any single author. The historical source is the product of the discourse in its time and place, and the historian's attention should fall upon the discourse rather than the document's author.

Theory summary

The **discourse** links with other discourses as messages about ideal behaviour (and its opposite, anti-ideal behaviour). The discourse is an activity, demands something be done. It is a 'doing', not passive. It commands 'do this, but not that'. Every individual negotiates their position in relation to this command, ranging from obedience, through hypocritical subservience, to outright rejection. The discourse is difficult to ignore. It is at the forefront of popular culture. However, it is not a material thing but a message contained in the sign – which is a material thing. Lots of signs deliver lots of discourses, which together constitute the real way in which knowledge is power.

The discourse is a central focus of postmodern History. The historian sees in it the exercise of power in a way that is characteristic of an episteme or epoch. To focus on discourse in an historical document is more important than merely researching the author of a document or other source – for s/he is doing little more than re-circulating the discourse, giving it some new words, but not seriously amending it. In studying discourse, the historian will be studying raw power in any society.

Application in History

The postmodernist historian invests heavily in the discourse. It is the key to new social history and to cultural history. Through it the historian can study political power at its base in any period and country.

The research method is called 'discourse analysis'. It was Foucault who formulated and inaugurated how this can be a method of History-writing and also suggested the initial agenda for research. He had three major interests as an historian: the history of madness, the history of sexuality, and the history of prisons.

In/sanity and sex

Foucault argued that madness was a social construction (a discourse) that went through four distinct historical phases. In the mediaeval period, madness was regarded as a special quality, even a holy quality. In the Renaissance, the second phase, it became seen as a form of high knowledge, as a revelatory experience, as ironical high reason, reflected in Shakespeare's use of mad characters and fools as mediums for revelation and insight in his plays. In the third phase from c.1650, madness was dramatically reconstructed as pure unreason, as a threatening and fearsome illness, something that had to be confined in asylums or bedlams, and something which 'rationality' claimed could be corrected by bizarre and tortuous treatments. Then, fourthly, in the eighteenth century the mad were defined as sick people, the object for the new practice of psychiatry that could claim to restore reason and rationality to the mad. In Foucault's eyes, this rationality still underlay psychiatry in the mid-twentieth century. But this was challenged from the 1960s by anti-psychiatry and some modern therapy that said madness was relative, not absolute – a condition of the mind on a wide spectrum that we should recognise in a less fearful division of sanity from insanity.

In this way, Foucault argued that discourses on madness changed with social context – with each episteme of knowledge. From a cultural equanimity in the mediaeval period, through vicious imprisonment to psycho-analytic treatment of the interior of the mind, the discourse of madness finally internalised the power of rationality within each individual. Foucault sought to demonstrate the same process of discursive power becoming internalised in his study of prisons. What he called the 'the fabrication of the disciplinary individual'[8] was the aim of the modern prison. The prison was not to punish (as in the Middle Ages), but to correct, and act as a fearsome reminder to the potentially deviant and miscreant to conform to acceptable discourses. The prison acted in the same way as the asylum in demanding in the punishment regime that the individual should acknowledge their deviancy and unreason.

The final and most personal internalisation of discursive power, arguably the ultimate internalised power, was in sexuality – what Foucault called 'bio-power'. In his final multi-volume study of sexuality, he said that the great Enlightenment project re-conceived the sexual nature of the human being, with the body acquiring two poles of interest: one as a medical entity that had to be explored and dissected as a machine, the second pole as a social machine that the individual him/herself had to discipline, make rational and useful to industrial-capitalist society (turning up to work on time, sober and compliant). From this, Foucault said an 'ascetic morality' of prudery and sexual restraint was imposed through a new use of a rational Christianity, promoted by a puritan bourgeoisie. 'This is why in the nineteenth century', Foucault wrote, 'sexuality was sought out in the smallest details of individual existences; it was tracked down in behaviour, pursued in dreams; it was suspected of underlying the least follies; it was traced back into the earliest years of childhood; it became the stamp of individuality – at the same time what enabled one to analyse the latter and what made it possible to master it.'[9] At all levels of society, sexuality became controlled through the power of gossip, respectability, the intense scrutiny of behaviour, and the criminalisation of homosexuality and minor misdemeanours of conduct. And by the end of the century, Freud and the emerging discipline of psychiatry portrayed sexuality (and its suppression) as the root of all human actions, intensifying interest and, ironically, prurience.

Women

The body emerges as a major focus of the postmodern historian. Discourses on the perfect body have changed radically according to period. The discourse on the body imposed **bio-power** upon the individual, and this has become a powerful concept for cultural historians. In particular, women's history pioneered study of discourses on the female body. Feminist history derived from the discourse an enormous conceptual and moral impetus.

Using bio-power as a tool for the analysis of discourses, women's historians were diverted from using *patriarchy* (the external force acting on women's subjugation) as their primary **category of analysis** to the *discourses* of women's inferiority and subjugation (as internal forces). This was the move from seeing women's subordination as mainly externally imposed (by male institutions) to internally imposed (by discourses internalised from culture).

In a 1976 book *Alone of All Her Sex*, Marina Warner studied the cult of the Virgin Mary and its discursive construction of ideal womanhood. She studied Mary in the five major roles that she has been given within discourse – as Virgin, Queen, Bride, Mother and Intercessor. Using imagery in early Christian statues as well as documentary evidence, Warner showed how the biblical representation of Mary was developed in these different themes. In analysing sermons by Bernard of Clairvaux during the years 1135–53, Warner demonstrated that the Christian discourse on sex portrayed a tension between sex and piety, between ecstatic sexual union where the man is attracted by female eroticism, and a pristine and self-denying soul unsullied with primal sexuality. Sex is rendered in this discourse as not sinful, but transitory, unable to attain the sustained bliss of heaven. Only one person ever attained this perfection: the Virgin Mary. 'Assumed into heaven, seated at Christ's right hand, she becomes the example for every Christian of his future joy. She was, according to Bernard, filled with love because she bore love itself in her womb.' In this way, Warner analysed the complex strands to the discourse on Mary. Her analysis showed how women were expected within Christian culture to look to the Virgin as their special example to be followed, though never completely emulated. She acknowledged that the myth of Mary had changed very dramatically over two millennia, but demonstrated how such discourse change was portrayed by the Catholic Church and her promoters not as innovation, but as a constant stripping down to an old and absolute truth. She cites Barthes who noted that 'in myth, things lose the memory that they once were made'.[10] Warner's work is a good example of how the historian needs to be aware of this quality of the absence of *memory* in myth, how it forgets where it originated in order to imply a universal quality. This helps to explain the power of myth as well as the difficulties in eliciting from the archive the answer to the question: 'When was the myth or the discourse born?'

Judith Walkowitz's 1992 book *City of Dreadful Delight: Narratives of Sexual Danger in Late-Victorian London* explored how discourse change occurred in the construction of anti-ideal woman. Hers was a study of prostitution in Victorian London which used the Jack the Ripper murders of 1888 to explore the development of intellectual and popular discourses on the vulnerability of women. Circulated in newspapers and academic debates, this vulnerability discursively banned the 'respectable woman' from being alone in 'dangerous' city spaces, and cast women in the lasting role of urban victims in modernity. She explored how the discourse on vulnerability was developed amongst male medical elites, matching the development of a popular discourse in newspapers and magazines of the period that argued that the respectable woman needed to avoid danger by being confined to the house or to the company of a man. This type of discourse analysis sits side by side with more conventional study of legislative and political history. Indeed, it was Walkowitz herself who published both types of study. Her earlier major study had been on the operation of prostitution *law* in Victorian Britain. With her move to discourse analysis, she was able as an historian to provide a sophisticated and rounded approach to an issue.

Discourse analysis of the changing construction of idealised (and anti-idealised) womanhood has explored changes to women's identity as circulated in all sorts of media. Considerable attention has been paid to the nineteenth and twentieth centuries when women's and family magazines, girls' magazines, novels and films, displayed the ideal woman in a domestic environment, shying from the worldly sphere, as a woman who should, ideally, not do paid work but be kept by a husband.

Discourse analysis is by no means limited to women's history. It is to be found applied across all branches of history. Discourses on race, ethnicity, religion, masculinity, social class and nationality in all periods of history are studied by historians. The literature is very large, and some examples from other areas crop up in later chapters.

For the student to do

Discourse analysis is probably the easiest way for a History student to incorporate a postmodern technique into his or her work. In the use of sources for critical commentaries or a gobbet study, there is invariably the opportunity to comment on the discourse or discourses than can be seen in a historical source.

Sticking with the example of women's history, here is what a British Christian magazine of 1844 said a woman should be:

Zeal and activity are, in their own places, excellent and essential qualities; but Christian women require to be very cautious, lest, even in the midst of praiseworthy exertions, they sacrifice those meek and lowly tempers which are so calculated to adorn and promote the cause they love and advocate. Female influence should shed its rays on every circle, but these ought to be felt, rather in their softening effects, than seen by their brilliancy. There are certain duties which sometimes call Christian women out of their quiet domestic circle, where both taste and feeling conspire to make them love to linger; such duties will, we humbly think, be best performed by those who enter this enlarged field, not from any desire of a more public sphere, but because, in obedience to the precepts of their divine Lord, the hungry are to be fed, the sick comforted, the prisoners visited.[11]

This is an obvious document for commentary and exploration of the discourse it pervades. It can be linked to the context of the Victorian period and the middle-class world from which it was drawn. It can be contrasted with working-class experience where a woman often had to work out of economic necessity. It can form the basis for showing the complexity of a single discourse, and how women (even bourgeois women) may have negotiated their way around it.

More broadly, the study of a series of sources from a period can form the basis for a research essay or dissertation. There are particular aspects of a discourse that can be pinpointed for study. Particular occupations had their own journals and magazines, and it can be an important task to explore the nuances of a discourse when it was circulating amongst certain groups. The beauty of discourse analysis is that it is conceptually quite quick to grasp as a method of inquiry, and can produce discerning and revealing additions to areas of historical knowledge. Seek out the topic that is interesting, and think about the types of source that would be suited to explore a period and place. Include visual and audio sources, especially from the twentieth century, as they are full of discourses. Later in this book, we look at some examples of visual analysis.

Guide to further reading

Theory

Foucault is not easy to read, especially not in M. Foucault, *The Archaeology of Knowledge* (orig. 1969, English edn, London, Routledge, 1997). Still, this is the book where he sets out how discourses operate within the wider system of knowledge. To understand it in the context of historical theory, the more readable R. Barthes, 'The discourse of history', in K. Jenkins (ed.), *The Postmodern History Reader* (London and New York, Routledge, 1997), needs to be looked at. But to get a digestible account, see the valuable A. Munslow, *The Routledge Companion to Historical Studies* (London, Routledge, 2000). Landmark discussions by a postmodernist historical theorist are Keith Jenkins, *Re-Thinking History* (London, Routledge, 1991) and his later *Why History? Ethics and Postmodernity* (London, Routledge, 1999).

On the theory of the author, the two principal (and, thankfully, fairly short and straightforward) texts are R. Barthes, 'The death of the author', in Roland Barthes, *Image, Music, Text* (London, Fontana, 1977), and M. Foucault, 'What is an author?', in P. Rabinow (ed.), *The Foucault Reader* (Harmondsworth, Penguin, 1984).

History

It is worth sampling at least one of Foucault's ground-breaking discourse analyses in M. Foucault, *Madness and Civilisation: The History of Insanity in the Age of Reason* (orig. 1961, London, Routledge, 1965); *The Birth of the Clinic: An Archaeology of Medical Perception* (orig. 1963, London, Tavistock, 1973); *Discipline and Punish: The Birth of the Prison* (orig. 1975, English edn 1977, Harmondsworth, Penguin, 1979) or *The History of Sexuality. Volume 1: An Introduction* (orig. 1976, New York, Vintage, 1990).

Good examples from women's history are M. Warner, *Alone of All Her Sex: The Myth and the Cult of the Virgin Mary* (London, Picador, 1976, 1990 edn.) and J.R. Walkowitz, *City of Dreadful Delight: Narratives of Sexual Danger in Late-Victorian London* (London, Virago, 1992). For a wider look at bio-power, see Thomas W. Laqueur, *Making Sex: Body and Gender from the Greeks to Freud* (London, Harvard University Press, 1990).

Notes

1 M. Foucault, *The Archaeology of Knowledge* (orig. 1969, English edn, London, Routledge, 1997), p. 107.

2 T. Eagleton, *Ideology: An Introduction* (London, Verso, 1991), p. 195.

3 Foucault, *Archaeology*, p. 99.

4 Ibid., p 107.

5 R. Barthes, *Mythologies* (orig. 1957, English edn, London, Vintage, 1993), pp. 129, 130–1, 137.

6 R. Barthes, 'The discourse of history', in K. Jenkins (ed.), *The Postmodern History Reader* (London and New York, Routledge, 1997), pp. 121–3.

7 M. Foucault, 'What is an author?', in P. Rabinow (ed.), *The Foucault Reader* (Harmondsworth, Penguin, 1984), pp. 118–20.

8 M. Foucault, *Discipline and Punish: The Birth of the Prison* (orig. 1975, English edn 1977, Harmondsworth, Penguin, 1979) p. 308.

9 M. Foucault, *The History of Sexuality. Volume 1: An Introduction* (orig. 1976, New York, Vintage, 1990), p. 146.

10 M. Warner, *Alone of All Her Sex: The Myth and the Cult of the Virgin Mary* (London, Picador, 1976, 1990 edn), pp. 129–30, 335.

11 *Free Church Magazine*, 1844 vol. 6, p. 171.

CHAPTER 4

Poststructuralism

The structuralism that had been laid out by Saussure (as well as others) reached a height of popularity in the 1950s and 1960s among historians as well as anthropologists and sociologists. This was based on the primacy he attributed to the spoken sign over the written one, and the implicit urge to find the 'authentic' original of any sign. But with increasing attention focusing on the sign and the discourse in those decades, the intellectual faults in it were becoming exposed by the early 1970s by those, like Roland Barthes, who were its keenest and most original advocates. His dissatisfaction led to the pioneering of poststructuralism.

Theory

Poststructuralism is an element of postmodernism, but in a sense it has a separate theoretical existence that allows many scholars to adhere to it whilst rejecting postmodernism as a totality. Poststructuralism as a coherent intellectual practice predates postmodernism. It was the term of choice to describe new cultural theory from the late 1960s and for much of the 1970s, and retains a separate body of support in the academy. But definitions get a little confused because of the way in which, over the past few decades, some scholars have conflated poststructuralism and postmodernism.

Structuralism

In the 1950s, structuralism established a dominance as the operating theory of radical social science. It was especially influential in France, signalling the beginning of French dominance in modern cultural theory – an influence that has continued right down to the early twenty-first century.

> **Box 4.1**   *Structure, structuralism*
>
> A structure arises in academic inquiry when a **category of analysis** is turned into a fixed **reality**. For a Marxist, social class is the primary category of analysis to be used in studying History, and the Marxist can be regarded a structuralist because of this focus on the structure of class. So, structuralism is the academic approach of regarding structures in the past (and present) as the key frameworks of academic analysis in subjects ranging from Sociology to History. It is challenged by poststructuralism (see Box 4.3).

As we saw in Chapter 3, Saussure argued in the 1910s that language is constructed of a sign, which is itself composed of a signifier and a signified. These have an arbitrary relationship, not founded on resemblance of either to the object (the referent). In turn, the signified is not the external object (or referent), but is only a *concept* of it. Because there is no link between the language system and outside 'reality', the language only operates because each speaker adheres to strict rules or structures for its use. If s/he did not operate in accordance with those rules or structures, there would be nobody to understand what s/he is saying. This means that the structures are pre-known to each speaker.

In Saussure's view, the signifier and signified for a given referent are founded on the principle of difference – of each signifier being different from another, and of each signified being different from another. Thus, a differential *structure* has been set up as the foundation for language. In this, each signified has an opposite, the whole conducted as a ruled-based system: male–female, black–white, good–bad, and so on. Each pairing includes a 'good' and a 'malevolent' signified, giving value and judgement to each signifier. So, each signifier comes laden with moral value. These are then used in combinations in syntagmatic or linear relations. Saussure gives as examples 'God is good', and 'If the weather is nice, we'll go out'. A syntagm is thus a methodical alliance of interconnecting signifiers that create a meaning (a larger sign) in the form of a chain (usually a sentence) in a text. At the same time, each signifier and signified has a paradigmatic relation with signs and referents not present – 'God' and its absent Other, 'the Devil', or 'good' and its absent Other, 'bad'.

Structuralism as an academic system arose out of this linguistic development. It became translated from language to culture. It focused on the syntagmatic oppositions in language, and how such oppositions were prevalent in all cultures. Structuralists in cultural studies and anthropology took to the study of divisions at one moment in time (synchronic study) rather than historical (diachronic study). The emphasis was on cross-sectioning culture rather than historicising it. The beauty of this approach was that because of the pairing of opposites, there could be a closure (a finality) to both the meaning of language and culture, and to the understanding of it by scholars. This approach was best exemplified by the French anthropologist Lévi-Strauss.

Box 4.2 *Claude Lévi-Strauss (1908–)*

Lévi-Strauss is an anthropologist who in the 1950s, inspired by Saussure, developed semiology as a way of exploring the structures of civilisation, using especially the notions of kinship, totemism and myth. From the late 1950s to the early 1970s, he fostered cultural research on the identification of binary oppositions as universals of the human mind. These, he argued, were apparent in all cultures (though often determined by natural factors such as geography and climate). These oppositions were represented for Lévi-Strauss in the myths, totems and rules of kinship that could not be understood in isolation from one another. If the entire language system was understood according to its rules and structures, including the universal rules, then each code of any culture could be comprehended. Moreover, this seemed to fit neatly with the presumptions of empiricism – namely that the object of study could be viewed by the observer externally at a distance, looking upon it as a closed system of meaning. Lévi-Strauss became a controversial figure for his views on women's place in culture, his apparent anti-westernism, and a sense that pervaded his work of progress being malevolent.

This synchronic approach, based on a study of structures at one point in time, led to Lévi-Strauss identifying certain key oppositions of all societies. The most controversial of those he identified was male–female, which he 'read' using structural semiotics as a binary opposition whose meaning in all cultures is that of the superiority of men over women. This approach naturalised the gender hierarchy as a given, and took the subordination of women as the root of culture. In the 1970s and 1980s, feminist scholarship reacted with vigorous hostility to this effective categorisation of women as cultural objects, not agents, in kinship and social relations. It seemed to demean women, not just in the culture concerned, but in the research too. But in terms of structural analysis, it provided anthropologists and some historians with a way of reading myth, attracting literary theorists and others.

Structuralism has had only limited impact in historical scholarship. One of the reasons is that the theory is in one sense essentially anti-historical. Lévi-Strauss, as its greatest exponent, deliberately eschews a narrative approach that permits historical change to be noted, but instead follows the study of myth through different moments of history simultaneously. On the other hand, the presumption that academic study of society could be undertaken from the point of view of the external observer fits readily with the views of the empiricist historian. It implies that there is a 'truth' to be known, to be understood through its pretty fixed rules, and to be accomplished by the better collection of data. In its emphasis on foundational structures in society and culture, and on closed systems to be understood from outside, structuralism has a strong affinity with Marxism. Louis Althusser (1918–90) came to prominence in France in the late 1960s alongside Lévi-Strauss and others with a commitment to social change built on a re-emphasis of the individual's subjugation to capitalist control through 'ideological state apparatuses' (including churches and schools, the family and media), and by a process that he called 'interpellation' in which the individual is summoned or hailed by ideology and constituted as a subject (of control). This was Marxist structuralism with a vengeance.

Structuralism and Marxism have in the eyes of postmodernist critics suffered from a denial of agency to individuals within cultures. People are seen as tools or victims whose cultural as well as economic lives are determined by the working out of impersonal structural forces. Though Marxist historians are more diachronic than synchronic (that is, more interested in historical change than in structures at a given point in time), they place emphasis on the structuring of society into social classes, and the working out of class struggle as the agent of historical change. Most postmodernist critics would wish to re-centre the individual as agent of action.

One of the leading structuralists was Roland Barthes. He is also considered one of the founders of poststructuralism. This is an important conundrum. In his works of the 1950s and 1960s, he sought to apply Saussure's structuralist analysis of closed language systems to elements of popular culture. Yet, he went on in the 1960s and 1970s to write less scientifically and more *playfully* (some have said) about popular culture and texts. He used language filled with irony and satire to question the role of the author, the existence of a fixed reality, and the structural elements of all sorts of texts – including the celebrated conflating of autobiography and biography in his book *Roland Barthes by Roland Barthes*. He became bored with the structuralist project of reducing all narratives to a common grammar. He found that the infinite number of narratives that could be written was offset by a tiny number of structures, and this limited inquiry. So, he moved literary studies from an emphasis on the *context* to the study of the *text* – from the external structures to the internal pre-figurations of the work. This was the ineluctable move from structuralism to poststructuralism. By the early 1970s he had taken many of the radical young theorists with him.

Poststructuralism

Poststructuralism is widely regarded as having its foundation amongst French philosophers and their students, and a key moment for its emergence was the student rebellion in Paris in May 1968. Many regard the emergence of poststructuralism as the most philosophically significant of any event in postmodernism. From it has been traced the agendas, the methods and the directions of development of other intellectual and ideological movements – including in the 1970s feminism, postcolonialism and the gay liberation movement.

In this way, poststructuralism is credited with the moral challenge to all forms of prejudice founded upon pre-figured structures and **essentialism** (the attachment of inherent qualities to individuals through structural belonging). It can also be credited with underscoring disability action, the challenge to religious bigotry, and the rise of multi-culturalism. Poststructuralism stands out from the postmodernist agenda for its setting of a moral agenda that has transformed many world cultures, but more especially that of western Europe, Australasia and North America, whilst also being the philosophical basis for postcolonialism.

In Paris in 1968, students rebelled against the French state. The rebellion failed. This gave a stimulus to poststructuralism in a number of ways. First, it became clear to many radicals, both during and after the failure, that the usual Marxist class analysis of social action (and indeed revolution) did not explain what happened – the emergence of radical groups and agendas apparently divorced from socialist agendas of action. Secondly, the structures of everyday life that had been initially accepted within the occupied Sorbonne were challenged – principally by female students who refused to conform to the stereotyped role expected of them of cooking and housekeeping for the male students. Thirdly, the ineffectualness of structuralist Marxism, embodied in the long refusal of the Marxist CGT trades union to join the protest, led to students brandishing placards saying 'Structures don't take to the streets!'[1] The Marxist agenda appeared

---

Box 4.3   *Poststructuralism*

Postmodernism argues that all knowledge is constructed socially – i.e.
a fact is not a fact until it is called upon by a human (in a History
book for instance) and is given (a) linguistic form and (b) narrative
form. These two things – language and narrative – are always socially
constructed by humans in given cultures and given times. They are
thus constructed as 'facts' within structures of politics, culture,
religion, gender, sexuality, and so on. No 'fact' exists independent of
a structure. But the postmodernist opposes those structures being
taken as 'real'. They are inventions of the observer. For instance, a
postmodernist will criticise a Marxist for regarding social class as a
real thing, and accepting it as a concrete phenomenon. The poststructuralist argues that we need to be aware of structures, using them as
devices to aid inquiry, but then we need to **de-centre** them and **problematise** them for study. So, 'social class' should be studied for the
origins of the concept and the language, how the meaning of the term
changed in different periods and places, and what messages of power
were conveyed by the term and the concept (messages of social hierarchy, for instance). Then it should be joined by other categories of
analysis (such as gender, race, and so on). In this way, poststructuralism seeks to prevent any structure establishing a monopoly in
study.

---

to be failing in Europe. Meanwhile, the weakness of Marxist theory in the
United States, the leading anti-communist nation, left anti-authoritarian
radical groups like feminists and the black civil rights movement receptive
to a new type of radical thought that could offer better History and
prophecy.

Poststructuralism filled this gap. It was born simultaneously as social
movements and as theory. There were five main movements involved. The
first was student rebellion, seen by many as the apotheosis of the rise of
youth in western culture after 1945. The second was second-wave feminism (or the women's liberation movement) as it emerged very suddenly in
1969–70, giving rise to struggles for equal opportunities in work, pay, education, and for an end to discrimination in language and depiction. The
third was the emergence of gay liberation in the late 1960s, heralded by
liberalisation of laws on homosexuality. Fourth was the collapse of many
European empires in the 1960s and 1970s (those of Britain, Portugal,
France, Belgium and Holland), making way for European awareness of the
structures of Orientalism and race prejudice embedded in western white

culture and intellectual thought. And fifth was the rise of black consciousness within the United States and western Europe, allied to liberation movements in developing nations and to the anti-apartheid movement in South Africa, in all of which race discrimination and racial stereotyping became challenged.

In each of these five movements, there were two important common features: the disturbance of structures, and the questioning of language – of the signs that carried prejudice. The hierarchies of superiority, assumed within western culture since the eighteenth century, started to be challenged: the hierarchies of class, gender, sexuality, national superiority, religion and race. In language, the signs used to convey discourses on those hierarchies, superiorities and prejudices became challenged through direct action and pressure group activity: challenges to sexist language and images (such as naked women in advertisements), words of homophobia (poof, queer), and words of racist denigration (coon, nigger, paki).

In theoretical development, many structuralist scholars became overtly critical of structures. Roland Barthes rejected the pseudo-scientific agenda of the structuralist data-gathering, and came to doubt the ability of the observer to adopt a disinterested and neutral position from which to recount and analyse any object of study. He became convinced of the need to move from reading the structures to exploring the variety of meanings. This has been described as the move from an analysis based on understanding a game like chess (with all its moves listed) to an analysis based on reading texts as if they were plays. The text becomes seen as needing to be played with, explored and deconstructed for the varieties and ambiguities of meanings it contains. In particular, poststructuralism shifted the emphasis squarely from the author to the reader. It is a reflection upon the act of reading a text that exposes its meanings, not reflection on the act of writing it.

Poststructuralism attacked many structures as irrational, illogical, empirically unfounded, or morally unacceptable. In the United States, some (perhaps many) historians supported poststructuralism in the 1980s and 1990s because the academic interest in culture was shifting from Marxism. By whatever routes, structures were exposed not as universal 'realities', but as socially constructed discourses.

However, not all structures are so clearly unacceptable. There are structures that in themselves may not be immoral, but which pose complex issues concerning analytical results. Take the issue of social class. Within British history-writing, social class has been the most elaborate, developed and commonplace structure of historical analysis throughout the twentieth century. In the 1950s, 1960s and 1970s, it formed the very framework within which the explosion of social and cultural historiography occurred, centred on a Marxist analysis of the construction and historical development of societies (including British society). It posited class as a seemingly concrete reality that was constructed in both economic and cultural terms. But in the 1980s and 1990s, British poststructuralism challenged 'social class' as both concept and object of historical study. This reflected a dissatisfaction shared by theorists on the political right as well as the left, and amongst feminist scholars. Society became seen in the 1980s as more nuanced and less structured than the traditional concept of class could account for. Yet, society was overlaid with varieties of identity. Identity became seen as more de-centred, unstable and complex, with the 'self' emerging as a more active and complex agent than the passive and 'class-simple individual' described by Marxism or even Gramscism. The traditional manual 'working class' seemed to be disappearing from late-twentieth-century Europe, and power became seen as diffuse, configured by categories of gender, race, sexuality, interest group, dis/ability, religion and age. Feminist scholarship did much to undermine the universalised category of class. If gender was socially constructed and variable by context, with no historically fixed notion of 'woman' or of 'man', so the same must follow for social class.

The French poststructuralists took their vision of the world further in the 1980s and 1990s. One important figure was Jean Baudrillard.

Jean Baudrillard, in exploring why popular action failed in Paris in 1968, moved on to see western society as becoming overwhelmed with signs which were substituting for the 'real', in what he called 'hyper-reality'.

Box 4.4   *Jean Baudrillard (1929–)*

A French-born sociologist and postmodernist, Baudrillard was a newly appointed lecturer at the Nanterre campus of the University of Paris when the student revolt broke out there in 1968. As a participant in those events, he became over the next two decades the great commentator of the postmodern condition that the revolt seemed to introduce, especially in the world of art. He is a key figure in cultural studies, especially as a poststructuralist analyst. His notion of the simulacrum – the fake without the original – is a key way of analysing postmodern society and the dominance of the sign. In this context, he said that 'History is our lost referential, that is to say our myth.' He is also a critic of ethnology and the harm he perceives it has done to world cultures.

The sign became prioritised over the signified, as western society lost central realities in the death of God, the destruction of the environment, and western destruction of primitive and non-western cultures. Taken together, this constitutes a loss of the past that becomes recalled increasingly through consumerist signs conducted by consumer industries. Signs come back to haunt us in what Baudrillard called the 'simulacrum', the fake representation. This process continues in western society's drive to name everything, and in the process the sign replaces the thing. Baudrillard says *the sign murders*, killing the 'real thing' and replacing it. We sense this loss and indulge a search for the authentic, which only generates the better simulation (television's dramatic reconstruction, computer-generated models and so on).

This is an apocalyptic vision in which the sign, instead of being a *representation* of the referent, becomes in modern culture a *substitution* for it. For Baudrillard, this reaches its apogee in the way that ethnology kills the 'real' in the developing world. The anthropologist is devoted to searching, recording, naming and packaging of world cultures through participant observation, for the purpose of creating the museum and the reservation. But anthropology murders the original through preserving it: the 'savages' become 'frozen, cryogenized, sterilized, *protected to death*'. Non-western cultures are laid waste, and the medium becomes a medley of messages indistinguishable from the 'real'. Power and authority in history was linear, but in postmodernity it has become circular. Baudrillard wrote:

... *one can always ask of the traditional holders of power where they got their power from. Who made you duke? The king. Who made you king? God. Only God no longer answers. But to the question: who made you a psycho-analyst? the analyst can well reply: You.*

Thus, Baudrillard says, 'History is our lost referential, that is to say our myth.' Our society in the postmodern world is consumed, traumatised, by 'the disappearance of history, and ... the advent of the archive'.[2] History is displaced by the intensity of hyper-reality in which media predominate in our experience. We are at 'this vanishing point' of the past where news is instant and 'real time' (24-hour TV news), so that it almost cancels out the flow of time and suppresses the sense of geography – of events happening in another place. History disappears because the simulation is so good, so perfect, that it supersedes the real. At this stage of Baudrillard's vision, the historian Alan Munslow has suggested, 'there no longer remains a foundational standard by which we judge the-past-as-history'.[3] Structureless-ness becomes a quality of our understanding of the past and of our present.

Thus, the undermining of structures in poststructuralism falls into three types of process. First, there is the desirable loss of immoral structures (of race and gender, for instance) – something for which the historian should work, reflect on and pursue, in part by historical research to uncover these structures in the past, expose their cultural and linguistic existence, and explore their impact upon discrimination in jobs, pay and so on. Second, there is the process of de-centring structures like social class which are not obliterated from study, but become in themselves objects of study (their development and circulation in different periods and countries) as power hierarchies with links to inequalities by income, culture, house, health and place of residence and so on, but which vary in nature and structure by period and place. And third, there is the loss of structures through the proliferation of signs in hyper-real postmodernity, as described by Baudrillard, and the loss of the past through the supposed perfection of the simulation that kills the original to create the simulacrum. Each of these intellectual pursuits can be found explored before postmodernism developed a name (within Marxist social history in the 1960s and 1970s, for instance). However, at that time the theorising tended to remain profoundly structuralist (seeking to add, refine, and grade the structures) and did not form the intellectual heart of the historical project (which tended to remain class struggle). With Baudrillard, the centre of analysis moves out of the structure.

In the final analysis, the structure is unavoidable. A sign only exists as a sign (with a discursive meaning) when it is linked to other signs, and that linkage requires a structure. No structure is benign, but is active and pointed, giving each sign its potency. The discourses or meanings of a group of signs are *held* in the structure. The point of the postmodernist position is that the scholar must be alive to the structure, perceive it, describe it, acknowledge which discourse it serves, and how it organises power. Then s/he must decide openly what to do with it – to morally reject and analyse it, to problematise and then use it, or to acknowledge its disappearance in postmodernity.

Application in history

Structures do not disappear from study in the poststructuralist vision. Far from it, they take on a new importance at centre stage as objects of study. By studying a structure – its intellectual construction, its applications, its modes of circulation in a culture – we can dispense with it as a **category of analysis** (at least temporarily), and then return to it if needs be to use as a research tool. It is the *awareness* of structures that is vital, and the continuous questioning of the structures that are used to locate, order, categorise, classify and utilise 'facts' from the past. In a broad sense, poststructuralism is a suspicion of the effectiveness and scientific presumption of structures, tables, statistics and data. Whilst we need them, we can constantly question them.

Class

The study of the history of social class in Britain was transformed in the 1980s and 1990s when historians like Gareth Stedman Jones and Patrick Joyce in Britain re-explored 'social class' not as a structure but as a discursive framework. Joyce has been studying social class for over two decades. He started in the early 1980s by applying broadly cultural Marxist approaches, especially influenced by Gramscist perspectives on cultural hegemony by capitalist elites on workers outside as well as within the factory. His work on the culture of the factory in Lancashire stressed the way in which there was deliberate cultural manipulation by capitalists to treat working-class culture as something different from middle-class or elite culture, in need of specific forms of control.

From the late 1980s, however, Joyce's work became 'linguistically turned', moving to problematise the concept of class in Victorian Britain, and bringing to the fore the notion of the 'common people' rather than 'the working' or 'middle' classes. He studied aspects of popular culture to show this – especially the music hall, where he focused on music hall songs and the interaction of audience with performers. Joyce argued that the notion of 'the common people' revealed the weakness of social class as a Victorian fixed structure, as something fluid yet powerful in English people's culture. Stretching across social classes, with an appeal that transcended occupation and gender, the 'common people' was an idea that gave a unity to society that the structuralist historian was likely to underestimate. As far as the middle classes were concerned, historian Dror Wahrman used magazines and journals to show how the creation of the myth of bourgeois British society, with its middle-class political identity, occurred in discourse, presaging and enabling the political and cultural transformation of Britain between 1780 and 1840. Returning to Joyce, he then went on to look at the self in nineteenth-century Britain, using case studies in the form of biographies to explore the complexity of personal identity in the nineteenth century. He showed the absence of a simple formulaic understanding of identity such as social class would allow. By the early 1990s there emerged from this an idea in British History research that the social and cultural historian was working towards 'the end of the social'. This is the idea that social history is misnamed, and that the historian's task is to look much more closely at the individual, at the rise of the self, at how the individual relates to society and its culture, rather than at society as a socially constructed entity. Individuals choose their own identities, and culture is the essential arena in which this occurs. Culture is thus not a thing produced by structures like class, but is the everyday life in which identities are assembled by each individual. (We go on to look at the theory of everyday life on pages 124–25.)

This development in the study of social class in British History has generated many new ideas and the restatement of more conventional Marxist approaches. In a sense it has brought the study of working people's history closer to other agendas – the history of gendered identities (with the study of masculinity now an important aspect of the history of class). But despite the continued interest in social class, and resistance to postmodernism in many quarters, it is probably true to say that the weakening of the *idea* of a class analysis of society (accompanied by the collapse of world Marxism since 1989) has challenged the role of social class as a category of analysis in some subject areas (including the social history of religion).

Postcolonialism

One of the major impacts of poststructuralist thinking has been in post-colonialism. In one sense, it is wrong to attribute a movement called poststructuralism to the formation of a movement called postcolonialism. Rather, the emergence of postcolonialism in the 1960s and 1970s has been one of the great markers of the development of poststructuralism.

Edward Said's book *Orientalism* published in 1978 contributed significantly to the intellectualisation of postcolonialism – the post-imperial understanding of non-white cultures in the present and under imperial domination in the past.

Said's book showed how western writers over many centuries constructed 'Orientalism' as an object of study. He revealed the intellectual processes by which 'the Orient' became an 'other' for civilised Europe, and how understanding languages, cultures, human moralities and philosophers was structured by Europeans essentially according to race. Said quotes a Scots Orientalist, Duncan Black Macdonald (1863–1943), who wrote in 1909: 'Inability, then, to see life steadily, and see it whole, to understand that a theory of life must cover all the facts, and liability to be

---

Box 4.5   *Edward Said (1935–2004)*

Edward Said was born in Jerusalem and was a campaigner for the rights of Palestinians in the years since the *nakbah*, or disaster of land loss after the foundation of Israel. He became an academic based in the United States, and was a leading teacher and broadcaster on postcolonial issues. He is credited with transforming the academy and the intellectual outlook of the liberal west by describing the nature of *Orientalism* (in his 1978 book of that title). This book demonstrated how racism was deeply embedded in western intellectual thought, framed in a structuralism that took race as the **category of analysis** for the study of world cultures. The book is a classic of the academy of the late twentieth century, by far the most profound and influential in political and academic terms. He showed the ability of interdisciplinary studies to produce ground-breaking research. He was a profound critic of supposed neutrality in the academy, arguing that academics must not 'camouflage' the social construction of their texts.

---

stampeded by a single idea and blinded to everything else – therein, I believe, is the difference between the East and the West.'[4] This is an **essentialist** structuring of intellect and culture according to race and religion. It recirculates and elaborates the category of 'Oriental' by Enlightenment categories of the 'other': inability to understand 'all the facts' implies empiricist failure, the reference to 'stampede' compares 'the Oriental' to an animal, and 'blinded' implies a reference to a closed mind. In short, this reflects how an academic discipline (and, one might argue, also government policy and European popular culture) was erected upon a structure defined by racism.

His book showed how signs of 'the Orient' appeared in western books, publications and even adverts to signify the inferiority of non-white, non-Christian races in the Middle and Far East. Said argued that, from the end of the eighteenth century, European writers and scientists came to expand understandings of 'the Orient' through 'distinctive colours, lights and people visible through their images, rhythms and motifs'.[5] Many other scholars followed this lead to dissect the signs used within British culture especially to represent 'the Orient' or parts of it, and the supposed innate qualities of the 'Oriental' people. A poster advertisement for Pear's Soap from the 1880s shows a black baby scrubbing with soap in a bathtub, being watched by a white baby as the blackness comes off – a sign that signified that white is desirable as well as superior to black.

Said went on to explore the meaning of these signs in discourse analysis. He illustrated how the European discourse on Oriental 'otherness' was embedded in texts about the non-white world in the eighteenth and nineteenth centuries, and lived on into the late twentieth century. He identified the 'Orientalist discourse' in western writing about the East. The Orient was not a *fact*, he showed, but a social construct of the European imperial imagination, refined and developed in all sorts of ways – academic, poetic, literary and even in advertisement. The discourse on 'the Orient' was that the black man was weaker intellectually, inferior in physique and stamina, given to riotousness and disorder, and needful of the European imperial enterprise to impose order, law, morals and Christianity. This was observable in the Indian-born English poet Rudyard Kipling (1865–1936) and his description of European colonial rule over 'new-caught, sullen peoples,/Half-devil and half-child' who frustrated imperial administration: 'Watch sloth and heathen Folly/ Bring all your hopes to nought.'[6] This was a profoundly pejorative discourse on the inferiority of other races, even if 'kindly' meant or well-intentioned within Christian or Enlightenment sensibilities. The postcolonialist historian argues that such discourses need to be exposed, rejected as morally unacceptable by us as historians and citizens, and then examined for their manner of circulation and the power they exerted in the past (and the present).

Edward Said's 1978 work *Orientalism* is based on a field of hundreds of books. His was a detailed research analysis of all sorts of written texts – academic books, tourist guides, imperialist memoirs – which he submits to an exploration of the dialectical impulses between authors and the discourse on the Oriental 'other' of the European imperial imagination. The texts of Said's study become read not for 'realities' but for what they reveal about structures of thought. Said puts the structural awareness of the poststructuralist into a textual format, showing the high degree of elaboration and nuance between 'the broad superstructural pressures' and what he calls 'the facts of textuality'. He shows that the pre-figured field of Orientalism – with its signs of the Orient, its discourse of Oriental inferiority and its structure of Occidental/Oriental (or European/Middle and Far Eastern) culture – was heavily drawn on by European books and articles in the eighteenth, nineteenth and twentieth centuries. The study of the 'Orient', he says, was built upon each new scholar borrowing the signs, discourses, and superstructure of preceding 'authorities', and then in turn becoming an 'authority' for his own age. Layer upon layer, Said says, the signs and discourses are regenerated, 'the ideas get repeated and re-repeated'.[7]

Through his analysis of signs and discourses, Said was assisting in the development of postcolonialism as what might be described as a poststructuralist approach to the history of the developing world. The structure of 'race' was being removed from History-writing as a *centred* or accepted 'reality' – as a universal structure that defined difference in the nature of the civilisation, the religion and the abilities of people of colour. Poststructuralism is by no means the only description of this intellectual development, as Marxism is very important in subaltern studies – the study of the peasantry in the colonial period of the developing world. But there is an underlying challenge to western structures being imposed on the historical study of former colonies. The structures are to be studied, not to be imposed.

Wider applications

The application of poststructuralism in History is extremely diverse. Foucault's historical work on madness, prisons and sexuality shows how the study of sign, discourse and poststructuralism could come together in historical analysis. His work here was poststructuralist in that he urged us to look away from the orthodox culprits in oppressive power.

Each of Foucault's studies sought to relocate scholarly interest in how power worked. Contrary to most left-wing approaches to power, he regarded it not as centred in the repressive state (as favoured by Marxists and structuralists like Althusser), nor even in the power of ideology circulated and culturally hegemonic in society (as in Gramsci's theoretical work). Rather, Foucault focused on power as lying outside the conventional structures into which power was conceived in historical inquiry. Like Barthes, he saw discourses as the source of power – the power of language located during modernity in knowledge (discourses) that normalised behaviour in the individual. But Foucault's ultimate poststructuralist agenda was in his study of **'bio-power'** as exemplified in his work on sexuality. In this he envisaged the most intimate, the most detailed and the most effective exercise of power was through the vast and intense circulation of detailed and imprisoning discourses on the conduct of the body and sexual behaviour, rather than through the imposition of the sexual discipline of church or state. Of course the state did come in to bolster this world – notably in the criminalisation of homosexuality in the late nineteenth century – but it came after the fact of discursive bio-power.

Poststructuralism has been a focus of specific debate in feminist history – indeed, much more so than postmodernism in general. In the late 1980s,

Joan Wallach Scott and Denise Riley promulgated a poststructuralist vision of women's history centred on gender as the category of analysis. This anti-essentialism overrode the primacy of biological sexual difference, and de-centred 'woman' from a unitary category to being a socially variable construction. This undermined the notion of a common female experience (now and in the past) that had lain at the heart of second-wave feminism for 20 years after 1968.

The consequence is that the poststructuralist agenda brings the sign and discourse into greater relief in historical inquiry. In one sense, poststructuralism provides a method of studying the historical record and of changing the interpretation of events. For instance, Edward Muir's study of the 'Cruel Carnival' in Friuli in Italy in 1511, in which carnival turned into revenge killings, uses conventional structures both to understand context and to narrate the history, but then uses poststructuralist approaches to situate the sources, understand the choices of individuals as active agents in unfolding events, and point to the absence of a single meaning to this episode. In this way, the historian has the ability to use poststructuralist approaches beside more 'conventional' narratives and explorations. The historian is not barred from studying structures, nor even from employing them as structures. But the postmodernist approach would be to incorporate into research a questioning of the origins, meaning and universality of structures.

For the student to do

Opportunities abound for small-scale as well as large-scale discourse analysis under postcolonial and poststructuralist umbrellas.

It is a common practice to explore how a particular group in society – be it unmarried mothers or drunken men, Afro-Caribbeans or Jews, gays or cross-dressers, or an occupational group – were represented in discourse in a particular historical source (magazine, novel, journal, court cases, charity literature and so on). This can then lead to assessment of the impact on public policy relating to these groups. The discourse may be analysed through both written and visual imagery, or could be discerned from the semiological analysis of rituals (such as religious rites, local festivals, floats, guising or mumming outfits, or annual dramas) we looked at in Chapter 2.

There are all sorts of structures that need exploration by historians – the structures of dis/ability, and perhaps the structure of time itself (which historians from Max Weber to the *Annales* school have been exploring for many decades). However, opportunities for dissertation work in poststructuralist analysis often relate to the issues of social class, women's history or postcolonialism. Work on the languages of class is always possible in the nineteenth and twentieth centuries – such as examination of the concept of the working class in British films, comics, television, and so on. Poststructuralist women's history puts women's common experiences at the forefront of analysis, and there are great openings in recovery of women's voices from different levels in societies. Postcolonial perspectives on the history of European colonies, slavery, or Black and Asian peoples in European or North American societies, offer vast scope for studies of assimilation (in work, leisure, politics or religion), alienation (in judicial systems for instance) and discrimination (in jobs, housing and education).

Yet, poststructuralism rarely operates as a category for analysis in postmodernism separate from some of the other techniques outlined in other chapters. Therefore, it is important to think about the alternative **categories of analysis** (gender, the self and so on) to be used in place of structures.

Guide to further reading

Theory

Poststructuralist theory lacks a central key text. But good guides include K. Jenkins (ed.) *The Postmodern History Reader* (London and New York, Routledge, 1997), and A. Munslow, *The Routledge Companion to Historical Studies* (London, Routledge, 2000). Baudrillard can sometimes be hard to read, though he is easier than Foucault. His seminal work is J. Baudrillard, *Simulacra and Simulation* (orig. 1981, English edn, Ann Arbor, University of Michigan Press, 1984) and see also J. Baudrillard, 'The illusion of the end', in K. Jenkins (ed.), *The Postmodern History Reader* (London, Routledge, 1997), pp. 39–46.

History

On poststructuralist approaches to, and influences in the study of, social class, see P. Joyce, *Visions of the People: Industrial England and Question of Class, 1848–1914* (Cambridge, Cambridge University Press, 1991); Patrick Joyce, *Democratic Subjects: The Self and the Social in Nineteenth-century England* (Cambridge, Cambridge University Press, 1994); G. Stedman Jones, *Languages of Class: Studies in English Working Class*

History 1832–1982 (Cambridge, Cambridge University Press, 1983) and D. Wahrman, *Imagining the Middle Class: The Political Representation of Class in Britain, c. 1780–1840* (Cambridge, Cambridge University Press, 1995).

Postcolonialism's key text is E. Said, *Orientalism* (orig. 1978, Harmondsworth, Penguin, 1985). To see some of the new ways it is being used by historians, see A. McClintock, *Imperial Leather: Race, Gender and Sexuality in the Colonial Contest* (New York, Routledge, 1995) and C. Hall, *White, Male and Middle Class: Explorations in Feminism and History* (Cambridge, Polity Press, 1992). On feminist history, see J. Scott, *Gender and the Politics of History* (New York, Columbia University Press, 1988) and D. Riley, *Am I that Name? Feminism and the Category of 'Women'* (Basingstoke, Macmillan, 1988).

To discover the mixed use of conventional structuralist and poststructuralist analysis, try E. Muir, *Mad Blood Stirring: Vendetta and Factions in Friuli during the Renaissance* (Baltimore, Johns Hopkins University Press, 1993).

Notes

1 Quoted in V.B. Leitch (gen. ed.) *The Norton Anthology of Theory and Criticism* (New York, Norton, 2001), p. 1459.

2 J. Baudrillard, *Simulacra and Simulation* (orig. 1981, English edn, Ann Arbor, University of Michigan Press, 1984), pp. 8, 30, 41, 43, 48.

3 J. Baudrillard, 'The illusion of the end', in K. Jenkins (ed.), *The Postmodern History Reader* (London, Routledge, 1997), pp. 39–46. A. Munslow, *The Routledge Companion to Historical Studies* (London, Routledge, 2000), p. 200.

4 Quoted in E. Said, *Orientalism* (orig. 1978, Harmondsworth, Penguin, 1985), p. 277.

5 Ibid., p. 22.

6 Rudyard Kipling, 'The White Man's Burden', *McClure's Magazine*, February (1899).

7 Said, *Orientalism*, pp. 13, 277.

CHAPTER 5

Text

From the mid-1970s, postmodern theory started to develop a very distinctive interest in the text. During the next 15 years, the text became the main focus of new theory, and this had an immense impact on academic research. A very important result was that textual analysis brought postmodernists together from different disciplines, especially from literary studies and History. This was to draw History more and more away from the social sciences, and more and more towards the humanities. The result was pressure to dissolve some of the recent divisions in History – especially that between economic, social and cultural history, and between all of those and other branches of History (covering everything from political and war history through to architectural and medical history).

At the same time, the distinctive method of the profession became increasingly challenged by the delivery in the 1980s of new historical research that was based on anthropology. Boundaries between disciplines began to be challenged, especially in the later 1980s and 1990s. The sign and the discourse were by then established focuses of new historical research, and the arrival of new theory on the text merely confirmed the erosion of boundaries between the humanities disciplines. History was discovering a new pivotal position between the humanities and social sciences, and its independence of method and theory was being eroded.

Theory

So far, we have come across four essential tasks which combine to define the postmodernist historian at work. Once the field of study is isolated, and the research theorised, there follows (1) empirical preparation, (2) decoding signs, (3) discourse analysis and (4) poststructural awareness of structures. These four come together with another task in the overall project of the postmodernist historian and scholar – the **deconstruction** of **texts**.

The text

What is a text? A dictionary will define it as a piece of literature, a book or an article. And that constitutes for the postmodernist a metaphor for something greater – all forms of narrative. In the postmodernist sense, a text is the material manifestation of a multiplicity of signs, discourses and structures. All three occur only within a text. If you recall, the **sign** gains meaning from its relationship with other signs and gives materiality to **discourse**, whilst discourse is a **knowledge** located (unavoidably) in structures that require awareness and critical reaction by the historian. So, the text is an ensemble of signs replete with discourses and structures. A text is thus a complex thing. The task of the historian is to approach the text as a package of all those three things (signs, discourses and structures), each requiring their relevant activity (i.e. decoding, discourse analysis, and imposing poststructural awareness).

What is the character of the text? The text is a *material* thing in the sense that there is something that the reader can see (or hear) in order to 'read' it. It might be a book, an article, a play, a building, a set of hieroglyphs on a wall, a medley of gestures, or a speech. There is a 'thing' that can be seen or heard. This makes it different from a discourse or a structure, but like a sign. However, two things taken together distinguish a text from a sign. These are what literary theorists call the qualities of textuality and intertextuality.

Textuality is the quality of the *non-real*. That is, it is composed of many signs, each of which is not a signified, and a signified that is not the object (the referent) but only a concept of it. A text excludes the 'real thing'. So, to take an example, one day the president makes a visit. The president's visit is an historical event which is not a text because the real thing – the president – is present. But the following *is* a text:

The president was in the city today and was given a warm reception at a retirement home for ex-servicemen, whilst later crowds greeted his arrival at an official reception.

This is a text because the real is not present. It is a report recounting the visit, composed of substitutes (words), not the things (the president, the visit). It is the absence of the *possibility* of the 'real', the indeterminate nature of language, but the presence of a meaning, that makes something a text. This was described by Jacques Derrida in possibly the single most famous statement of postmodernism as: 'There is nothing outside of the text.' By this he meant that when a reader is consulting a text, the text seeks to represent 'reality' only by trying to exclude it, by 'the absence of the referent'. Every attempt to get outside of the text ends up repeating the text, not jumping over the barrier between the text and reality. Derrida concludes that 'what opens meaning and language is writing as the disappearance of the natural presence.'[1] In other words, to make language into a text, it has to be opened to contain a meaning, and that is only achieved by removing the presence of the natural or real thing.

By doing so, however, certainty is also being removed. There is no closure in a text, only an illusion of it; to be open to a meaning, if certainty is removed, is to be open to *more than one* meaning. So, a text is always ambiguous in its meaning, though it works (i.e. fools the reader) by purporting to have only one. Two people may interpret a text differently because the signification it contains has *moved*. One reading of the text above is that the president of the USA is in Britain, and was met by cheering crowds of well-wishers. You may call upon a stock image of such types of visit, with flag-waving children and adults, and this will provide a **structure** for this reading. Opposing it, some people may call up a stock image of hostile crowds of demonstrators, shouting slogans of opposition to the president. So, the signification may shift from a discourse of approval to one of disapproval. Even more signification-shift may occur: is it the president of the USA, or the president of the ex-servicemen's association? Derrida says that differences in interpretation arise from each person viewing a text from two or more different structures, and because the illusion of closure (of certainty) has been deferred – even though the text appears to present a closed or certain statement.

Thus, Derrida perceives the meanings within a text as having the capability of *différence* (differing by structural or synchronic variation between meanings) and the capability of *différance* (deferring by a process of postponing, in an historical or diachronic change). Note the change in spelling. Each signification within a text is thus related to an 'other' or opposing signifier. The 'other' is absent, but is implied within the same structure of meaning. And there is also a sliding away (the deferring) of certainty concerning time. For Derrida, signs are in incessant play over their meaning, tantalising and confusing. This causes humans to impose some arbitrary certainty – or else we would never be able to cope. (This is why many postmodernists refer to the 'playfulness' of the sign and of the text.) Closures have to be imposed upon signs within texts to give us usable meanings (perhaps to stop us going mad from the uncertainty).

> **Box 5.1**   *Jacques Derrida (1930–)*
>
> French theorist, born in Algeria, part of the group that included Barthes
> that has attained fame as the core of postmodern philosophy, Derrida is
> considered the father of deconstruction. This is described as a way of
> 'reading' things (books, objects, actions) that looks beyond the obvious to
> concealed meanings, undermining the certainty of the one meaning in a sign
> or group of signs. Derrida perfected the critical reading of literature and
> other signs. His most famous book, *On Grammatology* (1976), argued that
> a language is made by the exclusion of the real, that nature disappears from
> text. This led to him making the most famous statement of postmodernism:
> '*il n'y a pas de hors-texte*' (there is nothing outside of the text). This state-
> ment has been hotly debated, with critics claiming that Derrida seems to
> suggest that the world is a text and not real, whilst his defenders say it
> means getting outside of a text is impossible as that only creates another
> text. To describe a fact, you need to use another fact. In other words,
> humans are trapped in language in order to understand the world. Derrida
> has been a revered figure of postmodernism in the late twentieth and early
> twenty-first centuries, much in demand at conferences and events.

Intertextuality is the quality of a text having borrowed from previous
texts, historic antecedents, which give every text a place in a history of
signs, discourses and structures. Nothing is original in the text. Recalling
Foucault from Chapter 3, 'the author does not precede the work'. No text
is in itself completely original in its combination of sign, discourse and
structure. That lack of originality leads to intertextual borrowing. We
write essays and letters in certain styles which we know of because we have
learned of the style of words, the sorts of things to say, the layout of the
page, and so forth. This is not plagiarism (where entire passages are replicated exactly), but the use of common styles in ways familiar to ourselves
and to the people who read our texts.

Narratives

Texts do something more than merely the sum of their parts – texts tell
stories or narratives. Narratives are things we all recognise, often by the
terms *fiction* and *non-fiction* (the way, for instance, bookshops divide up
their stock). In History there is also the division between historical fiction
(usually the work of novelists) and non-fiction (the work of historians,

whether academic or not). This was a division that came to maturity in the course of the nineteenth century.

Narratives are the unavoidable by-product of writing. They are made by humans, and are assembled in ways that allow us to sequence signs, discourses and structures. Thus, a narrative is in itself historicised, putting things into an order, and taking time to read. This makes it, in Foucault's view, a characteristic of the Enlightenment: if hierarchic order (a parallel to social rank) characterised the knowledge system in the episteme of pre-modernity, History characterised the knowledge system in the episteme of modernity. Examples of historical narrative pre-date the Enlightenment, of course, but Foucault considered that they did not reflect the character of knowledge until then. Thus, the encyclopaedic and hierarchic lists of things were emblematic of the Renaissance, whilst the narrative history book was emblematic of the Enlightenment. Of course, this act of ordering is an act of including and excluding things, and of making things intelligible by the construction of a story. Even when the story is not written in prose, but in a photograph or a newspaper headline, we can still understand it.

However, the narrative has important characteristics that should be analysed. From the 1960s to the 1980s, narrative theorists like Northrop Frye and Umberto Eco were exploring universal narrative modes – in Frye's case, arguing that the Bible provided the universal model for emplotment of written human stories. Even if that may not be acceptable to all historians, narratives have tropes (ways of using words in non-literal expressions, such as in metaphor or irony), and different plots, arguments and ideologies. The narrative is a poetic and aesthetic construct, and one that has an important impact upon both the use and the status of 'evidence'. It contains putatively 'factual' content that requires checking. So, it matters that the narratives of the past, and the narratives generated by historians, are studied.

Metanarratives

The most important stories are the big ones. Jean-François Lyotard has been one influential theorist of the big story.

Lyotard has contributed to forming the idea of the **metanarrative**. This grand or master narrative is a story that shapes other narratives. The term is applied especially by postmodernists to those narratives intellectualised or generated by the European Enlightenment that were re-circulated in its wake at home and abroad. These include the metanarratives of 'the power of reason', 'scientific method', 'white racial superiority', and the virtue of

---

Box 5.2   *Jean-François Lyotard (1925–98)*

Another member of the French theoretical circle, Lyotard is noteworthy for promoting discussion of postmodernism, for coining the phrase 'the postmodern condition', and for announcing the death of 'grand narratives'. His long essay, *The Postmodern Condition* (1977) is the nearest thing to a postmodernist manifesto, arguing for the end of the Enlightenment project, the universalist aim of its knowledge, and the failure of its political project in democracy and human rights. As part of his assertion of the distinctiveness of the postmodern, Lyotard argued that the Enlightenment had been intolerant of that which could not be captured by 'reason', and had sought to suppress all that could not be expressed by modernity's signs. To go beyond this narrowness and intolerance, the postmodern would cultivate a sensibility for the sublime – for the things in art and culture that are irreducible to reason, that are transcendent, beyond measurement and calculation – the things that are soul-stirring but unsignable.

'rational religion' (as many British clergy called Christianity in the early nineteenth century). In diluted or pure form, these metanarratives provided for over a century the foundation 'truths' underlying hundreds if not thousands of smaller narratives in all branches of European learning, popular culture and government. But according to Lyotard in 1979, they were disintegrating in the mid-twentieth century. He said: 'the status of knowledge is altered as societies enter what is known as the postindustrial age and cultures enter what is known as the postmodern age'. This transition, he said, started at least in the late 1950s, and was faster or slower depending on the country. For Lyotard, the decay of metanarratives defined the postmodern episteme: 'I define postmodern as incredulity toward metanarratives.' He went on: 'The narrative function is losing its functors, its great hero, its great dangers, its great voyages, its great goal. It is being dispersed in clouds of narrative language elements – narrative, but also denotative, prescriptive, descriptive, and so on.'[2] The argument is that reduced dependence on metanarratives makes the historian bound to be more sensible of their existence in older history books and in the historical sources that s/he is using. To progress the discipline, there has to be a dispensing with the metanarrative.

But does this mean that there are no metanarratives now? This is a moot point. Most postmodernists would argue that the instability of meaning in postmodernity implies an inability for a metanarrative to become established – since a constancy of meaning, and an absence of any credible or believable opposing narrative, is required for it to exist. Hierarchies of knowledge, race, gender and all essentialist presumptions are being constantly de-centred and constantly problematised (i.e. they have not gone, but are not allowed to be accepted as normal) in ways that make them widespread discourses of our contemporary society. This renders no cultural ground sufficiently fertile for a metanarrative to take intellectual root. That is a postmodernist's aim.

Deconstructing the text

The text is thus a complex thing. Analysing it is often called by postmodernists '**deconstruction**'. This involves more than one skill. I will list these, but not necessarily in the order of employing them.

First, deconstruction is the act of establishing empiricist issues – date and author of a text, its different versions, and the accuracy of any data contained in it. There will also be issues of content that may need verification or substantiation. Second, there is the business of decoding signs in the text. Third, there is identification and analysis of discourses. Fourth, there is the identification of structures, which may require the actions of rejection, de-centring, or conscious deployment of them. Fifth, there is the task of identifying the text – its intertextual origins, its manner of circulation, and how it relates to the signs, discourses and structures within it. What style does it adopt, and how does this style relate to its signs and discourses? Sixth, there is the task of identifying the ambiguities of meaning, and opposing meanings. This involves what is often called 'reading against the grain', reading at 90 degrees to the meanings within the text. This involves going into the text as a reader to comprehend the possible closed meanings, and then standing back and re-reading them together, comparing and contrasting them. Seventh, there is the task of identifying modes of trope, emplotment, argument and ideology. And eighth, there is the task of isolating any foundational metanarratives underlying a text.

The deployment of these eight analytical tasks constitutes deconstruction. It sounds like a step-by-step scientific exercise, the type eschewed by postmodernists. I have adopted this style solely to ease understanding, and not to imply that deconstruction consists of checking off tasks in a numbered list. Deconstruction is a much more creative, often aesthetic, and exciting undertaking. For one thing, the eight tasks can occur in any order, and often almost simultaneously. For instance, discourse analysis is close to the analysis of metanarratives, as the first will often arise from the second. And it is usually the case that these eight tasks are reported by historians in their research without a consciousness of them as separate items. So, the itemisation here is to help to understand the tasks, not to prescribe the tone or the method of doing them.

A few concluding remarks on the theory of deconstruction. Deconstruction is a reaction against the notion that there is or can be a certainty of meaning in a text. It is a rejection of the notion of there being a true and authentic voice to be heard, if only the reader is able to contextualise and research sufficiently the origins of the text and its author. Instead, deconstruction works on the notion that signs and discourses rely on the relationships between them, on structures of meaning, and use literary modes to convey, enhance or alter meanings. The literary modes are in themselves neutral, though they can distort. By contrast, those structures of meaning often bear moral or ideological meanings, and are unavoidable in some form, though we can renegotiate our position in relation to them. As we saw in the previous chapter, some structures may be debarred for moral reasons (like racism), some can be de-centred (like class) and some structures are lost in the intensity of signage in hyper-reality (we lose the plot, in other words). Structures implicate the readers in those structures. To observe is to interact with structures, and the observer is inside, not outside, the text. But once the observer inside the structures has become aware, then s/he can move outside. This movement in and out of the text's structures of meaning is the necessary work of the deconstructionist.

This may be a difficult notion to understand immediately. One way of understanding what is meant is to think back to the discourse analysis of the historical source on ideal womanhood from 1844 on page 72. In describing the discourse on the ideal woman in the 'domestic sphere', the historian can move into the text to describe its content in 'the voice' of a contemporary reader and supporter – in the voice of a Victorian Christian who believed and adhered to the discourse. This would be 'reading from inside the text'. Then, the historian can move outside the text and describe the discourse from a twenty-first-century viewpoint of non-believing. We may not be detached exactly, but we are removed from the discourse, so will present it in a different way. The result of this in-and-out movement will be an enhanced sense of the narrative, a greater awareness of how it works to an inside reader, and a better sense of its impact in the past.

Equally, the historian must move in and out of metanarratives to understand them. Just as signs in a text operate through a playfulness (what semiologists call 'freeplay' from Derrida's usage of the word 'jeu'), so the analyst him/herself can or should or even must also adopt a 'playfulness' as part of the process of analysis – such as adopting the voice of characters in order to convey readings of signs. The historian must also appreciate some of the skills of the literary theorists, being able to understand the structure of narrative and its elements. This brings the work of the historian close to that of the literature specialist. It also, incidentally, historicises the work of the literature specialist, bringing what is called 'the new historicism' to literature studies.

The past is a text

One of the most controversial implications of the postmodernist position is that the past itself is a text, and nothing but a text. The historian is involved in reading the past as if it were one large text.

Roland Barthes was one of the first in 1967 to present the historian's work in this way. His concern was to challenge the positivistic and deterministic aim of history-writing that dominated in France. This French tradition, he said, saw everything that happened before the Revolution of 1789 in the light of its having led up to the events of that year. There was in all French written History, he argued, an assumption of the endpoint of 1789. This approach he criticised, saying that 'all history with an endpoint is a myth'.[3] In this he was not saying it was untrue, merely that the historian was incapable of doing more than reading the past as if it were a large narrative text with an endpoint. In 1971, he told an interviewer: 'The teaching problem of today is to upset the notion of literary text and to manage to make adolescents understand that there is text everywhere, but also that everything is text.'

This approach was further developed by Derrida in his statement: 'there is nothing outside of the text'. This is not a denial that the past happened, merely a denial of the historian's ability to describe it in anything other than a text. Every postmodernist acknowledges the existence of reality, and every postmodernist historian acknowledges the existence of the past. The best way to express the approach is this. The past exists as an infinity of events. Those events constitute a 'reality'. However, our ability to recall events only in texts transforms those events into fact-statements and narrative-statements that divorce them immediately from the reality of the past, and puts them in a relationship to each other that they may not have had. The implication is, of course, that the human mind, including that of the skilled historian, is unable even to *read* the past as anything other than a text. We think in texts, read in texts, write in texts. Narrative surrounds human intellect. There may be a sublime to contend with, as Lyotard said, but this is not something that can be easily distilled into words and a History book.

This position was not new in the 1960s. Friedrich Nietzsche said in the late nineteenth century: 'There are no facts in themselves. It is always necessary to begin by introducing a meaning in order that there can be a fact.' An event that happened in the past only becomes 'a fact' when it is recalled (summoned up) by the historian, and in that summoning there is a pre-figured meaning already in place. The summoning is done with a purpose, an intention, with a place for that fact in the historian's work. The discourse is already in existence, and it exists in the form of a text. It is this postmodernist reasoning that explains the summary conclusion that there is nothing outside of the text. Barthes agreed in 1967: 'The fact can only have a linguistic existence, as a term in a discourse, and yet it is exactly as if this existence were merely the "copy", purely and simply, of another existence situated in the extra structural domain of the "real".'[4]

Reading history: the text as primary source

The postmodernist position is that there is essentially no difference between the text as primary source, and the text as secondary source. However, I shall consider each in turn.

Primary sources are used by historians to gain material or data with which to investigate the past, and to write articles and books about their chosen topic. These primary sources take various forms: archaeological remains, buildings and material artefacts, hieroglyphics and drawings, published books, newspapers and journals, official government reports and parliamentary proceedings, manuscript files containing memoranda and letters, memoirs and autobiographies, statistics, tape recordings, video and film records, and so on. The postmodernist position is that these all constitute texts.

The postmodernist does not limit the range of forms that a text may take, nor privilege one form of text over another. So, a book or a journal is no more important nor more reliable than, say, a memoir or an oral history interview or a music lyric. Now, this assumption has to be approached through empirical investigation into the factual reliability of different sources, and there may be cause for arguing that a source that originated close to an event has the greatest chance of reliability, perti-nence and unsullied character (as in a law court, putting the contemporaneous account ahead of the later memoir). However, the sig-nificance of a source to an historian may not lie in its factual reliability, but in its display of values, ideologies, interpretations, and so on. Moreover, factual misconstruction may be significant – a source that gets facts wrong is often highly significant in an historian's eyes. This means that there is nothing intrinsic in the *form* of a source that endows one with greater significance than another (a document over a film, a drawing over an interview). Equally, there is nothing in authorship that attributes greater value in terms of meaning to one author over another.

In this sense, the postmodernist approach to texts is very democratic. Because there is no external reality in our summoning of events to become fact-statements in a History narrative, there is no text that can claim to be any 'better' than any other. All views of an event, all perspectives on a subject, are *in principle* equally valid and potentially useful to an historian who is exploring expressions of views and perspectives. All views were equally shaped by the forces of structures and antecedent discourses. Indeed, one of the consequences of this is the privileging by many social and cultural historians of the texts neglected by conventional or traditional history. This is not new. The great claim of the new social history of the 1960s and 1970s was to look at history from the bottom up. But postmodernist history from the 1980s onwards would claim to go further in avoiding having to empirically test every source in a reliability exercise. Empirical testing still has its place, but people's voices have to be heard not just as sources of information to add to the big narratives about the past, but as narratives that aid in constructing small narratives and help in other ways (such as understanding personal identities). If the task is no longer to address grand narratives, but to look increasingly for the little ones, then the sources of the unconventional, of the ordinary, of the mundane attain a new interest. Their meanings have been neglected, and that makes them more urgent for the historian to look at.

Writing history: the text as secondary source

Postmodernists have a special concern to reveal the historian's writing as being no different as a literary construction from a novel. The contrary position, that of the privileged truth of the historian, creates what Roland Barthes called in the 1960s 'the reality effect'. It is worth quoting Barthes at length:

... in 'objective' history, the 'real' is never more than an unformulated signified, sheltering behind the apparently all-powerful referent. This situation characterizes what we might call the realistic effect. *The*

signified is eliminated from the 'objective' discourse, and ostensibly allows the 'real' and its expression to come together, and this succeeds in establishing a new meaning, on the infallible principle already stated that any deficiency of elements in a system is in itself significant. This new meaning – which extends to the whole of historical discourse and is its ultimately distinctive property – is the real in itself surreptitiously transformed into a sheepish signified. Historical discourse does not follow the real, it can do no more than signify the real, constantly repeating that it happened, *without this assertion amounting to anything but the signified 'other side' of the whole process of historical narration.*

This narrative style of history, favoured by the History profession, Barthes went on:

... draws its 'truth' from the careful attention to narration, the architecture of articulations and the abundance of expanded elements (known, in this case, as 'concrete details'). So the circle of paradox is complete. Narrative structure, which was originally developed within the cauldron of fiction (in myths and the first epics) becomes at once the sign and the proof of reality.[5]

This equating of History-writing with fiction-writing raises serious concerns amongst critics that postmodernism sidelines the issue of 'truth' altogether from the profession. But the 'reality effect' is a powerful facet of the History subject. The historian asks for his/her narrative to be accepted because it is a good narrative in which the 'real' and the signified seem to be united.

This assault on objective history was taken up in the 1970s by Hayden White.

In an influential essay on 'The Fictions of Factual Representation', White argued that historians have traditionally constructed the past in stories without thinking through the conceptual presuppositions that they, as individuals, brought to it. Those presuppositions were the products of their time and place, and the discursive environment in which they worked. He argued that language and protocols arising from it shape the writing of history, and the choices made in what he describes as a 'poetic act'. There is no necessary relationship between the structuring of the narrative and the historical evidence, and though this does not diminish the significance of varying quality in historical research in a given field of study, one historian cannot be more 'authoritative' than any another. The term 'authoritative' is much used in reviews of History books, implying a

> **Box 5.3** *Hayden White (1928–)*
>
> Hayden White is an American philosopher of History. Since the 1970s, he has been the leading figure in debate regarding History as a literary exercise, and regarding History books as texts. In his 1973 book *Metahistory*, he argued that History should not regard itself as a science. He argued that the historian has the same types of choices as any writer, and is making them on poetic grounds. White put forward a structuralist scheme for analysing History books for their inner literary structures. Poststructuralist critics have argued that his approach is too crude, and is based on a notion of 'deep structures' in academic work. For all that, it is White who has formulated the most accessibly the problem of the historian's choice of how to write History. That choice instantly removes the historian from the world of science, and puts him/her in a world of literary inquiry and technique.

closure and a finality of judgement and raising one historian over all others. In general, the postmodernist has difficulties with the principle of there being the possibility of an authoritative work on major historical issues. This is because there is a subjectivity that the historian brings to the writing of history that is identical to the subjectivity of the primary source. This does not diminish the importance of an historian's empirical skills, quality of hypotheses, moral judgements, and deconstructive powers. Nevertheless, the historian needs to reflect on his or her pre-figuring of a topic.

White argued that historians' narratives are pre-figured by trope, by plots, and by ideological arguments. These, he said, were first distinguished in History-writing by Giambattista Vico (1668–1744) in the eighteenth century. The tropes White identified were:

- *metaphor* (where one thing is described as being another, carrying over its associations – like the aeronautical linkage in 'the British economy took off in the eighteenth century')

- *metonymy* (the substitution of a thing by a symbol of it, a name for the anonymous people, place for event, thing for people, as one signified stands-in for another – the British Crown; the American White House; 'Hiroshima introduced the atomic age'; 'the government said nothing'; 'British Tommies went off to war')

- *synecdoche* (where a part of something is used to describe the whole, or possibly vice versa, as in 'Queen Elizabeth I never gave her hand in marriage' and 'factories took on more hands')

- *irony* (saying one thing while you mean or want to suggest the opposite, though the inversion of meaning often requires additional information or another sign, such as a smile or inflection of voice – as in 'British weather is wonderful', or saying in an empty lecture, 'It's crowded today'. Irony is less used by historians because of the possibility of confusion.)

The modes of emplotment White listed are romance, tragedy, comedy and satire. Understanding the presence of these in a narrative depends on familiarity with the signs, discourses and structures, and this makes the historian's task one of sensitivity to a period and theme. He listed the mode of argument as formist, mechanistic, organicist or contextualist, whilst the mode of ideological implication he offered was anarchist, radical, conservative or liberal.

White's early work was quite structuralist in approach – though he (and others) noted a deliberate irony in this. He moved in the later 1970s and 1980s towards thinking about narrative in other ways. He argued that historians' work is not *really* about facts: 'What is at issue here is not, What are the facts? but rather, How are the facts to be described in order to sanction one mode of explaining them rather than another?' Some historians want a technical terminology to make it a science, others consider that 'ordinary language is the safeguard against ideological deformations of the "facts"'. From this, White said, what historians fail to recognise is that 'ordinary language itself has its own forms of terminological determinism, represented by the figures of speech without which discourse itself is impossible'.[6] White went further in the 1980s, arguing that historical events are not 'real' because they occurred, but because they are remembered and placed in a chronological sequence. But to be considered 'a historical account', facts further need to be locatable *outside* the chronology –

... in an order of narrative, that makes them, at one and the same time, questionable as to their authenticity and susceptible to being considered as tokens of reality. In order to qualify as historical, an event must be susceptible to at least two narrations of its occurrence. Unless at least two versions of the same set of events can be imagined, there is no reason for the historian to take upon himself the authority of giving the true account of what really happened. The authority of the historical narrative is the authority of reality itself; the historical account endows

this reality with form and thereby makes it desirable by the imposition upon its processes of the formal coherency that only stories possess.

White adds that what distinguishes the second from the first (chronological) narration is the moralising of the story. Together, these qualities constitute the character of the historian's narrative form. White calls it 'allegory' (an extended metaphor), thus distinguishing it from scientific accounts (though historians might spuriously claim that quality). Thus, what an historian is doing, says White, is telling a story to mediate between events and their context, thus symbolising something wider than the events themselves. On the other side of the coin, White argued that historiography is a representational practice highly suited to political ends – not just because it deals with patriotism or morality, but because it produces notions of continuity, wholeness, closure and individuality that every 'civilised' society wishes to see itself as incarnating.[7]

There are three major implications for the historian in this mode of thinking. First, the past is a text like any literary production (a novel, a poem) which needs to be treated like a literary production. Secondly, the present is also a text that affects the subjectivity of the historian. And thirdly, the History book is a text resulting from the interaction between the first two – the texts of past and present. So, just as structures are unavoidable, so are narratives. Just as poststructuralism problematises, de-centres and despatches structures (but not all of them), so deconstruction of text does not dispense with narratives. If the narrative is unavoidable, says Lyotard, the little narrative is better than the big narrative, and the littler the better. As Keith Jenkins has written, 'it is the smallest narratives and least imperial of genres whose rules and procedures are the least determined and determining'.[8] The postmodernist privileges the unclosed, open text, that makes the least firm, the least 'realist' and the least grand claims to authority, authenticity and finality. These facets tend towards what Barthes termed 'degree zero of writing', but that may – as he concluded – be unattainable. We cannot recall a fact without narratising it. But we can be very aware of the choices of narrative modes we have made, and explain them and what they might do to the narrative.

Application in history

The application of textual analysis for the historian lies in both the reading and the writing of history.

Cats again – Deconstructing the massacre story

In Chapter 2 we looked at the remarkable piece of History-writing by Robert Darnton – his study of a document that recounted a trial and massacre of a cat in Paris in the 1730s. Darnton's account was criticised by a French historian, Roger Chartier. Chartier focused attention away from the symbols to the text.

Chartier praised Darnton for innovative 'work of such engrossing interest', in which 'the society of *ancien régime* France springs to life, in which men and women of 300 years ago become flesh-and-blood beings who think and suffer, cry or laugh'. But he charged Darnton with being too quick to conduct semiological analysis (that is, analysis of the signs and symbols used by the print workers in the mock trial and massacre). Chartier said that Darnton sought to *reconstruct* the incident from the document but, first, failed to *deconstruct* the 990-word document, and second, assumed that the text was what it purported to be – namely, a factual, face-value text written some thirty years after the event. The result, Chartier postulated, was an error of interpretation.

Chartier re-analysed the document. He looked at the signs of cats, sorcery and carnival in the story, and he noted the presence of some satirical elements that he thought Darnton had missed – some anti-clerical allusions, for instance – and considered that it was not 'a strictly carnival rite'. This led him to conclude that there was not only one text (the massacre) to be interpreted, there was actually a second text – the print-worker Contat's account. Chartier argued that Contat's text may not be a neutral account by a former worker who was present at the mock trial and massacre of cats. Rather, it may be in the form of a well-known Parisian genre of *exposé* of the goings-on in various professions and trades. Contat himself existed, but we do not know if he was the author of the document. Chartier noted the curious absence of an authorial 'I' in the text, so that we do not really know who is speaking. If the story was in the form of a revelation of a trade, designed to amuse, shock and sell pamphlets, the account may have been much more what we might call 'tabloid journalism' than eyewitness account. This means that the amount of 'play' of specific signs in the text becomes a difficult task for the historian to judge relative to the general idioms of carnival in early-modern France. Is this story something akin to a satirical exaggeration, like a revue sketch in a modern comedy show? Is this a story full of irony? Just what did hanging cats mean in that culture? Chartier concludes that the massacre probably took place, but not necessarily as 'Contat' described it in the text. It became a text performing other discursive functions. In this light, the account could well have other layers of meaning that were very different in terms of the power being expressed. Whether Chartier is right or not in his re-analysis, his criticism was that Darnton had in part failed to consider what texts were present requiring textual analysis.

So, deconstruction is something that highlights the text as a whole as well as the signs within it. At its best, deconstruction is informed by wide empirical and contextual knowledge, and energised by methodical insight. This does not necessarily always mean that it is 'right', but when done well it does cast new light on old problems of historical understanding of the past.

A story of disputed identity

A second example is also from France. In 1983, the historian Natalie Zemon Davis dissected a celebrated story concerning a peasant, Martin Guerre, who disappeared in 1546 from his village in the Basque region of southern France, only for a man claiming to be him to return to the village and live with Martin's wife for many years. However, relatives accused this man of being an impostor after he tried to sell off family land. He went through two trials but, amazingly, the wife stood by him. Only when the 'real' Martin returned to the village in the final days of the last trial was the unmasking ensured. The story was written up by the prosecuting lawyer involved, and widely referred to by others. Davis came to write her study after assisting in the production of a film about it starring Gérard Depardieu.

The historian's work here involved all sorts of skills. One was in decoding signs. A narrative of the case in 1588 by the French philosopher Michel de Montaigne (1533–92) told how one of the men had a wooden leg. Here, Davis showed that the historian needs to be alert to signs that the developed world of the twenty-first century may not only *not understand*, but may not recognise as signs at all. Montaigne dwelt on the image of legs in his description of the story's many characters – a prince's gouty legs, the thin legs of the French and the thick legs of a German, and the deformed legs of a pleasure-giving lame woman. Once alerted to this, it is clear to the historian Davis that Montaigne ascribed significance to the wooden-legged Martin Guerre and disabled legs generally. Davis decoded deformity as understood by Montaigne as a sign of difficulty in comprehension, perhaps an insoluble riddle. One of the two Martin Guerres was an impostor, and Montaigne knew the popular saying of the time that lies come on a limping leg – for you could not travel far on them. Indeed, Montaigne saw himself as deformed – that is, a mystery: 'The more I frequent and know myselfe, the more my deformitie astonieth me and the lesse I understand myselfe.' Montaigne was gaining philosophical mileage out of the issue of deformed legs in a way distinctive in the culture of the period. Thus, something apparently semiologically 'innocent' in a story may be a sign to which the historian must be fully alert.

This was a long process that was very well documented. The prosecutor, Jean de Coras, wrote an account of the trial that became a bestseller. This provided the historian Davis with the material to deconstruct the discursive world of the courts and the bourgeoisie. She describes how the means of the imposture was attributed by the prosecutor not to the man's inventiveness but to magic and an evil spirit. This showed how the place of other-worldliness was vital in the cultural world of the prosecutor and his mostly middle-class readership. Textual analysis of the narratives gave Davis the opportunity to explore how such a crime was characterised in prosecutor Coras' legal format of Text and Annotation. But she notes how it also offered him the opportunity to discuss wider social issues – marriage, the wedding of children before puberty, impotence, desertion and adultery. In addition, Coras used his account to convey a Protestant message. As a law book, it became a bestseller, written in vernacular, not Latin, and full of contradictions. Davis says: 'Here is a law book that calls into question the workings of the law; an historical account that raises doubts about its own truth. This is a text that moves among the moral tale, comedy, and tragedy. Heroes seem villains and villains seem heroes, and the story is told in two ways at the same time.' And of course, the book titillated for the apparent ability of the impostor to fool a wife in bed. As a narrative, Davis shows that Coras' account reversed the tradition of tragicomedy into a 'comictragic' format, where the hero-villain is executed. Davis shows the power of this moral story through its playful teasing with the conventional emplotment by inverting the usual genre of the legal fraternity. Davis says of Coras' narrative: 'The tragedy is more in his unmasking than in his imposture.'[9]

The case raises all sorts of other issues, too. Ahead of the subject of our next chapter, the case arouses historical interest in the changing construction of 'the self'. How in the sixteenth century, at a time without photographs, passports, fingerprints or DNA, could a person's identity be established beyond doubt? Imposture is the sublimation of one self and the creation of another, and Davis uses this to explore the composition of the self in sixteenth-century terms. Most interesting in some ways were the wife's actions – a woman who accepted the impostor, but who recanted the moment the real Martin Guerre appeared at the final stages of the second trial. One of the key aspects of the story was that, before his disappearance, Martin Guerre was impotent. The first man to return to the village claiming to be him was evidently not, though he seemed to be accepted by his wife as the real Martin. Indeed, she gave evidence that he was who he said he was. Many questions arise from this, not all of which we can answer. At the end of the day, the impostor was hung on a gibbet erected outside the house of the real Martin Guerre.

Images as texts

The deconstruction of texts is not limited to words. The use of images from the past is a well-known element of historical research, but it has acquired new capabilities with deconstruction.

One of the most interesting examples is a study by Brian Maidment. He studied popular British prints between 1790 and 1870 – prints that were sold both in journals and separately as one of the key media of the day. People hung prints on their walls at home (often containing religious homilies or scenes), whilst others were like cartoons, interpreting events of the day. Before photography became widespread after about 1860, the print was an important medium of popular culture.

Maidment developed important conclusions from the study of common incidents and themes in the prints. One print he studied portrayed an incident much talked about and drawn in British magazines – the burning of the Albion Corn Mill at Southwark in London in 1791. This building and its destruction became an object of anxiety, especially amongst the elites, over popular protest against industrialisation. One print showed three plebeian men apparently dancing and rejoicing as the mill burned, and has been conventionally interpreted as portraying elite fears, together with the plebeian resistance to industrial development and to rising bread prices (especially less than two years after the fall of the Bastille in Paris).

But Maidment re-reads the picture, pointing to the instability of meaning in the signs and discourses. He suggests that the burning mill is a symbol of high hopes dashed, and displays the crestfallen rich mocked by jovial men (with one holding a child's toy windmill as a casual sign of 'the pleasures of popular carnival'). He describes it as more a celebration of urban street life and a theatrical gesture than a polemical attack on potential plebeian rebellion, concluding that the artist may be torn between mocking and celebrating popular reaction. Such instability of meaning reflects the difficulties for popular art within commercial publishing, using both vernacular and genteel tradition to reflect 'a complexly symbolic event'. The search for simple meanings in prints is fraught with danger, Maidment argues, when meanings 'remain disconcertingly unstable'.[10] This may have been a print floating between literal and satirical meaning. This interpretation may be reinforced by noting the date of publication shown beneath the print – 1 April, which was then, as now, a day for pranks. Is the drawing a prank? Is the depiction of the burning bringing out its prankish quality?

This type of work is now common amongst historians. David Hopkin has examined prints of the same period, 1766–1870, but from France, looking at the common depiction of soldiers. He argues from this that in French culture there is an exploration going on of the relationship between peasant and soldier. Popular art, said Hopkin, picked up on the stories of well-known folktales, modernising them to address the issues of a society in which male peasants were called on to serve as soldiers. He argues that soldiers in these prints came to represent an 'absent other', or an alternative way of life to rural society – the type of representation that every society has. In this way, Hopkin explores the way in which the prints constituted an important medium of popular culture.

In a similar vein, Bob Scribner's study of propaganda woodcuts in the German Reformation two centuries earlier gives a sophisticated reading of images depicting popular culture (especially carnival). He shows them as complex texts, rich in meaning to the sixteenth-century reader. In the process, he studied both content and form, revealing the ironic Protestant usage of image in the midst of a religious revolution against imagery (which labelled it as Catholic idolatry) and in favour of the printed word. In this manner, he shows how the medium – the image – was itself subject to controversy in certain societies and how popular culture was always subjected to pressures from elites. In this way, power was at stake in the circulation of texts.

New ways of writing History

The ways of writing History are becoming increasingly varied, reflecting in part a consciousness of tropes and narrative method.

A central, simple method is that of 'thick description'. This was a term coined in 1973 by the American historical anthropologist Clifford Geertz in his conception of culture as 'essentially a semiotic one' in which the distillations and simplifications of the texts of historical actors are avoided in favour of 'thick-description ethnography' that may 'draw large conclusions from small, but very densely textured facts'.[11] Postmodern theorist Richard Rorty says that thick description is a method of democracy itself:

The method is to redescribe lots and lots of things in new ways, until you have created a pattern of linguistic behaviour which will tempt the rising generation to adopt it, thereby causing them to look for appropriate new forms of non linguistic behaviour ... It says things like 'try thinking of it this way' ...[12]

Another method is the historian's use of 'playful' techniques – including the use of the fictionalised account (and conversely the increased appreciation of the modern novel for providing historical insight). This diversity becomes endorsed through the postmodernist notion of the unknowability of the past – that it is an unordered and chaotic thing, sometimes referred to as a 'sublime'. As Keith Jenkins puts it, 'the past in all its sublimity can never be grasped fully in narrative form'.[13]

This absence of ability to represent the past in narrative, in a text, means that the historian should rely more openly and enthusiastically upon the use of metaphor. Metaphor is central to nearly all historical writing, but there is a case for expanding its reflexive use – that is, confessing that our modes of description are metaphorical and not some representationalist literalness. Rorty argues that metaphor develops new language games, that crazy writing opens up new ways of looking at social systems and new knowledges. He suggests that it is apparently crazy people who spark revolutions. Be that as it may, there is greater tolerance of new styles of writing in History now than 40 years ago. Autobiographical writing, the writing in the 'voice' of historical characters, and the use of participant observation are all now commonplace in social and cultural history.

An example of autobiographical writing is Carolyn Steedman's *Landscape for a Good Woman* (1986), based on the author's emotional engagement with her mother's life. In the book she recounts not just her mother's story, but explores her own relationship to her. Biography and autobiography are inextricably merged in an act of historical scholarship and very personal family discovery. The exploration is a story of discovering a parent as one gets older, and perhaps learning most after she dies. From the study, Steedman goes on to examine other issues in historical scholarship.

An example of an alternative form of writing comes again from Natalie Zemon Davis in her study of three seventeenth-century women – one

Jewish, one Catholic and one Protestant. At the start of her study, Davis constructs an imaginary conversation between herself and her three subjects in which they offer critiques of the book that follows. The writing in voices of imagined or real historic characters used to be the sole domain of the novelist. The historian is now starting to see utility in it too.

In such ways, new forms of writing, drawn from other textual examples (the modern interview, the autobiography and so on) are brought in to the work of the historian.

For the student to do

The deconstruction of texts is in many regards not dissimilar to what every student of History already does. But deconstruction, the constituents of which are itemised on page 99, extends the list of issues and deepens the aims of engaging with the primary source.

Deconstruction should become second nature, an everyday task of the historian confronting historical sources. It should be incorporated in historical writing – in essay, project and dissertation – wherever there are texts to be analysed. It may also need to be used in handling secondary sources too – in reading historians' narratives. A project cannot be selected specifically just to permit deconstruction. But cultural or social history, and the types of project outlined in the chapters on signs and discourses (pages 55–6 and 72–3) , provide good opportunities. At all levels of operating, the historian should be prepared to deconstruct.

The use of new or alternative ways of writing is also not beyond the realms of student work in History, though it has to be approached very carefully and with limited ambitions. The danger is that in inexperienced hands, it can become self-indulgent and lose track of other historical skills. But under good guidance, it may be very useful.

Guide to further reading

Theory

Understanding textual theory for the historian is best explored through the 1967 essay by Roland Barthes, 'The Discourse of History', in K. Jenkins (ed.), *The Postmodern History Reader* (London, Routledge, 1997) and Hayden White, *Metahistory: The Historical Imagination in Nineteenth-century Europe* (Baltimore, Johns Hopkins University Press, 1975). J-F Lyotard, *The Postmodern Condition: A Report on Knowledge* (orig. 1979,

Manchester, Manchester University Press, 1984) is difficult. Keith Jenkins's work is a key postmodernist reflection on History-writing from a British perspective: try K. Jenkins, *Why History? Ethics and Postmodernity* (London, Routledge, 1999) and his *On 'What is History?': From Carr and Elton to Rorty and White* (London, Routledge, 1995). Important reflections on the historian's task come in R. Chartier, *On the Edge of the Cliff: History, Language, and Practices* (Baltimore, Johns Hopkins University Press, 1997); H. White, *Tropics of Discourse: Essays in Cultural Criticism* (Baltimore, Johns Hopkins University Press, 1978) and H. White, *The Content of the Form: Narrative Discourse and Historical Representation* (Baltimore, Johns Hopkins University Press, 1987).

On the Bible as the basis for human stories, see N. Frye, *The Secular Scripture: A Study of the Structure of Romance* (Cambridge Mass., Harvard University Press, 1976) and his *The Great Code: The Bible and Literature* (Toronto, Academic Press Canada, 1982). The importance of History to literature studies is theorised in P. Hamilton, *Historicism* (London, Routledge, 1996). On Derrida, see the entry on him in V.B. Leitch (gen. ed.) *The Norton Anthology of Theory and Criticism* (New York, Norton, 2001).

History

The cat massacre story is critiqued in R. Chartier, *Cultural History: Between Practices and Representations* (Oxford, Polity Press, 1988), pp. 95–111. The study of imposture is in N.Z. Davis, *The Return of Martin Guerre* (Cambridge Mass., Harvard University Press, 1983). On 'reading' visual sources, with excellent examples of visual deconstruction, see B. Maidment, *Reading Popular Prints 1790–1870* (Manchester, Manchester University Press, 2001); D.M. Hopkin, *Soldier and Peasant in French Popular Culture, 1766–1870* (Woodbridge, Royal Historical Society/Boydell, 2003) and R.W. Scribner, *For the Sake of Simple Folk: Popular Propaganda for the German Reformation* (Cambridge, Cambridge University Press, 1980).

For autobiographical history-writing, see Carolyn Steedman, *Landscape for a Good Woman* (London, Virago, 1986), and for the use of imagined conversation see N.Z. Davis, *Women on the Margins: Three Seventeenth-Century Lives* (Cambridge, Mass., Harvard University Press, 1995), pp. 1–4.

Notes

1 J. Derrida, *Of Grammatology*, cited in V .B. Leitch (gen. ed.) *The Norton Anthology of Theory and Criticism* (New York, Norton, 2001), pp. 1825–6.

2 J-F Lyotard, *The Postmodern Condition: A Report on Knowledge* (orig. 1979, Manchester, Manchester University Press, 1984), pp. xxiv, 3.

3 Quoted in A. Stafford, *Roland Barthes, Phenomenon and Myth* (Edinburgh, Edinburgh U.P., 1998), pp. 137, 67.

4 R. Barthes, 'The Discourse of History', in K. Jenkins (ed.), *The Postmodern History Reader* (London, Routledge, 1997), pp. 121–3.

5 Ibid.

6 H. White, *Tropics of Discourse: Essays in Cultural Criticism* (Baltimore, Johns Hopkins University Press, 1978), p. 134.

7 H. White, *The Content of the Form: Narrative Discourse and Historical Representation* (Baltimore, Johns Hopkins University Press, 1987), pp. 20, 24–5, 44–7, 56–7, 87.

8 K. Jenkins, *Why History? Ethics and Postmodernity* (London, Routledge, 1999), p. 84.

9 N.Z. Davis, *The Return of Martin Guerre* (Cambridge Mass., Harvard University Press, 1983), pp. 103, 108, 113, 122.

10 B. Maidment, *Reading Popular Prints 1790–1870* (Manchester, Manchester University Press, 2001), pp. 27–52.

11 G. Geertz, *The Interpretation of Cultures* (London, Hutchinson, 1975), pp. 9–10, 28.

12 Quoted in K. Jenkins, On *'What is History?': From Carr and Elton to Rorty and White* (London, Routledge, 1995), p. 102.

13 K. Jenkins, On *'What is History?'*, p. 135.

CHAPTER 6

Self

Is the individual an agent or a victim of history? How much is the individual a 'free agent' to behave as they wish, and to change the direction of history? How much is the individual moulded by powerful forces beyond their control, and swept hither and thither by them? The individual in the past, and how s/he is represented in written History, is a major issue for all historians.

In the late 1980s and 1990s, historians started to engage with the nature of the self. In this, the theorist and the historian started to come together to a greater degree than before. Indeed, much of the new conceptualisation of the individual has been carried on by practising researchers who have confronted the individual in the archive. For this reason, the section Application in history below contains as much that is theoretical development as practical application.

Theory

We have seen a trail of activities for the postmodernist historian. Culture should be deconstructed through its signs, discourses, structures, literary modes and foundational metanarratives. That alone implies a lot of work. But there is more. We move on in this chapter to see that postmodernism raises fundamental issues about the relationship of culture (comprising those elements listed above) *to the individual*. This is where postmodernism gets personal. The linkages here are complex and sophisticated, but the study of the self is the most daring, exciting and innovative area of modern humanities research. What postmodernism does is bring discourse and experience together.

The development of theories of the self, as used by historians, owes a great deal to the work of practising and researching scholars in the field – from anthropology, psychology, literary studies, linguistics, women's and gender studies, and religious studies. It is not easy to point to a body of printed works that lend a notion of a coherent theoretical core to 'the self in history'. Core theorists are less important than practising scholars, and the scholarship is constantly changing.

The social construction of the individual

For many scholars, the central concept in this field is the notion of *the socially constructed nature of the self*. (This makes the concept exactly like those of discourse and text.) An identity is the product of self-perception by the individual (how we see ourselves in a mirror, and how we respond to what we 'see'), and perception by others in society (our response to what others think of us). Therefore, the identity of the individual is something constructed within its social and cultural environment. This social construction involves an interaction between culture (and especially discourses) on the one hand, and the individual's bodily and material experiences on the other. Cultural, corporeal and material elements come together in the construction of identity.

The study of the self in the western academy started from the core modernist notion that has been described as **essentialism**. This is the notion that within each person there is an innate identity (defined by breeding, sex, sexuality, dis/ability, race and class) waiting to be developed, that the individual will develop along those given lines, and that we can and must analyse the self in terms of such essentialist qualities. Essentialism is the attribution of structuralist-defined qualities to the self. Though many scientists and social scientists during and since the Enlightenment explored and challenged essentialism, it was sustained in the nineteenth and early twentieth centuries in popular culture, literature and in 'official' discourse. Government policies of the period were often racist, for instance. From the mid-twentieth century, the postmodernist and poststructuralist conception of the self has rejected essentialism – in part because it is often immoral (amongst other things, racist and sexist). This was publicised in 1948 by the French philosopher Jean-Paul Sartre in the existentialist motto 'existence precedes essence' – the nature of our self comes before our race, religion or gender.[1] But the rejection is not complete, and in some areas is still a theoretically challenged notion. Some structures are not automatically discarded. Postmodernists always **problematise** those structures – they question, explore, examine, try removing them from analysis, and then replace them in analysis.

There is no single and coherent theory of the self to which historians turn in their work. Rather, there are a number of diverse theoretical roots that contribute. In some areas, there are major disagreements between theorists. I will briefly introduce seven key intellectual roots for the study of the self.

One root is Marxist theory and Marxist historiography. Historical interest in the social construction of the individual developed in many countries in the 1960s and 1970s through left-wing-inspired research into oral history and the study of autobiography as an historical source. The drive to provide 'history from the bottom up' was a mainly socialist historical agenda to rediscover (or recover) the voices of the powerless – initially the working classes and the poor, but increasingly also the voices of native peoples, women and ethnic minorities. In Britain and many European countries, this started within a Marxist and Gramscist theoretical framework concerning the subjugation of the individual to the forces of class struggle, and the significance of true and false consciousness as factors affecting the destiny of proletarian revolution. The self was envisaged as buffeted by irresistible external forces of class struggle – both economic and increasingly (by Gramscists) cultural forces. The individual was pictured as swept along by the tides of history. But the theory in this field started to be affected very quickly by the experience of researching historians. They developed a natural affinity with, and respect for, the interviewed subject – for the plebeian, native person, woman and so on. This meant that it was not sufficient to regard the individual as the *victim* of history.

The issue became increasingly for left-wing social historians to have regard for the individual as *agent* of their own choices in life – of their own destiny. More and more attention came to focus on signs and discourses, and a strain of cultural Marxist theory has argued that the floating sign is actually a class-contested sign. As early as 1929, the Soviet theoretician V.N. Volosinov argued that signs are social productions, socially negotiated around an underlying material reality, and as such give rise to different class meanings: 'Sign becomes an arena of the class struggle.'[2] Raymond Williams (1921–88) revived this approach in the 1950s, and it was transformed in the 1980s into a cultural Marxism that responded directly to postmodernism. In this, the social individual has been perceived as the product of subjectification of the discourses of social classifications of class, gender, religion and nation, and thus emerges as the site for contest between those discourses. The social individual is thus 'a space' or site for negotiation, deconstruction, or resistance to the 'ideal forms of dominance' surrounding a sign.

A second root for theory of the self developed in psychology around the figure of Jacques Lacan.

Box 6.1   *Jacques Lacan (1901–81)*

Lacan was a psychologist and theorist who was a member of the Parisian cultural theorists that included Barthes, Foucault and Althusser. His writings are amongst the most obscure of modern cultural theorists, as he wrote in irony, with little structure, playing with words, and using strange grammar. But he was important. He posed a radical challenge to the Freudian establishment in psychology, suggesting that the psyche had three dimensions: the symbolic, the imaginary and the real. His central contribution, from a postmodernist viewpoint, was that he prioritised the textuality of the mind over Freud's verbalisation. 'The unconscious is structured like a language',[3] wrote Lacan. His view was that in the unconscious mind, there are signifiers without fixed links to signifieds, and with no links to external referents. The mind is a text of signs, many of them words, that requires to be read. It has all the properties of the text – signs, discourses, textuality, intertextuality, and embedded structures that compose a reality by which the individual understands the world, and his/her place in it. The human mind must have structures to locate, order and comprehend the welter of signs that it has to absorb. From Freud's verbal science to Lacan's literary humanity, this has extended postmodernism into the heart of a science.

Lacan's approach challenged, and continues to challenge, Sigmund Freud's dominant conception of the human mind. Freud encouraged recognition of the mind's chaos of verbal associations, requiring scientific modelling by the analyst. Lacan encouraged envisaging the unconscious mind as composed of an ordered text, requiring the analyst to 'read' it. The mind is thus, for the Lacanian psychoanalyst, a text requiring deconstruction like any other text. Meaning is derived in the relationship of each word to other words – in difference, in oppositions and parallels. For those readers familiar with Freud, Lacan re-translates dreams from the Freudian mechanisms of condensation and displacement into the literary modes of metaphor and metonymy (that we encountered on page 105).

Lacan's central argument is that the unconscious is the 'kernel of our being'. This makes the self not the traditional stable, unique, separate and conscious entity described by Freud, but an unstable and fragmented conglomeration of signifiers, each of which pre-date the self. In short, the code precedes the message. The signifiers are absorbed into the psyche's

'Imaginary' during infancy through the child seeing their image (in a mirror, for instance) and imagining the relation between I (the beginnings of the self) and the mirror's reflection of the body, with the child learning signifiers more or less empty of meaning. At 6–18 months the child develops a 'Symbolic' dimension of relations, of articulation, in which these signifiers start to attach to signifieds – the start of an endless process of slippery linkages between signifiers and signifieds in the human mind. So, the infant acquires subjectivity and sexuality through interaction with society, rather than through innate human qualities. Lacan's approach is not without challenge in modern cultural theory. Julia Kristeva is distinctive for promoting the importance of the corporeal body for subjectivity, suggesting how sensory and bodily components of a self pre-date the linguistic structures. So, there is still great debate and flux in thought between Lacanian and non-Lacanian approaches.

A third root of the theory of the self was formed through the influence of Lacan's work upon Barthes. In the 1970s he translated the notion of the text from literature and history to the individual and his/her self. He condensed the idea of the self from Lacan, seeing the text not just as an act of analytical reading, but as a personal and projective act of consumption. We each of us activate an identity by projecting a text of our self through speech, bodily actions, written words, our work and so on, thereby creating a text of our self (for others and ourselves to read) in which the relationship of the Imaginary to the Symbolic (in Lacan) allows no demystification of literary language. There was no 'real' or 'true' literary language, no language without meaning, no possibility of 'writing degree zero' as Barthes had originally thought in the early 1950s. Barthes progressed from the Lacanian understanding of the self, where the signifier precedes the signified and the code precedes the message, to perceive the production of texts (including writing) as an act of filling a gap, of attributing signifieds to pre-existing signifiers, not an act of making meaning of a void. Thus, the self was constructed (during growing-up especially) by the mind making textual linkages between detached signifiers (already captured by the mind) and signifieds (coming into vision during maturation). Barthes gave substance to his approach by writing an autobiography as biography, by showing that there was no authorial reality, no quality of the autobiography that was different from the biography. This means that there is no single version of a life, of an identity, of self. Different people will see an individual differently. As sociologist and literary theorist Liz Stanley has written: 'Because memory inevitably has limits, the self we construct is necessarily partial; memory ties together events, persons and feelings actually linked only in such accounts and not in life as it was lived; it equally necessarily relies upon fictive devices in producing any and every account of the self it is concerned with.'[4] The selves invoked in autobiographies, as Stanley adds, 'are actually invocations of a cultural representation of what selves should be: these are shared ideas, conventions, about a cultural form: not descriptions of actual lives but interpretations within the convention'. In short, the autobiographical memory is intertextual, discourse-responsive, and inhabited by signs with no fixed referents, and the individual will also have no single version of his/her life, providing different versions of themselves at different times, in different contexts, and to different questioners. This is **intersubjectivity**, which we discuss later in this chapter as a method for the researching historian.

A fourth and critical root for theoretical development of the self has been feminist theory. The notion of *différence* is central to gender, and many (male) postmodernist theorists including Derrida, Lacan and Baudrillard have located 'woman' as central to conceptualising postmodernity. But each has been highly criticised by feminists for remaining phallocentric, for taking patriarchy as a given and not actually being interested in *women* (rather than the abstract 'woman').[5] The notion of *différence* is very controversial within feminist theory. On the one side it is argued by an historian like Joan Wallach Scott that it is poststructuralist to put gender forward as a category of analysis in front of class and others. However, for the psychoanalyst and literary theorist Julia Kristeva the postmodernist position de-centres the single difference of femininity, the singularity of womanhood, in an effort to avoid the creation of a new closure – what has been described as a new totalitarianism.[6] In either respect, the canon of recent feminist literary theory has been extremely influential in History and the development of the study of the self. Simone de Beauvoir in *The Second Sex* (1956) made an influential exploration of gender as a social rather than a biological construction, and from the late 1960s second-wave feminism used language to challenge patriarchal structures. This challenge came in various forms. One was the feminist reaction against the perception (and self-perception) that women were articles of exchange – a construct associated with Lévi-Strauss and structural anthropology (drawn from Freud and elsewhere) that woman was a commodity, traded in and transacted by men, in a commerce that transcended time and cultures. Another development of many radical feminists of 1968–80 was locating women as part of the tradition of working-class liberation, associating women's subjugation to the structures of society in a way familiar to many early-twentieth-century radical feminists.

But socialist feminism gave way in influence in the 1980s and 1990s to poststructuralist feminism in which agency passed much more to the individual woman. Feminist poststructuralist theorist-historians like Joan Wallach Scott and Denise Riley stressed the reliance upon language as the individual constructed her identity. Women speaking for themselves through personal testimony are using language (signs, discourses), and so deploying cultural constructions in their own identity. From this, feminist theory gave rise to the notion of gendered selves – that women and men construct themselves in different ways. Liz Stanley denies that to claim that the female author is 'alive' and not 'dead' is some 'naive clinging to the wreckage of bourgeois humanist essentialism'.[7] Scott's position is that the personal testimony of an individual cannot represent a truth independent of discourse. Experience cannot exist outside discourse; agency cannot exist independently of language. The objective of the historian working with personal testimony becomes, in the words of Kathleen Canning, 'to untangle the relationships between discourses and experiences by exploring the ways in which subjects mediated or transformed discourses in specific historical settings'.[8] Some theorists argue that poststructuralism and anti-essentialism imply the erosion of gender difference. In any event, it is important to note that subjectivities are very rarely constituted through a single and unified dominant discourse. What makes a woman is not just *one* discourse on being a woman – there will be many, and some that are not necessarily distinctive to women.

A fifth root is the rise within recent historical research of an acceptance of the self as a universal construct of human cultures, but a construct changing in nature according to time and culture. There has been a long-standing modernist notion of the non-universality of the self, locating the self as a product of modernity and western culture. Scholars from many disciplines have argued that subjectivity (the basis of the self) was tied to the rise of the rational and the modern from the Reformation or, later, the Enlightenment. For instance, linguistic philosopher Charles Taylor linked the rise of sense of self to the Enlightenment-induced decline of magic and 'disenchantment of the world', whilst historical anthropologist Stephen Greenblatt linked articulation of the self or concept of the individual (as evinced in autobiography) to modernity – one that was alien, for instance, to Renaissance culture. This seemed to explain, for example, how the early-modern historian is often a commentator on the collective character of early-modern society – guilds and corporations, Italian confraternities, with their signs, symbols and rituals – rather than the individualism of Enlightenment culture. The same impact occurred in anthropology and its treatment of non-western and developing cultures. However, this approach is now less influential in History. It is criticised, firstly, because it is a product of structuralist thinking, secondly because it is derived from a whiggish notion of historical progress, and thirdly because it is essentialist (including imperialist, sexist and even racist) in confining the self to western culture. Postmodernists are not alone in this challenge, but they certainly de-centre and problematise such structures.

A sixth approach emanates from the French religious historian and philosopher Michel de Certeau who, in the late 1960s and early 1970s, followed Barthes in exploring the role of *process* in identity and in the historian's work – the making of history, history as a 'doing'. Equally, he explored production – the economic making of things – and reclaimed from Marx a sense of history as a 'practice'. Marx said: 'Life involves, before everything else, eating and drinking, habitation, and many other things. The first historical fact is the production of the means to satisfy those needs, the production of material life itself. And this is a historical fact, a fundamental condition of all history, which today, as thousands of years ago, must daily and hourly be fulfilled.'[9] In 1984, Certeau consolidated this fragment from Marx together with postmodern ideas (notably from Foucault) and new Marxist ones (from Bourdieu) in a book *The Practice of Everyday Life*. In this, he argued that day-to-day '"ways of operating" constitute the innumerable practices by means of which users reappropriate the space organized by techniques of sociocultural production'. Certeau conceived this as the people's means of resistance, what he called 'the network of an antidiscipline'.[10] He postulated that everyday practices, such as talking, reading, walking, shopping and cooking, were 'tactical in character', part of the individual's negotiation with the disciplines of power, part of the resistance, part of the construction of self. He also cited writing, speaking, reading, religious belief and even death as areas of everyday practice. Within such patterns, Certeau concluded (in an echo of Foucault's 'silence of a murmur') that 'the murmuring of everyday practices' (the small constitutive acts of our daily lives) are not mere parts of functionalist capitalist practice: 'They do not form pockets in economic society.' On the contrary, 'Far from being a local, and thus classifiable, revolt, it is a common and silent, almost sheeplike subversion – our own.'[11]

A seventh and last root I shall cite is performativity theory. Here again, as in Barthes and Certeau, everyday practice emerges as a site of self in a move away from abstract units of knowledge (as in discourses). Where Foucault and others tended to undertheorise the *circulation* of discourse, Derrida emphasised the performative speech acts which rework, tease and stretch language with every usage. As we speak, we don't merely recirculate, but minutely alter, refresh and reassemble language, discourse and signs. Judith Butler continued this approach in 1990 in her *Gender Trouble* in which she argued that gender is *practised*, not merely received and negotiated as discourse, in everyday activity, ritual and learning. Every individual feels his/her way into gender roles, making them unfixed and uncertain. The very notion of 'identity' becomes with Butler an interpretative danger that ensnares analysis in a struggle to define the capture of the individual – that male and female are Enlightenment-project polarisations. She argues instead for 'resignification' of received meanings, and a loosening and multiplication of categories by which we constitute the individual in analysis. Subversive acts, like cross-dressing, should destabilise categories of identity and desire, undermining essentialism, and transgressing (or troubling) the boundaries of male and female. In this way, queer theory is promulgated, and performativity allows research (in both present and past) 'in which gender does not necessarily follow from sex, and desire, or sexuality generally, does not seem to follow from gender'.[12] So, gender becomes a practice, not a pre-figured or constitutive category (such as 'woman'). We make our gender.

To summarise, here we have seven roots for the theory of the self in modern cultural theory. First, we have the Marxist location of a cultural class struggle within (and for the control of) the individual. Second, there is the Lacanian textuality of the mind. Third, there is the Barthesian notion of the discursive construction of the self, in which the text (and its discourses) precedes the existence of the self. Fourth, we come to the feminist conception of the gendered self as dominant in all personal accounts. Fifth, we have an acceptance of the self as a universal characteristic of all societies, and not as a marker of the advancement of European and Enlightenment culture. And sixth and seventh, with de Certeau's theorising of everyday life and Butler's of performativity, we have an emphasis on the personal, practical and mundane in daily routine in the construction of the self.

This is not an exhaustive list of influences, but it gives an idea of the arena for postmodernist formulation of the self. It is a sophisticated area of theory, and we should expect it in the future to become more sophisticated, better distilled, and certainly more influential in the work of the historian, though it is already having great influence.

Application in history

This section discusses more recent theoretical developments, mostly since 1990, alongside practical applications. The two are inseparable. The practitioners of written History are starting to emerge as theorisers.

The empiricist historian has traditionally approached the self largely through the study of biography. This has three main usages in written History. First, the biography of the individual has long been used as a way of understanding historical change – what might be called the heroic interpretation of history. Using the lives of the powerful (such as Alexander the Great, Napoleon, Hitler), biography explores how the attributes of a given individual, from their morality to their technical skills, have changed the course of history. Second, the individual has been studied to look at the *mentalités* of the age, the ways of thinking of a period or a group within a period and place. Third, it has been used as a source of information – as a memory with a bank of details witnessed by the person during his/her lifetime to add to the known facts about events in the past. The postmodernist notion of the self affects these approaches.

Memory

Historians used to take a rather dim view of the human memory. Until the 1960s, there was an interest in the memories of the influential elite – of politicians, diplomats, monarchs, intellectuals and so on. The autobiographies, memoirs and contemporary biographies of such people provided useful information about the facts of history that they experienced, and about attitudes of the elites, political parties and different nations towards those events. But memory itself was not terribly trusted by the historian. The human memory was seen as fallible (getting dates and the order of events wrong), as liable to selective editing, as biased (often propagandistic in format in the knowledge that others would read it), and perhaps as always self-justificatory. The memories of the non-elites and the less educated were treated especially badly, being seen as unreliable and poorly formulated intellectually, and they were usually ignored because they were from the least powerful, least interesting and frankly 'unimportant' people. Such were the memories of the working classes, most women, ethnic minorities, many native peoples, and the mentally and physically disabled.

But historians' attitudes to memory changed in the last 30 years of the twentieth century – so much so, that memory is now a jewel of the social and cultural historian. It started in the late 1960s in an empirical project of radical historians, interviewing living people initially as informants – as sources of evidence of the life of the subordinate groups in society (especially women and the working classes in Europe). In the 1980s and 1990s, the stress of oral history interviewing moved towards exploring the memory as a construction in itself that told, firstly, of how subordination was accomplished in cultural terms, and secondly of how the memory was constructed by interaction with discourse and myth in society. This oral history method was advanced most notably in Italy by the work of Luisa Passerini, who in the late 1970s and 1980s undertook work amongst people in Turin concerning their experience of Fascism. Some historians, especially of the left, have focused their attention specifically on collective memory and how groups, peoples and nations construct their collective histories. From this, some historians became interested in the relation between the collective and the individual memory, and how they were formed. The interaction of memory with discourse and myth became highly developed in work by Alistair Thomson in which he interviewed former Anzac soldiers in Australia about their wartime experiences in the twentieth century. He showed that the memory they constructed of wartime was overwhelmingly determined not by their own experiences (their 'real' memories) but by popular and government-inspired discourse *since the war* about the heroism of the Anzacs. They recounted to Thomson stories of particular battles in which their own memories were superseded by how they were redrawn in Australian national culture. In Thomson's words, 'Memory is a battlefield.'[13] And it becomes so through being an important site for (in this case) national discourse.

This does not mean that memory is automatically overwhelmed by circulating discourses. Far from it. People's minds, conscious or unconscious, are not passive vessels for containing discourses. Rather, the individual constructs their own identity by drawing on the discursive construction of the self available in society at large – so a woman will draw upon the ideal of the perfect woman (and its embedded opposite, the anti-ideal – angel and harlot at the same time), situate themselves between those paradigms of the discourse, and reflect this in their oral history testimonies. In a study of how British women recalled their lives during the Second World War, Penny Summerfield showed the power of two dominant but seemingly opposing discourses – the modernising woman and the traditional woman – in testimony: the first saw the war as a welcome liberalising of women's roles, the second as something to be endured before resumption of normal or traditional female roles. By analysing oral testimony, she was able to show how women's narratives could adopt various and changing positions in relation to those discourses, sometimes floating from one to the other as different periods of life were being recounted. Summerfield concluded that: 'personal narratives draw on the generalized subject available in discourse to construct the particular personal subject. It is thus necessary to encompass within oral-history analysis and interpretation, not only the voice that speaks for itself, but also the voices that speak to it, the discursive formulations from which understandings are selected and within which accounts are made.'[14]

There has been an interacting study between how women narrate their lives in oral testimony and in auto/biography. Almost uniquely in recent cultural theory, the theory has developed through historical practice – through research into experience. Feminist literary theory has contributed greatly to understanding the texts with which the historian deals, creating in feminist history more than any other area of the humanities a convergence of interest between the historian and the literary specialist. The sociologist and literary theorist Liz Stanley has studied women's autobiography. She raises a key issue – that the chronological autobiography is quintessentially male in form, and alien to the ways of female memory. She suggests that in some past memoirs, women felt compelled to adopt the male chronology and its implicit thematic framework of advancement, progress, and upward movement of the individual. But when freed from such compulsion, or fighting against it, female autobiography has distinctive features that Stanley traces: 'The self is fractured, changing, alterable and frequently an object as well as a puzzle to the subject whose self it is.' In addition, the self is not represented as 'the unfolding or development of a coherent, mature and completely actualised unique self'.[15] A girl's childhood, as historian Carolyn Steedman notes, is often adult in self-understanding, much more than for a boy, and often confuses adult men into infantilising a girl's sense of self; to be crude, girls grow up faster than boys, whilst men falsely treat girls as immature.[16] Indeed, in my own study of nineteenth- and twentieth-century British Christian culture, I found that the conversion was discursively constructed as a masculine phenomenon (involving very male physical display of muscular strength, and the weakness of the converted man before his Lord), reflected in personal testimony of the conversion as a male need, whilst a woman was depicted as innately religious, and this may be observed in testimony as well as in discourse.

Stanley goes further and suggests that there are important issues for the investigating historian or literary specialist in reading auto/biography and conducting oral interviewing of those from times or places (or perhaps sub-cultures) where the understanding and even the practice of sexual encounters (and the types of sexual encounter) were not the same as those of the present-day historian. We have modern categories of sexuality which we use to pigeonhole people (gay, heterosexual and transsexual). But Stanley shows, through a close reading in autobiography, testimony and book inscriptions, that such categories were unknown a century ago, and that lesbianism, for instance, was often categorised as 'friendship'.[17] So, personal testimony produces no single authoritative reading, for changing structures are invoked, and the reader's reading can change greatly too. Clearly, also, the structuring of narratives of the self is highly variable. For instance, Christian narratives fade in the secular age of the late twentieth century (even in the recounting of religious lives). Intertextuality changes as the self changes. New models are borrowed from television soap operas or from tabloid newspapers to provide ways of thinking about our lives and ways of narrating our lives in biography or oral testimony.

The self that emerges in recent scholarship is far from solely definable as postmodern. There are controversies, for instance over the categorisation of structures in the self. Are male/female, black/white, able/disabled and gay/straight structural categories? Is using such structuralism in the construction of the self inevitable, and thus inevitable in the reading of others' construction of *their* selves? This is an ongoing debate of some intensity in feminist and black scholarship. For the historian, it raises issues of how much to draw upon structures to pigeonhole individuals from the past. It also raises the issue of just how can we discover the nature of the self in the past. How do we source the information?

Re/deconstructing the self: the witch and the child

Reconstruction and deconstruction are often portrayed as jarring opposites. In this section, we see the two techniques coming together in postmodernist work on the self.

In 1994, the historian Lyndal Roper dissected the trials and confessionals of Regina Bartholome, an accused witch in Augsburg in Germany in 1670. Regina's testimony (mostly acquired without torture) is a fantasy of her association with the devil, but it is also a vehement rage against paternal figures – the exclusively male council of inquiry, God, and her father who failed to protect her. A fantasy of witchcraft emerged, relating, Roper argues, to the psychic conflicts of womanhood. Roper says that, working within their own masculine fantasies, the interrogators turned on every detail of Regina's account. A culture obsessed with the power of the devil, fathers and women 'enabled a combustion of interests to occur, flaring up into interrogations under torture and the production of those sadistic, masochistic stories which so whetted their contemporaries' appetite for tales of the relation between women and the Devil'. Roper shows the enduring power of the sense of self during the early-modern period where many historians had argued for its construction only within later modernity. She uses the notion of real physical difference to explore the nuanced texts of autobiography, seeing the confession of Regina as a 'theatre of the mind' in which the individual's inner conflicts are projected into fantasy and acted out in her relations with others. 'If gender is to be a category of social explanation, it must bridge the gap between discourse, social formation and the individual sexed subject.' Roper concludes: 'Bodies are not merely the creations of discourse. What we have is a history of discourses about the body; what we need is a history that problematises the relation between the psychic and the physical.' But this is not a claim to return to the 'real' in history. Indeed, Roper explicitly says that to understand women's confessions before a witchcraft trial there is no gain in the strategy of 'teasing out the "real" from the fantastic' in such accounts.[18] Rather, this is a call to show that the construction of an auto-biography, an account of the self, cannot be left to the study of discourses alone.

Historian Carolyn Steedman analysed how female children and women have, until the very recent past in Britain – the mid-twentieth century – dis-played an economic understanding of the self. Steedman analyses a passage from an 1849 encounter between social investigator Henry Mayhew and an eight-year-old watercress-seller in East London. In this, the girl described her own life in economic terms – how she struggled to keep a poor family through street earnings, her shrewdness and streetwise econ-omic sense. The girl understood her self, her virtues and her very identity, as an economic operator on the streets and within her distressed family. This approach is one that we, living in a society where child labour is banned as a social evil, find alien. Toys, the symbol of childhood to which Mayhew and perhaps we might expect the child to respond, feature only briefly in the girl's account. But the economic metaphor is a powerful one in her testimony. The girl defined herself in terms of earnings, economic operations, and her hard and clever labour, and with a surprising intensity. Steedman says that 'her labour was not an attribute, nor a possession, but herself'.[19] Steedman's book disturbs our sense of the criteria of judgement, the expectations with which we approach historical encounters with people. The economic sense of the self, especially the child self, seems quite alien to the bourgeois conceptions with which most historians are infused. As Steedman demonstrates, there are stock, pre-figured narratives of the childhood self with which the investigators, both in the 1840s and now, are familiar. We tend to draw on ideas of working-class struggle with an external oppressor, solidarity in the working-class community, and the juvenilisation of a child's identity. By contrast, the working-class female subject has a different narrative, certainly down to the middle of the twentieth century.

To a great extent, the development of this work on the personal testimony of people from the more distant past drew on the example of oral history, which records and analyses testimony from the living. Focusing especially on subordinate groups – notably women, and religious, ethnic and sexual minorities – those traditionally without voices in written History, oral history as a technique has developed tremendous new theory and method. Using its principles, documentary History has used *third-hand accounts* not just to deconstruct, but, as in Roper's example above, to reconstruct testimony. This uses evidence given to lawyers, courts or visiting journalists, where testimony was translated into the format (sometimes the different language or dialect) of the legally literate, or a different social class, or a different gender (sometimes all three). In relation to feminist work this often involves putting the woman's experience in the past back together again after it has been dissolved by (often) men and patriarchal institutions such as judicial or church courts. Once assembled, the reconstructed voices are ripe for the historian to deconstruct.

One development in oral history has been especially important – historians' awareness of **intersubjectivity**. This is the principle that in an interview between an interviewer (the historian) and an interviewee (the subject of historical inquiry) there are actually two selves, or subjectivities, present. The interviewer presents a subjectivity, composed of his/her sex, age, dress, manner of deportment and, of course, the way of asking the questions, and this constitutes a culture of signs and discourses that is understood by the interviewee. The interviewee will be responsive in his/her testimony to this presence in all sorts of ways. It is commonly observed that young female oral history interviewers obtain better accounts from older men of the working of machines, since a man speaking to a younger man often assumes knowledge of the workings of technical equipment. A woman interviewing an older man about parenting is often more able to elicit favourable comments on 'new man' qualities like tending babies. If this undermines some of the empiricist aims of oral testimony, it certainly opens up the self to quite deep exploration. The sensitivity of personal testimony to the subjectivities present is quite extraordinary, and a fascinating tool in the development of oral history in the twentieth century.

But, by precisely the same token, testimonies from the sources of the dead – in court records, in autobiographies and even in diaries – can be 'read' with the same sensitivity to the subjectivities present. A good example is historian Carlo Ginzburg's use of witchcraft interrogations in Italy in 1575. He used the accounts of these encounters to exploit the gap between the image of witchcraft within the interrogators' questions and the actual testimony of the accused. This then permitted him to reconstruct the nature of the *benandanti* 'sleep-walking' cult of the time. Intersubjectivity shows the constant reconstruction of the self at every interview, bringing the historian closer to the methods of both the literary specialist and the anthropologist.

A new research method and ethic respects the people being researched by historical inquiry. Patrick Joyce applied the study of the self to understand nineteenth-century British society through the lives of two men, Edwin Waugh and John Bright and, through them, opened up the study of the 'social' as a way of discovering how democracy was imagined. The reconstruction of lost voices is often undertaken by historians when the weak and powerless met power the most – in courts of law. Lynn Abrams has used court records in nineteenth-century Germany to open up the language of verbal abuse, cited in cases of marital breakdown, to explore discourses on femininity, whilst David Nash has looked at cases of blasphemy in British courts, applying Foucauldian perspectives to show how light can be cast on this aspect of religious belief and authority. The increasing byword in such research is that of respect for the interviewed subject. This is signalled by increased scrutiny of oral history projects by college ethics committees, the use of approval forms, and ensuring the informed consent of those being interviewed.

Reconstruction has another basis within deconstruction – in the new study of everyday life, and the parallel emergence of performativity theory. The study of everyday life (much of it originally inspired by the *Annales* school) has moved forward a conventional interest of social history, but this has been re-theorised by performativity and Certeau's ideas in exploring the role of ritual and consumption, space and place, on identity and the construction of the individual. This is already familiar territory in anthropology and geography, but historians have much to learn.

Reflexivity of the historian

The personal position of the historian becomes critical in postmodernist study. This is not entirely new. As Edward Said points out, the Italian Marxist Antonio Gramsci wrote in the 1940s: 'The starting-point of critical elaboration is the consciousness of what one really is, and "knowing thyself" as a product of the historical process to date, which has deposited in you an affinity of traces, without leaving an inventory.' Therefore, added Gramsci, 'it is imperative at the outset to compile such an inventory'.[20]

Reflexivity is an acknowledgement by the historian in his/her narrative of the personal political issues that s/he brings to the study. In oral history, it is an acknowledgement of the subjectivity that is brought to the inter-view and that is 'read' by, and influential upon, the interviewee in his/her testimony. It is also an acknowledgement of ideological, ethnic, religious and sexual issues. It banishes claims to neutrality and situates the study in the context of other historians' writings and research. It is not the preserve of the postmodernist, but it is certainly an obligation upon him/her.

Reflexivity goes further than this. One vital development has been the increasing use since 1990 of the personal in history. The implication of the past and present as texts, and of the historian as the mediator between the two, is that the historian is personally involved in the production of History. The historian thus becomes a central figure, and this 'personal' can take the form of autobiography, the use of family experience, and the playing with literary genres – such as writing a study of a theme by 'authoring' accounts from different characters in an historical event. This has been especially important amongst feminists of the 1960s and 1970s in their exploration of their experiences as girls growing up under the older discursive world of the 1950s, and in the understanding of their relation-ships with their mothers. Carolyn Steedman's searing account of autobiographic remembrance (laced with the guilt of the grown-up, moved-away child) of her mother's very difficult economic circumstances, followed by an academic analysis of the narrative features in the construc-tion of the working-class woman's self. Steedman undermines the certainties of the traditional structures of 'the working-class life' in English socialist historiography in their applicability to women and girls. 'Women are the final outsiders,' she wrote. Using her mother's story as seen through the daughter's eyes, Steedman seeks in her own words to find for women a self based on 'a psychology where once there was only the assumption of pathology or false consciousness to be seen'.[21] But there is no central 'alternative' scholarship model here. Franca Iacovetta's work on Italian immigrants to Toronto shares in this 'autobiographical turn' of the his-torian, though in a more conventional form of historical scholarship, raising the usage of postmodern insights within (amongst other things) a materialist, class-based Marxist tradition.

The overlap between writing research-based history, biography (of a parent especially) and autobiography enriches as well as textures the history of the recent past. The memory is no longer merely the source-spring for the historian in search of the hero, the *mentalités* of the time, and 'hard' data. The memory is a thing in itself, a window onto both causation and negotiation of the individual within their historical context. Study of memory, above all, is the first step to returning agency to the individual. And in doing so, the historian can see the cultural processes that impact on human action and historical change.

Yet, it must be said that most historians are rarely as reflexive as scholars in other disciplines, such as anthropology. A major controversy of that discipline is the extent to which western scholars can write about and understand non-western societies. Do Enlightenment paradigms of thought, such as Marxism, have an inappropriateness to the peoples of developing nations where the economic and social structures of the west are perhaps irrelevant? Does a scholar have to belong to the culture, or colour, of the cultures s/he is studying, or even speak the language? (For instance, as an historian of Scotland, must I know the now-decaying language of Gaelic to research in Highland history?) Explicit controversies of this kind are starting to affect the History profession, but there have been larger issues within social and cultural anthropology (especially historical anthropology) that may come to impact on the postcolonial studies of the historian. One example in the 1990s was the Sahlins–Obeyesekere controversy over whether a westerner could interpret the Hawaiians' encounter with Captain Cook in the eighteenth century.

At the end of the day, different scholars can bring different skills (including languages, statistics and deconstruction skills) to the same topic of research, and nobody can or should be excluded. The study of the experience and testimony of the neglected individual in the past can be privileged. However, the same privilege cannot be extended to a single 'authoritative' voice of research scholarship. If essentialism is being eroded from historical theory and narrative, then it needs to be eroded from scholarship entirely. Historians should not be barred from doing research because of their race or gender.

Agency

The greatest difficulty any historian has in his/her work is in ascribing *agency*. By this is meant saying what or who caused history to happen, and an acknowledgement of who has the freedom to cause historical change. It concerns the freedom of the individual to make choices that change history.

There is no easy or single solution to the conundrum of how far the individual is historically responsible. The postmodernist historian appears to be in a double bind. On the one hand, postmodernism seems, on the face of it, to suggest that the discursivity of culture prescribes, or limits, the choice of human actions. Every culture is composed of discourses concerning human actions (orders effectively to 'do this, but not that') and, in effect, all possible actions are socially constructed and limited in number. This seems to suggest the individual is limited in what he or she can do to change history. Further, the textuality of all knowledge means that there is constant intertextual borrowing – including by individuals in constructing their sense of self and their personal testimony. So, the individual seems to be described as incapable of much or any originality, bound by the context in which he or she lives either to obey or to refute discourse (the refutation thereby becoming in itself a discourse). The conformist and the nonconformist (the conservative and the rebel) are then equally entrapped by the discursivity of culture. If culture forms the primary venue for hierarchies of power to be exerted, circulated, challenged and overturned, then this means that there is a constant enslavement to cultural choices. What room is there for the agency of the individual?

On the other hand, the postmodernist wants to be a radical, a democrat and anti-authoritarian. S/he is building on all the work of Marxist and Gramscist historians to construct a 'history from the bottom up' that empowers the individual of the past. The postmodernist historian thus seems to get into a major conceptual difficulty here. How can the individual be ascribed agency while being at the same time ensnared inescapably in culture?

Foucault certainly diverted attention towards how the individual was more the victim than the author of history, buffeted by the discourses which said 'do this and avoid doing that'. But others who have contributed to postmodernist theory have been much more willing to empower the individual through his or her own agency. Each individual has to negotiate through discourse within the context of their body and their material environment. Lacanian psychology sees no submissive, manipulated and passive self. The individual self has vital decisions to make in handling the traumas of life. S/he must decide how to deploy the self as an independent agent in society (as sociologist Nikolas Rose says) 'in which life and its contingencies become meaningful to the extent that they can be construed as the product of personal choice'.[22] The postmodernist self is arguably a more active agent than the Freudian one.

But two things in postmodernism seem to be denials of agency: the death of the author (giving primacy to pre-existing culture), and an acceptance that the self is a modern idea of the west (thus denying agency pre-1700 and outside the west). Concerning the second of these, Lyndal Roper's study of the accused witch of the sixteenth century challenged historians' acceptance of the self as a creation of eighteenth-century Enlightenment culture. But as far as the first is concerned, the most systematically challenging work has been that of postcolonial subaltern studies. This school of work denies in stark terms that the rebel against colonial and imperial European power (in, for example, India), between the sixteenth and twentieth centuries, was in any sense ensnared by culture. 'When a peasant rose in revolt at any time or place under the Raj,' wrote Indian scholar Ranajit Guha in 1983, 'he did so necessarily and explicitly in violation of a series of codes which defined his very existence as a member of that colonial, and still largely semi-feudal society … To rebel was indeed to destroy many of those familiar signs which he had learned to read and manipulate in order to extract a meaning out of the harsh world around him and live with it.' Here is a merger of Gramscism with postmodernism. The peasant rebel, in Guha's terms, is 'an entity whose will and reason constituted the praxis called rebellion'. Historiography has an 'affinity with policy' that, says Guha, 'reveals its character as a form of *colonialist knowledge*'. A history of rebellion that merely becomes 'a datum in the life-story of the Empire' fails to focus on insurgency: 'The rebel has no place in this history as the subject of rebellion.' For Guha, this effect is enforced by the historian ascribing 'causes' to rebellion: 'To know the cause of a phenomenon is already a step taken in the direction of controlling it.' And in seeking those causes in the history of colonies, the historian is drawn inevitably closer to the reasons ascribed by the colonialist witnesses and secondary witnesses. This is another denial of agency. It extends, ironically, to two classes of would-be postcolonial historians. The first is the critic-historian of empire who ascribes rebellion to the 'failures' of empire, as if empire should succeed or inevitably could not succeed, thus denying agency to the individual peasant or even the 'masses'. The second is the radical historian who retrieves the history of insurgency from imperial historiography and tries to 'arrange it along the alternative axis of a protracted campaign for freedom and socialism', thus amounting to 'an act of appropriation which excludes the rebel as the conscious subject of his own history and incorporates the latter as only a contingent element in another history with another subject'. In these attempts, the historian becomes 'a prisoner of empty abstractions'.[23]

This is a powerful critique. And it does not stand alone. The death of the author is taken by many to infer that the postmodernist position also implies 'the death of the subject'[24] (meaning the denial of the agency of the individual). Interest in resistance (of the rebel), as in subaltern studies within postcolonialism, is a readjustment that shifts the locus of the problem back to a kind of middle ground inhabited by the power of the individual. The individual is in constant, everyday resistance. The practice of everyday life, as Certeau has argued of the individual in western culture, is relocated by subaltern studies historian James Scott to the colonial rebel's daily resistance to imperial rule.

This is an important lesson for the historian. It is to focus upon the resistance, and not upon either the hegemony of structures or upon the poststructural. The lesson is that power is *not just language*, but is in the resistance to power when language may not (yet) be formulated by the inarticulate rebel. Rebellion can precede the language of rebellion. Consequently, there is in Guha an argument that the radical historian must champion the resistance, not the power.

This issue of agency is approached in a different way by British symbolic anthropologist Anthony Cohen, but his conclusion strikingly converges theoretically with subaltern studies. 'In treating the self as socially constituted,' Cohen says, 'social science has denied "authorship" to the individual, seeing identity either as imposed by an other, or as formulated by the individual in relation to an other. Both views imply the insubstantial nature of selfhood.' He argues that all signs and discourses are interpreted differently by people. The point of discourse, he persuasively argues, is that those diverse meanings amongst individuals lead society to the construction of a common discourse – not the other way around. In other words, the meanings precede the discourses (just as the rebellion may precede the language of rebellion). We must not doom people to be forever portrayed as 'perpetrators rather than architects of action'. As with the subaltern studies position, Cohen warns of structuralist determinism of individual action – arguing that people of a certain race or class or gender must think and act alike. Anthropology suggests that societies have a tension – a dialectic – between the self and the society, not one that is necessarily resolved, but one constantly in play in social relations and whose aim is 'the balanced self'. In echoes of both Certeau's everyday life and of poststructuralism, Cohen points out that social science tends to see the self as defined by society rules rather than by society practices. Society, he urges, is a set of forms – of actions – rather than a set of rules or meanings. The meanings are in the self; all society is providing is the forms. The self is filled out, elaborated or, as one academic put it, 'made competent' by culture, but is not something subjugated to it.[25]

This conclusion might be reinforced by a 'textualist' counter-argument to the subaltern studies' view of the resistance of the individual. It could be said that the notion of resistance is part of a new narrative that the subaltern student is creating, which in itself regathers and retotalises the historical subject. The implication of all this is that the individual is constantly being summoned to inhabit different narratives which inevitably tend to totalising answers. It is natural that every narrative tends to totalisation – towards a closure and completeness. It is inescapable. So the postmodernist must constantly bounce off one totalising narrative against another. For instance, the rebel peasant needs to be constantly positioned in different narratives, and playing off the one against the other brings thickening of the description (*après* Geertz) from which emanate more understandings.

This is a highly suggestive theorising of what postmodernists should be striving for. It helps us to rethink the link between discourse and the individual by shifting the meaning out from the abstract to the personal. Clearly, the absence of a single discourse or meaning is important in studying the self and society. The meaning that the individual adheres to and circulates through everyday action is part of the constant redrafting of society – a hybridisation of discourse – and the one through which the individual scribes his/her self upon society. Equally, though, it is important not to ascribe 'big meanings' to all human actions. Individuals act through accidents, aberrations, alcohol, drugs, learning disabilities or mental instability. An individual's action may seem to an historian to have major premeditation, but may be accidental and have no link, discourse or ideology.

This means that there can be no one, totalising historical aim for the historian. If postmodernism has undermined the treatment of the totalising power (of the state, the institution, the political party) and substituted for it the power of language in culture (discourse), then these critics remind us to beware the alternative totalising of power in language. Yet, as Cohen makes plain, asserting the primacy of the self does not make 'culture' or 'society' redundant in analysis. Culture and society are still necessary concepts. We cannot escape them.

For the student to do

There is much virtue in the History student seeking to place the individual at the forefront of their writings about the past. The individual concerned should not be just the ruler and the elite. To focus on such people is hardly a novel technique. The heroic interpretation of History (that the hero made History), which was so influential in the nineteenth and early twentieth centuries, was greatly challenged from the 1950s by left-wing social science (which argued that society made the individual). In the 1990s, the postmodern idea emerged that two selves make History – the self in the past and the self in the present (the historian). The reflexive inquirer now engages with the ordinary individual of the past.

The History student can think about reconstructing stories of individuals previously unrecognised in written History. In the 1980s and 1990s, gay History as well as women's History did much to recover the voices of those marginalised or even unheard in their own times. There remain many to study. A classic group is the disabled – a group that is not a 'group' with similar physical or mental conditions, but which in certain times has been so regarded. The History of the experience and representation of disability is only just beginning to feature in scholarship. But there is still much to be researched about individuals whose stories, buried in archives, or on oral history tapes, or still in their heads, provide the opportunity for being reconstructed and deconstructed. Such work can be done on a single live individual who is willing to be interviewed or asked to write down their memories and can, with his/her consent, be studied.

After all, the History book is not dissimilar from the oral history interview. In that, the oral historian is undertaking data gathering from the memory of the respondent, while possibly also exploring discourse reflection, intertextuality and intersubjectivity. By the same token, the archival historian is undertaking data-gathering from the document of a person of the past, discourse analysis and textual deconstruction. But s/he should also be thinking about the subjectivity that s/he has brought to the desk of the archive, and that is eliciting results in the selection, editing and ways of 'reading' the past. The scholarship of the deconstructing historian should not be all postmodern; equally, the scholarship of the empiricist should not be all empirical. The History student can try to bring some of this consciousness and sense of responsibility to her/his work.

Guide to further reading

Theory

Excellent on many of the issues in this chapter are entries on Kristeva, Lacan, Butler, Gramsci, Greenblatt, in V.B. Leitch (gen. ed.) *The Norton Anthology of Theory and Criticism* (New York, Norton, 2001). On the Marxist root of the self, see N. Volosinov, *Marxism and the Philosophy of Language* (London, Seminar Press 1973) and E. Yeo, 'Language and contestation: the case of "the People", 1832 to the present', in J. Belcham and N. Kirk (eds) *Languages of Labour* (Aldershot, Ashgate, 1997). On Kristeva, see L. Curti, *Female Stories, Female Bodies: Narrative, Identity and Representation* (Basingstoke, Macmillan, 1998). On autobiography and feminist scholarship, see L. Stanley, *The Auto/biographical I* (Manchester, Manchester University Press, 1992); L. Stanley and S. Wise, *Breaking Out Again: Feminist Ontology and Epistemology* (London and New York, Routledge, 1993) and K. Canning, 'Feminist history after the linguistic turn: historicizing discourse and experience', *Signs: Journal of Women in Culture and Society*, vol. 19 (1994).

On ideas on everyday life, see M. de Certeau, *The Writing of History* (orig. 1975, New York, Columbia University Press, 1988) and M. de Certeau, *The Practice of Everyday Life* (Berkeley, University of California Press, 1984). For an example of anthropological practice in this realm, see D. Headon, J. Hooton and D. Horne (eds) *The Abundant Culture: Meaning and Significance in Everyday Australia* (St Leonards, NSW, Allen & Unwin, 1994).

On anthropology and the self, see N. Rapport, 'Individualism', in A. Barnard and J. Spencer (eds) *Encyclopaedia of Social and Cultural Anthropology* (London, Routledge, 1996), pp. 298–301; S.M. Low and D. Lawrence-Zúniga (eds), *The Anthropology of Space and Place: Locating Culture* (Oxford, Blackwell, 2003), pp. 31–2 and A.P. Cohen, *Self Consciousness: An Alternative Anthropology of Identity* (London, Routledge, 1994). For the debate over who should write the history of non-western peoples, see M. Sahlins, *How Natives Think: About Captain Cook, For Example* (Chicago, University of Chicago Press, 1995).

On reflexivity of the historian, see F. Iacovetta, 'Post-modern ethnography, historical materialism, and decentring the (male) authorial voice: a feminist conversation', *Histoire Sociale/Social History* 32 (1999), 275–93.

History

Five of the very best histories of the self, written on very different individuals in very different ways, are L. Roper, *Oedipus and the Devil: Women, Sexuality and Religion in Early Modern Europe* (London, Routledge, 1994); C. Ginzburg, *The Night Battles: Witchcraft and Agrarian Cults in the Sixteenth and Seventeenth Centuries* (orig. 1966, London, Routledge & Kegan Paul, 1983); C. Steedman, *Landscape for a Good Woman* (London, Virago, 1986); P. Joyce, *Democratic Subjects: The Self and the Social in Nineteenth-century England* (Cambridge, Cambridge University Press, 1994) and P. Summerfield, *Reconstructing Women's Wartime Lives: Discourse and Subjectivity in Oral Histories of the Second World War* (Manchester, Manchester University Press, 1998). See also L. Passerini, *Fascism in Popular Memory: The Cultural Experience of the Turin Working Class* (Cambridge, Cambridge University Press, 1987).

On subaltern studies within postcolonial History, see R. Guha, 'The prose of counter-insurgency', in N.B. Dirks, G. Eley and S.B. Ortner (eds), *Culture/Power/History: A Reader in Contemporary Social Theory* (Princeton, Princeton University Press, 1994). On the nature of intersubjectivity between the historian and subject, and how power, authority and responsibility should be handled, see L. Sitzia, 'Telling Arthur's story: oral history relationships and shared authority', *Oral History Journal*, 1999, vol. 27. For a fascinating speculative commentary on identity and mental health in a colonial setting, see James Mills, *Madness, Cannabis and Colonialism: The 'Native-only' Lunatic Asylums of British India, 1857–1900* (Basingstoke, Macmillan, 2000).

Other examples cited which use studies of reconstructed ideas of the self, focusing on language, are L. Abrams, 'Whores, whore-chasers and swine: the regulation of sexuality and restoration of order in the nineteenth century German divorce court', *Journal of Family History*, vol. 21 (1996); D. Nash, *Blasphemy in Modern Britain: 1789 to the Present* (Aldershot, Ashgate, 1999) and C.G. Brown, *The Death of Christian Britain: Understanding Secularisation 1800–2000* (London, Routledge, 2000).

Notes

1 J-P Sartre, *Existentialism and Humanism* (orig. 1948, London, Eyre Methuen, 1973), p. 26.

2 V.N. Volosinov, *Marxism and the Philosophy of Language* (London, Seminar Press 1973), p. 23.

3 Lacan quoted in V.B. Leitch (gen. ed.) *The Norton Anthology of Theory and Criticism* (New York, Norton, 2001), p 1281.

4 L. Stanley, *The Auto/biographical I* (Manchester, Manchester University Press, 1992), p. 62.

5 Veitch (gen. ed.), *Norton,* pp. 1282–3.

6 L. Curti, *Female Stories, Female Bodies: Narrative, Identity and Representation* (Basingstoke, Macmillan, 1998), pp. 20–1.

7 L. Stanley, *The Auto/biographical I*, pp. 16–17.

8 K. Canning, 'Feminist history after the linguistic turn: historicizing discourse and experience', *Signs: Journal of Women in Culture and Society*, vol. 19 (1994), pp. 374–5.

9 Marx quoted in M. de Certeau, *The Writing of History* (orig. 1975, New York, Columbia University Press, 1988), p. 13.

10 M. de Certeau, *The Practice of Everyday Life* (Berkeley, University of California Press, 1984), pp. xiv–xv.

11 Ibid., pp. 200–3.

12 J. Butler, *Gender Trouble*, quoted in Veitch (gen. ed.), *Norton,* p. 2497.

13 A. Thomson, 'The Anzac legend: Exploring national myth and memory in Australia', in R. Samuel and P. Thompson (eds) *The Myths We Live By* (London, Routledge, 1990), p. 73.

14 P. Summerfield, *Reconstructing Women's Wartime Lives: Discourse and Subjectivity in Oral Histories of the Second World War* (Manchester, Manchester University Press, 1998), pp. 15, 259.

15 Stanley, *Auto/biographical I* , pp. 63, 85.

16 C. Steedman, *Landscape for a Good Woman* (London, Virago, 1986), pp. 128–9.

17 Stanley, *Auto/biographical I*, pp. 214–35.

18 L. Roper, *Oedipus and the Devil: Women, sexuality and religion in early modern Europe* (London, Routledge, 1994), pp. 3, 15, 21, 231–3, 240.

19 Steedman, *Landscape*, pp. 129, 136.

20 Gramsci quoted in E. Said, *Orientalism* (orig. 1978, Harmondsworth, Penguin, 1985), p. 25.

21 Steedman, *Landscape*, p. 144.

22 N. Rose, 'Assembling the modern self', in Porter R. (ed.), *Rewriting the Self: Histories from the Renaissance to the Present* (London, Routledge, 1997), pp. 241, 244–6.

23 R. Guha, 'The prose of counter-insurgency', in N.B. Dirks, G. Eley and S.B. Ortner (eds), *Culture/Power/History: A Reader in Contemporary Social Theory* (Princeton, Princeton University Press, 1994), pp. 335–6, 358, 360, 365.

24 Dirks, Eley and Ortner, ibid., 'Introduction', p. 14.

25 A.P. Cohen, *Self Consiousness: An Alternative Anthropology of Identity* (London, Routledge, 1994), pp. 15, 21, 28–9, 30–2, 73, 109, 113–14, 117, 133.

CHAPTER 7

Morality

Is studying History about moral issues? It has already been argued in this book that the answer is 'yes'. In the 1990s and early 2000s, some theorists argued that the nature of History as a subject is a moral project, but that professional historians failed to recognise this. We explore this further.

Theory

Morality

The central moral implication of postmodernism is that morality is not, cannot be and should not be founded on empiricism. Many historians during the twentieth century, especially those attached to empiricist method, argued that an understanding of history provides an understanding of ethical issues. They saw the past as informing our understanding now of the moral conditions through which humanity has traversed. Moreover, because of this it was implicit that the present day provided a superior version of morality than the past. In other words, an empiricist line of thinking is that experience has taught humanity its morality. Thus, knowledge of the history of the slave trade, and of the Jewish Holocaust, defines our own moral position on these issues. As a result, citation of historical examples peppers moral exposition and exhortation. The certainty of morality, of its correctness, becomes verified by the catalogues of history's manifest and self-evident moral wrongs. So, an empirical historical foundation is seen as the pre-requisite of a well-argued morality.

The postmodernist position is different. It argues that morality is divorced from empiricism. It argues that there can be no logical recourse to the past as an empirical resource by which to justify a moral position. It argues that morality comes from *a sense of the immoral*. This may be gained from history, but the decision to make it an immorality is a non-empirical one. Immoralities are declared, not proven. The past does not make one action immoral and another moral. The decision as to what is acceptable behaviour and what is not acceptable behaviour has to be taken by each generation, and by each person within each generation.

There are a number of **epistemological** and practical reasons for arriving at this position. First, morality changes. It is not a constant, but changes by era, by country, by culture and sometimes within a society by ethnography, social class and age of the people. For example, young people of the twenty-first century in many nations in the world are considerably more sexually liberal than their grandparents, but are likely to be considerably more environmentally conscious. This absence of constancy is especially noticeable for those alive in the last 60 years as western society has undergone the most dramatic shift in its sexual, racial and legal morality. These have been profound, epoch-forming shifts in morality. This absence of certainty and constancy breaks any link between history, empirical certainty and morality.

A second reason is that facts are always open to dispute since they are representations of historical events and, as such, are ripe for constant re-evaluation or rebuttal in the light of new research, hypotheses and perspective. So, the *facts* of history cannot be allowed to be the decisive factor in our construction of human morality.

The third reason is that because the past has always to be rendered in narrative to be part of written History, we cannot rely on a given narrative as constituting 'reality'. This opens the way to many different accounts and interpretations of the past. People's confidence in morality will tend to be undermined if it is based on facts and narratives that are so obviously uncertain. There will always be dissidents, even if such dissent is in itself immoral or unfathomable (as in the case of Holocaust deniers). It must be emphasised that this does not mean that the Holocaust cannot be proved to have happened. But the deniers exist. They are mad, bad or both. But they are allowed to exist by the lack of epistemological certainty in the construction of a single 'reality' that all must philosophically (not politically) adhere to. It is obscene, but it is unavoidable.

A fourth reason is that many of us in the early twenty-first century recall a time of unusual transition in morality that has deeply affected how we work as historians. Many of today's historians were raised in the seemingly unchangeable puritanism in sexual and leisure life of the late 1940s, 1950s and early 1960s, accompanied by a heavy-handed discipline imposed in school, home and national life. This gave way in a convulsive liberation in the later 1960s and 1970s in which a new moral culture was constructed from which the ethics of today's society have developed. Personal experience of that moral change has shown many of today's historians how much of our world is socially constructed upon shifting meanings of language and identity. They have come to appreciate that morality is a social construction, rather than an historical constant. This changes their outlook from that of many earlier historians.

All of this means that moral values are not fixed and unchanging, and that knowledge of the past cannot buttress our sense of what is good and just. History can inform, and help us to judge. But the decision that something is immoral requires declaration, not an inductive reasoning drawn from spurious lessons of history.

The secular character to postmodernity

The postmodern condition has an important religious dimension that bears on the work of the historian. The de-Christianisation of Europe since 1960, and the de-centring of organised religion from the politics, state apparatuses, popular culture and everyday life of most of the people of western Europe and many of those elsewhere, mark the creation of a secular character to our condition. This informs the character of History-writing now. Historians now routinely speak of the decline of Christendom in western Europe (though markedly less so in other continents). Secularisation has created this dominion, marked in most of Europe (but not all of it) by minimal levels of church attendance, high multi-culturality, the dominance of non-religious rhetoric in culture, and the removal of motifs and symbols of religious certainty. This has led to the decline of prophetic, apocalyptic and transcendental explanations in History books – including their decline in national Histories of many countries. The secular condition is far from universal. Most countries of the world, including the United States, sustain strong religious cultures which still influence their written History, underpinning their sense of 'mission', prophecy and destiny. Even a leading postmodernist theorist, Richard Rorty, asserts the role of the United States as a liberal context for the perfection of the postmodern condition.[1] To a European ear, this reeks of a postmodern patriotism – a belief in constitutional destiny and leadership, an acceptance of an almost holy symbolism to words like 'freedom' and even 'democracy'. Such a thing has mostly gone from western Europe where patriotism, like religion, is now more lightly worn by most people – itself a sign of postmodernity.

This has impacted on the way that History is studied and written in places touched by the secular condition of postmodernity. Historians in some places tend to think differently about their own countries' histories, and not just about religion or spirituality. They think differently about notions like human progress and the politics of the present, tending to perceive 'progress' as a conceptual problem and the people of the past as not intrinsically less wise or less moral than we. They look differently upon the agenda of History research. Environmental history is a case in point, which in Europe has benefited from strong government and popular acceptance that human-induced environmental degradation (including global warming) is under way. So, the religious condition of Europe also affects its moral condition, and this impacts upon the way in which historical scholarship is developing.

The past as not-history

This does not mean that the postmodernist sees History as amoral or immoral. All History-writing, all History research, everything the professional historian and the student of History are doing, is morally charged. History is never neutral. We are informed by our concerns with moral issues, political and ideological issues, and with the here and now. History-writing is the history-record of the present – of its contemporary disputes, its passions, its obsessions.

There is, then, a seemingly ineluctable end-game of postmodernist logic to contend with. If History-writing is about morality, and if the past cannot make our morality, then History-writing is redundant. This seems like a piece of thinking with a far-reaching conclusion.

The Dutch postmodernist historian Frank Ankersmit argues that it is possible for everyone to go to the archive to check the veracity of the statement of an historian. An individual 'fact' can be checked, and empirically proved right or wrong. So, individual statements by the historian can be legitimately empirically tested – not necessarily all of them, but those claimed to be based on verifiable, indisputable facts. However, Ankersmit states that this does not apply to an entire text – to a whole book or article. He says that the History book is not based on objectivity or truth. At the level of the text, the writing of History is a discourse infused with morality (incorporating ideology and other things). The historian can write many more true statements about the past than s/he can find in the archive. The result of historians' writings is the production of millions of 'facts-as-statements'. This then creates the problem of selection. So, Ankersmit says that what the historian is actually doing is selecting some facts for inclusion in some statements about the past. The really important products of the historian are not the 'facts', but the statements, which combine together to make large hypotheses. It is these that the historian produces, that shape the text, and then shape the type of publisher that a given piece of research is sent to for publication. Moreover, the statements and hypotheses make the reputation of an historian, rarely the facts. Equally, it is these statements and hypotheses that are difficult to disprove. And, as Rorty pointed out, it is because the 'small' facts can be checked as 'true' that the empiricist historian has traditionally depended on the inference that his/her statements and hypotheses are also 'true', and, even more, that we are able to know 'the truth of the past'.[2]

This means that historians are rarely dependent in their narratives on the truth of a single fact. However, it does happen that the reputation of an historian can be challenged or even destroyed by an error of fact in the archive (as in recent celebrated cases concerning the Holocaust and American gun culture). In some cases where some facts have proved to be wrong, the rest of the work of an historian has been damned (and the historian him/herself damned as well) when many felt there was little justification for sweeping condemnation. So, the issue of good/bad History-writing in general tends to get reduced to the policing of the profession, and not really to the importance of verifiable facts in an argument. Ankersmit argues that this makes the historian more vulnerable over the facts than over the text s/he constructs. It becomes relatively easy to make statements and hypotheses, but not easy to present facts. This is ironic, because it is the statements and hypotheses that are the really important part of what the academic historian does. And that makes the text of the historian a discourse, and the facts within it become signs of that discourse. The fact-signs may be true in themselves, as events, but in the discourse they are lifted from *historical* context and put into the *historian's* context of her/his discourse. A new status is attained. They become something additional to what they were. They are no longer dormant events of the past, dormant items on a sheet of paper in an archive box. Their enclosure by the historian into his/her text makes them discursively active in the present.

This changes the discursive quality of a fact from one period to another – from the past to the present. Thus, as Ankersmit says, every work of History-writing should be judged on two levels: on the empirical verification of the statement (the modernist method), and the appropriateness of the historian's text (narrative). The first is judged by empirical judgement, testing the archive. Judging the historian's texts is in some branches of history an issue of empirical verification, where the facts in the case are still matters of open and lively dispute. But for the vast majority of historians in the vast majority of fields of study, empirical verifiability is not an issue. It is the second level of judgement, the appropriateness of the historian's narrative, that is by far the dominant form of dispute between historians, by far the most important issue in the training of History students, and consumes the vast bulk of space in History books and journals. And the judgement here is only carried out by placing one historian's text against another historian's text. Judgement of 'facts' plays little or no part in this, since the external referent (the past) cannot be drawn into this process because it merely creates yet another text. Historians are perpetually condemned to judging their work largely by comparing their narratives against each other, not against the past. (Incidentally, this means historians are not like scientists who can judge each other's work by replication of an entire experiment or observation.) So, for the most part, we are always judging the historian, not the past. The referent, the past, slips further and further away as the historian's hypothesis gets bigger. The more complex the hypothesis of the historian, the closer it comes to the sweep and breadth and disconcerting certainty of the **metanarrative**.

The logical consequence is that empirical verification becomes less valid as a means of judging History as an entire discipline. This creates for Ankersmit a 'radical undecideability'. For him, as for the American postmodernist Richard Rorty, this uncertainty is the foundation and the protection of political freedom. Democracy is based on the absence of a single past. If only one past existed, he or she who claimed to know it would be the danger to democracy and to freedom. The unknowability of the past becomes something to celebrate, not something to denigrate or fear. Relativity thus becomes, for some postmodernists, the very basis of political freedom. More particularly, **relativity** is the product and character of the postmodern condition of the late twentieth and early twenty-first centuries (wherever in the world that condition can be said to have taken root). Our very liberalisation of personal morality in western Europe since 1945, the decline of nationalism and the way in which racism, sexism and essentialism of all sorts have been made immoral and illegal, are a product of this process of denying certainty now and in the past world. We continue to draw on the past to explain, elaborate and infuse our own passions and ideologies. Relativism is not a licence for 'anything goes'. But by passing the responsibility from History facts to our own moral choices, postmodernity becomes the basis of the humanistic desire for personal freedom.

From this Ankersmit wrote in 1989 that 'Autumn has come to Western historiography'. By this he meant the closing down of any attempt to recover, reconstruct or invent the essence of the past. The western tradition that traces History as an upward movement is now, in the postmodern condition, no longer held as a universal or underlying metanarrative. Indeed, a great deal of what the postmodernist historian is doing is to recover the lost passages of the past condemned by modernism during the eighteenth and nineteenth centuries – the evils of European imperialism, for instance. There are topics that are now studied that were once ignored. The sense of righteous mission in European written History started to wither in the mid-twentieth century. Ankersmit speaks of how postmodernism has killed the modernist tree of knowledge that formerly reached skywards. The historian's gaze has shifted. The creation of totality, objectivity, truth and a synthesis of the whole of history is no longer, broadly, attempted. As Ankersmit puts it, we privilege not the tree of history, but its leaves.[3]

The sense of presentism, of writing about the past according to our contemporary concerns, is not new, but is much more alive and admitted now than was previously the case. Environmental history grew in little over ten years from nothing to one of the major investments of historical research because of global warming. It is also worth observing that the postmodern condition shapes the profoundly areligious and deeply secular History written and researched in western Europe, and the loss from historiography of the various religious senses understood by previous generations of people and historians (the sense of the apocalypse, moral order, and national imperial mission in God's name). Insofar as religion is still on the contemporary agenda of historical research, it tends to be in the guise of the history of sectarianism, fundamentalism and the rise of new age spirituality – each derived from pressing policy concerns of our modern world.

The disappearance of empirically historicised moralities has, for some theorists, other implications. In the 1960s and 1970s, Michel de Certeau argued that the western tradition of History rests in the overturning of previous systems of knowledge, whereas non-western traditions tend to absorb past and present traditions. Thus, the western sense of History is itself a sense of 'the other' – of death, of loss – and one which is analytically understandable through a Freudian perspective. More recently, Elizabeth Ermarth argues that linear time, the basis of historical understanding, is redundant in the postmodern condition. There are other rhythms in her view than chronological time. The 'postmodern narrative language undermines historical time and substitutes for it a new construction of temporality that I call rhythmic time'. She sees historical time as modernist, western, Euro-centric, and male. Historical time is the most 'commanding metanarrative in western discourse', and is the final frontier of the modernism–postmodernism switch or episteme change. The argument runs that postmodernism subverts historical time as we know it – concepts of division like mediaeval, modern, and even postmodern. She urges that the postmodern approach should be to problematise our linear sense of time. 'Time, in other words, is not neutral and absolute but a function of position.'[4] Some decades ago, Barthes argued that the succession of events that a reader encounters in narrative (in History books, novels or journalism) is not fundamentally chronological in its origins. The action of reading involves the passage of time, and that forces us to encounter the order of its elements as a chronological succession. This happens with written and aural texts, with films and videos, and is a facet of the form – the narrative – adding to the 'reality-effect' of historiography identified by both Barthes and Foucault. Barthes spoke approvingly in 1967 of attempts 'to "dechronologize" the "thread" of history and to restore, even though it may merely be a matter of reminiscence or nostalgia, a form of time that is complex, parametric and not in the least linear'.[5] Incidentally, the passage of time is not a facet to be found in the reading of the still photograph, in which time is neither located in the reading nor in the signifieds, creating what Barthes considered an unusual and disturbed semiotic system.

For Ermarth, what postmodernism puts forward is its own discourse. It is an exercise in looking to the future. Historical thinking, she says, is disappearing as postmodernism undermines the historian. The modernist historian constrains the future by defining linearity from the past, through the present, to an ordained future. She challenges the notion that 'history' exists as a separate 'space': 'A postmodernist would never speak of "historical reality": not just because 'reality' doesn't exist except as defined locally but also because history doesn't exist either, except as defined locally.' She predicts that History as a subject will remain as a site of experimentation – what she describes as 'The postmodern idea of theory as a guerrilla tactic.' She goes on: 'The practice of postmodern theory ... requires a fine sense of play and a total willingness to live without discursive sleep.'[6] This means, as I understand it, that the historian – the scholar – is never free from thinking reflexively, is never free from being aware of their own and everything's discursivity, and of the need to use all playful narrative and research techniques – irony, comedy, satire – to explore the past. Closure is never attained nor attainable. This is 'a future of interminable play', as Jenkins puts it.[7] If you de-centre and withdraw the metanarrative, then historical narratives must become more playful as the signifiers lose their attachment to referents.

Ermarth has no worries that a future without linear history would become so relativistic as to allow future immorality on a grand scale. She sees modernist History as the cause of many evil events because it passed the sense of victimhood from generation to generation – the sense of victimhood in nations, in ethnic groups and in religious groups. History teachers taught victimhood. She means that modernist History has given certainty of exploitation, subjugation and discrimination to peoples who define themselves by race, religion, region or language. History has given to them rituals of resistance, remembrances of events of persecution, and annual calendar days when confrontation with their 'oppressors' is recalled and re-enacted. Thereby, History perpetuates internecine conflict in today's world. History reinforces and perpetuates the sense of being victims, giving little or no quarter to 'outside' views, to compromise, to forgiveness, to tolerance of difference. In this view, modernist history is used to define, infuse, irritate and inflame. The troubles of the contemporary world, and most of its wars, are invariably based on the clashes of different Histories. And the way out, in Ermarth's view, is via a postmodernist History that puts on us, in the present day, the responsibility for declaring what is just and moral. We as historians must promote awareness of what different Histories are written to underpin the sense of victimhood and maintain violence in today's world. We must defuse the power of metanarratives that charge one account with truth and another with falsity. In short, we should raise awareness of the importance of rejecting History in favour of the present.

In this way, History as a subject itself becomes accused of being a moral problem. By facing up to it, we can defuse national, racial and religious conflict, marginalise the voices of the intolerant, the chauvinist, the racist and the bigot, and give air to the multi-vocal Histories of postmodern society. This will not obliterate the bigot, but it should obliterate a society's dominant culture of bigotry. Where modernist History allows intolerance to flourish, postmodernist History should dissolve it. Truth and reconciliation, the work of healing in post-apartheid South Africa and post-Troubles Northern Ireland, are processes based on revealing all empirical 'truths' about all the small facts of the past, and reconciliation of the major certainties – the metanarratives by which opposing sides lived.

Postmodernism, if it works, defuses the discourses which have scarred the past.

There was a massive rejection of all sorts of Histories in the 1960s and 1970s. These were metanarratives engrossed in 'official' and popular representations of the past, supported by professional History books. They constituted national cultures infused with medleys of uncontested certainties concerning superiorities of race, religion, nation, gender, sexuality and dis/ability. One that was rejected was the Christian History of Britain that was taken to confer identity and moral worth – the history of our forebears' devotion to Christianity and to particular Christian churches. In the secularisation of European culture from the mid-twentieth century, Christianity was de-centred and marginalised. Another History that was rejected was sectarian identity – the Catholic–Protestant division in much of England and Wales, and in the United States. There was the rejection of the moral History of Enlightenment Europe – the History that had infused moral correctness, respectability, female sexual abstinence and male sexual hypocrisy into the culture of the nineteenth and early twentieth centuries. There was the rejection of the History of gender stereotypes which had underpinned sexual inequality and inspired feminist historical scholarship. There was a rejection of racist History which had approved of European empire and imperialism, apartheid in South Africa and racial segregation in parts of the United States. Multi-culturality was not something born whole in the 1960s, nor is it something completely achieved since then. But it is something that has totally transformed the intellectualising of the west European world since the 1960s, and is making considerable inroads elsewhere.

It must be emphasised that this process is not complete. There are some places (in Europe as in many other continents) where certainty in History narratives matters too much – the Balkans and Northern Ireland come to mind. In the eruption of the American-led 'war on terrorism' since 9/11, metanarratives are still profoundly in evidence in many quarters, and the relations between religious traditions of Christianity, Judaism, Islam, and Hinduism remain at the forefront of international debate. Yet, God and patriotism tend to be worn more lightly (if at all) in modern History scholarship. The postmodern condition is the process of overturning written Histories which continued to be manifestos for victimhood, war and hatred. This is a moral task. One challenge for the postmodern historian is to maintain the popularity of History as it takes the linguistic turn. Postmodern History cannot defuse the historicised justifications of regional and global conflicts if it cannot position itself in popular culture. We have to be out there.

Application in history

The historian is motivated by a variety of factors.

Intellectual problems can be interesting and stimulating on their own, attracting the student and scholar just because of the need to solve a problem about what happened in the past, what caused it, or what conceptual system is most apt to understanding an historical phenomenon. Many historians fall into studying topics by accident – through getting a research job, or through an unexpected encounter with an area of study.

However, moral choice is often a reason for starting to research an historical topic, and for adopting a particular interpretation. Historians invariably choose to research the history of war, racism, bigotry or sexism because they have adopted a moral position. The examples of historians' work that have been given in previous chapters have often been the product of deep interest on the part of the researcher in the moral history of something that is a concern now, in the present. But less and less are historians researching the past for the sake of its issues – for the sake of sustaining old **metanarratives** that divide nation from nation, and race from race. We live in a multi-cultural society and strain to perfect multi-culturality – the mixing and toleration of cultures distinguished by different religions, rituals, family structures, leisure practices, gender roles and relations, music and attitudes. History then becomes employed to explore the longevity of previous cultural hegemonies, and the barriers to multi-culturality in the past.

We study the history of patriarchy, and of women's subordination (through discourse and experience), because we want to know how they lasted so long and how they came to be contested. For the same reasons, we study the past of sectarianism and religious conflict, of imperialism and its legacy, the secret forgotten histories of subordinate, pre-Christian peoples whose heritage was obliterated by the metanarratives of powerful (usually western) nations. So, ironically, postmodern History involves the recovery of lost identities, of lost metanarratives, of subordinate peoples, of nations suppressed by empires of one sort or another, of forgotten religions destroyed by the great Euro-centred Christian mission. This is a process of lost peoples recovering their freedom from neglect and forgottenness, not one of re-empowering to some new national pre-eminence. It is, if you like, a spiking of the balloons of the pent-up frustration of decades and sometimes centuries of cultural subordination to the metanarratives of others.

The postmodernist would be hesitant about the creation of new metanarratives, however. Postmodern History is a process of the weak and the subordinate reclaiming their histories (their pasts) in order to deflate their Histories (their metanarratives). These may not disappear, but the process is a settling of the historical passions. It is the act of historical reconciliation. The voices of the powerless are being heard as a process of historical egalitarianism, a mobilisation of postmodern moral curiosity into modernity. The voices of ordinary men and women are recovered from all manner of records to reveal the discourses, experiences and activities of the culture in which they lived.

For the student to do

Many issues of moral concern can motivate the History student – race, religion, class, gender, dis/ability and so on. However, moral issues for historical studies can lurk in topics that we may not always think about. Here is one example.

Globalisation is a process that has become of immense moral and political interest – especially to the radical, the young and the churches within both western and developing nations. The dominance of world markets by multi-national companies, the unequal trading links between the developed 'north' and underdeveloped 'south', are of massive moral concern to very many institutions of liberal democracy. For historians, there is an obvious role in writing the history of multi-national capitalism that has led to this – the drive of those economic principles of capitalist development, of rational-economic action, that have proved so powerful as material forces in the shaping of our modern world. This includes traditional business history, as well as the radical left-wing economic History of the Marxist.

Equally, though, there is an interest amongst others in approaching topics that in a different way pose the moral question about this development. Why have flea markets survived in the midst of the developing nations, attracting large numbers of the aspiring and wealthy middle classes, when there are plenty of other big business outlets at which to spend their money? Such a topic can involve investigating the history and nature of the flea markets – institutions where low-value and second-hand goods are bought and sold. These markets of small capitalist transactions are thriving in places where economic development is most advanced.

These are venues that attract tens of thousands of people. Explaining this requires a non-traditional economic history theory. The flea market has addressed new issues of moral identity untouched by global capitalism. People living in the midst of sophisticated capitalism have sought out the identity, and not just the bargains, to be found in the flea market. Customers and even some vendors seek this through participating in such markets and the 'fair trade' principle is applied to many goods brought from the developing nations to sell there. There is also a wider moral worth conceived in participating in something that speaks of community, commonality and co-operation. The flea market shows little sign of disappearing, and it seems to fly in the face of traditional economic theory. To undertake a study of flea markets, the History student must traverse from the skills of empirical history (tracing the origins and development of these markets) through to discourse analysis, postmodern economic theory and social anthropology. The result is a set of usable explanations concerning the moral and cultural dimensions to many people's modern economic identity. If you like, there is a postmodern economic history to contend with, based, in large part, on moral issues. It tackles the seemingly irrational economic relations in postmodern society.

Wherever the modern agenda of moral concern touches, there History must be. For every student, there may well be a set of distinctive moral issues. Such a drive is important not merely for shaping the study, but also for motivating the student. Motivation is important in everything that is done in education and learning, and moral motivation can be extremely effective, highly justified, and immensely satisfying.

Guide to further reading

Theory

The best sympathetic guides to the moral issues of postmodernist History are K. Jenkins, On 'What is History?': From Carr and Elton to Rorty and White (London, Routledge, 1995); Keith Jenkins, Why History? Ethics and Postmodernity (London, Routledge, 1999) and M. de Certeau, The Writing of History (orig. 1975, New York, Columbia University Press, 1988), esp. pp. 287–307. On the photograph and the passage of time, see R. Barthes, Camera Lucida (orig. 1980, London, Vintage, 1993) and L. Stanley, The Auto/biographical I (Manchester, Manchester University Press, 1992), pp. 20–42.

History

A great way to start to find material on a particular moral topic is to go online on the web. Using a search engine, explore sites that construct the moral issue that interests you. From there, find out who the leading History scholars are, and move to academic websites where there will be booklists and guides to definitions and specific theoretical matters. You can start to construct an idea for a history essay or project. Guidance from a tutor is very important early in this process. S/he will want to ensure that there is a do-able History project, composed of a reasonable research question to ask, a historiography from which to start background reading, and historical sources with which to research the topic.

Notes

1 See K. Jenkins, *On 'What is History?': From Carr and Elton to Rorty and White* (London, Routledge, 1995), pp. 117–18. This and other books by Jenkins have been important to large parts of this chapter.

2 Ibid., p. 100.

3 Cited in Jenkins, *Why History?*, pp. 153, 155.

4 Quoted in Jenkins, *Why History?*, pp. 163, 166.

5 R. Barthes, 'The discourse of history', *Comparative Criticism*, 3 (1981): 7–20.

6 Quoted in Jenkins, *Why History?*, p. 174.

7 Ibid., p. 176.

Criticism of postmodernism in History

Why is postmodernism spectacularly controversial in History?

Since the 1980s, academic subjects in the humanities and social sciences have been developing postmodernist techniques with great speed – notably literature, anthropology and cultural studies, but also geography, sociology and religious studies. In the sciences and medical sciences postmodernism has made only a very slight impression, despite attempts by some scholars to persuade scientists of its significance to their work. Yet, in all of academic life, it is in History that the greatest controversy has arisen. Some historians have attacked postmodernism and postmodernists with a vengeance. The History world has been splitting apart, postmodernism setting many historians against each other. In the 1990s especially, accusations were flying – accusations of ignorance in theory, of failure to read books properly, of not understanding argument, of endangering the History discipline, of intellectual betrayal to the schemes of non-historians, of disrespect for historical evidence and traditional historical skills, and of moral relativity. Though some of these tensions have eased at the beginning of the twenty-first century, there is still a distinctive energy to debate over postmodernism in the History profession.

 Why should this controversy be so much greater in History than in other branches of learning and the civilised arts? There are three general reasons for this state of affairs. First, postmodernism presents a theory that seems to destroy the barrier of distinctiveness around History as a discipline, threatening its existence as a subject and historians as a breed. Second, postmodernism is accused of putting 'culture' (including popular culture) above every other aspect of history, and of being thereby more interested in 'representation' than in 'reality'. Third, postmodernist historians are criticised for apparently abjuring moral judgement of the past by adopting or condoning moral relativism – the notion that morality changes with the ages, and that the historian is unable to confer moral blame upon historical figures because they lived under different moral rules. These arguments are complex. This chapter provides a brief guide to how critics have shaped their commentary and how I feel they are wrong.

The critics come from a variety of positions. There have been empiricist, conservative, Marxist and liberal critics. There have been critics who perceive History as an arts and humanities subject, and those who perceived it as a social science subject. But interestingly, the critics seem to have come together in the 1990s and 2000s to perceive postmodernism as 'a common threat' to History as a subject. They have tended to share ideas of what History should be as a subject much more than was the case in the 1960s and 1970s when Marxists and conservatives, arts and social science historians, were in constant dispute over what methods the historian should use, what the aims should be of doing the research, and what skills the historian required. This means that divisions between them have tended to pale in significance compared to the divisions between all of them and postmodernist historians.

There are many historians who use some of the techniques described in this book, and indeed have been innovators of them, but who yet decry postmodernism. They object to the name, oppose some of its key attributes, and refute the suggestion that the concepts and methods can be claimed as postmodernist. There is much merit in this argument. What has been described in this book is by no means the sole preserve of postmodernism, and postmodernists cannot claim that they have been the originators of all this work. Indeed, there is a very strong sense in which the name 'postmodernism' arrived after much of the theory. However, that does not detract from the theoretical connections that run through from the sign to the study of the self within postmodernism. This is not to claim, in a kind of imperialism, that the poststructuralist, the feminist or the postcolonialist is a postmodernist. Each scholar positions him/herself in relation to the theory, and nobody else does that for them.

So, there is a range of positions with regard to postmodernism. On top of that, it is worth observing that postmodernists are not a coherent and totally agreeing group of scholars. This is not a theory with an extended central manifesto to which all sign up. There is a great deal of variety in attitudes to how to understand postmodern theory, and there is no single authority on this. It is inherent in postmodern theory to de-centre 'realities' and metanarratives. Postmodernism is no exception to this.

Facts and empiricism

Many critics take exception to the way that many postmodernists describe empiricism, the Enlightenment and modernity. The tendency to speak of reconstruction as a central output of empiricist method divides the critics. Arthur Marwick recoils from being called a 'reconstructionist', saying, 'Historians no more replicate or reconstruct the past than natural scientists replicate or reconstruct aspects of the natural world and the physical universe.'[1] Marxist historian Willie Thompson accepts the term, though, saying, 'All historical accounts are reconstructions', but then qualifies the nature of the reconstructions, saying that they 'can never reveal the full reality of whatever is being investigated'.[2] The postmodernist case is that amongst empiricists of all hues tends to rest an unacceptable underlying assumption that the past can be represented as a verifiable reality verified in historians' statements. Such objectivity is unattainable. However, few historians would subscribe to a purist reconstructive view. There is a greater acceptance, indebted in large measure to the theory described in this book, that the issues of language, description and subjectivity preclude History from producing research that is a neutral and complete reconstruction of what happened.

'Facts', says the philosopher Terry Eagleton, constitute 'a resource much despised by the postmodernists'.[3] This is the heart of the critique of postmodernism. It emanates from the political left, right and centre, from Marxist and from conservative, and even from some feminists, within the humanities and the social sciences. It is seen by many as the simple, effective and fatal *coup de grâce* in debate. If the postmodernist denies facts, there can be no academy, no knowledge, no purpose, no past.

The undermining of the notion of 'facts', say critics, starts with semiology, though it is rarely expressed that way by anti-postmodern historians. Indeed, much of the major impact of semiology upon the History profession is seen to come further down the theoretical trail – after semiology had instigated the study of discourses, poststructuralism and texts. So critics of postmodernism rarely isolate semiotics and the study of sign-systems *alone* for their reproach. Amongst all the volumes of criticism of postmodernist history, there is barely any detailed discussion of these subjects. It is usually in the combination of semiotics with discourse analysis and the study of the text that the complaints come. For instance, there is a general acceptance amongst historians of *signifier–signified–sign* as a trilogy of related 'things', and they are treated with a general casual acceptance, even by empiricists. These terms feature frequently in the works of historians from many different intellectual positions, though without much concern for explaining theoretical origins or placement. So, an historian using 'sign' or 'signifier' as words in their books or articles is little indication that s/he is a postmodernist (nor even a semiotician).

However, there is a concern when the empiricist historian approaches the issue of signs when they are linked with the concept of 'reality'. Richard Evans posits that 'signs – words, language, concepts, arguments, books – do bear some relation to material reality', and does so as part of a larger argument about the common-sense acceptance of the ability of the historian to represent reality. He attacks the postmodernist position that the sign is only one representation of 'reality', and not capable of being a *true* representation of it. Evans asserts that 'The past does speak through the sources, and is recoverable through them.' He remains convinced that historical method, 'based on the rules of verification laid down by Ranke', evidenced in footnotes and bibliographical references, provides the subject with a foundation of materiality and reality.[4] A critic like Thompson seems to go further to denigrate the postmodernist historian as 'relativist' or, worse, 'hyper-relativist' over facts and reality.[5] The target of the critics' comments is thus not so much the value of semiology as such, but is rather that signs have a stronger link to 'reality' than the postmodern theoreticians allow. There is unwillingness on the part of the opponent of postmodernist history to let go of the capability of the fact to represent reality, and for the fact to be the basis of written History. Despite this kind of 'common-sense' argument, critics are less concerned with what the semiology system is (how it operates and so on), and more with what postmodernism in general is arguing about the absence of an external reality beyond sign-systems.

The problem with discourse

Critics of postmodernism fall upon discourse with great vigour. Their criticism comes in four main arguments. First, some of what passes for discourse analysis is what professional historians have long been doing anyway. Second, the discourse of history (of the professional historian's narrative) is an absurd notion that stipulates that 'reality' does not exist, only discourse. Third, to see discourses in all historical evidence and all historiography is absurd. Fourth, the 'death of the author' argument constitutes a postmodernist abdication of research interest in the origins of the historical document.

In relation to the first criticism, it is, of course, true to say that many of the techniques favoured by the postmodernists were not invented by them. There are scores of examples of discourse-analytical techniques deployed before postmodernism became anything approaching a coherent philosophy of history. This may be said of Darnton's work on the cat massacre, Marina Warner's study of the Virgin Mary and Edward Said's study of Orientalism. Sometimes a scholar like Darnton is a critic of postmodernism and would not wish to be classified under that banner. Even Karl Marx, it has been pointed out, wrote about the importance of language in historical study, and the wrapping of the new in what he called the 'borrowed language' of the old.[6] In response, postmodernist historians can surely lose no credit for *not* having invented discourse analysis. But it *is* to their credit that, in large part due to the running development of modern cultural theory, it has become better theorised, more methodologically sophisticated and linked to a wider framework of cultural theory and research method.

In relation to the second criticism, many critics challenge that discourse analysis tends to substitute consideration of words for 'real' history. Labour historians have been especially critical of colleagues who have allegedly turned their backs on the reality of economic suffering, oppression and class subjugation. As Bryan Palmer put it, 'Critical theory is no substitute for historical materialism; language is not life.'[7] Barthes' discourse of history is one that is caricatured by Richard Evans as absurd. He lampoons the Frenchman's notion of the 'referential illusion' to reality in historical discourse: 'The illusion [according to Barthes] lay in the fact that the past was only imagined to be out there, waiting to be discovered: in practice [Barthes said] it was an empty space waiting to be filled in by the historian.'[8] This may suggest that Barthes was merely asserting the ultimate unknowability of the past. From a postmodernist perspective, that is the case as the past in a 'real', uncontestable version is impossible. But there is a tendency for anti-postmodernist criticism to charge postmodernists with asserting the *non-existence* of reality in favour of discourse. This Barthes never did, and few practising postmodernist historians would agree to that proposition. He credited the past with existing, but it was the *representation* of the past (in historiography) that had to be imagined and completed by the historian.

Discourse is now a word that adorns the pages of many History books. It is often used with a casualness about theory, but still with a basic agreement that the theory emanates from Foucault, that it is central to contemporary historical research, and that it is legitimate for any historian – postmodernist or not – to use it. A postmodernist may argue that better theorising is always important, but at the end of the day the written History produced is valuable, justifiable and takes forward the under-standing of the past.

The reaction to discourse in historical study produces some unsubtle and some subtle critiques. Amongst the unsubtle is philosopher Terry Eagleton's defence of Marxism from the onslaught of discourse obsession – in large part for its enticement of the revolutionary left to what he calls post-Marxism. He presents his case through a satire on the case of the galley slave wanting to escape slavery, who, if he met a postmodernist dis-course theorist, would have it suggested to him that 'being lashed to ribbons by the emperor's captain' shows that his desire to escape is not a 'mere passive reflection of social reality' and 'that "oppression" is a discur-sive affair'.[9] A postmodernist would suggest Eagleton is wrong in his analysis, first, because discourse as an internal oppression was less signifi-cant before modernity than after, and slaves in galley ships were there as an imprisonment, not as a consequence of concurrence in submission to discourse (making the interesting discourse the one about the sanctity and utility of slavery held by the enslaving elite, not by the slave himself). And secondly, the postmodernist would absolutely *not* deny the power of the slave's social reality as a materialist motivation for escape. What would be of discursive interest would be if he was the agent for circulation of a dis-course of rebellion amongst his fellow slaves on this and other galleys (since the slave cannot be alone in the promulgation of and adherence to a discourse – there has to be a society for its circulation). So, Eagleton's cri-tique fails through poor historical modelling coupled with a mistaken understanding of the nature of the postmodernist notion of the *socially constructed* discourse.

A good example of the more subtle response to the failings of discourse theory comes from historian Lyndal Roper in her study of an individual in a not dissimilar predicament of material oppression – a woman on trial for witchcraft in sixteenth-century Germany. She is one historical researcher who argues that the historian should not see all elements of the world as purely discursive constructions of language and culture. She argues that gender should not be seen only as a product of cultural and linguistic prac-tice, but that 'sexual difference has its own physiological and psychological reality'. If discourses are about controlling the individual, then there is a gap when gender is approached. The history of the body is not complete or satisfactory if it is seen solely as the individual's negotiation with circu-lating discourse. It is also about the individual woman's experience of her body – of rape, incest, sexual explorations and so on – which produces psychological consequences. 'We experience our body through mediations of discourse and perhaps other things,' as Roper says, but it is wrong for the historian 'to write as if there were nothing but a historically constructed body'. She sees discourse analysis as not capable of providing the fullness of account of historical causation. Indeed, she observes of some gender history writing: 'The contradictions of femininity in sixteenth-century Germany bear an uncanny resemblance to those of twentieth-century Britain.'[10] This is finely tuned and historically informed criticism. It shows that the discourse must not be regarded as alienated from material reality, but embedded in it. The historian can start to achieve this by focusing on the self – the experience, predicament and tribulations of an individual like the accused witch – as the way to explore the contradictions between discourse, materiality and mind.

The 'death of the author' argument has caused problems for some historians. Edward Said, who acknowledged his debt to Foucault for theoretical approaches, found fault on this point: 'I do believe in the determining imprint of individual writers upon the otherwise anonymous collective body of texts constituting a discursive formation like Orientalism.' Yet later, Said admits the power of the discourse over the author: 'In time such knowledge and reality produce a tradition, or what Michel Foucault calls a discourse, whose material presence or weight, not the originality of a given author, is really responsible for the texts produced out of it.' The result is that the pre-existence of Orientalism as a field of inquiry and explanation 'tend[s] to diminish the effects of the individual scholar's production'. Said goes on: 'The result for Orientalism has been a sort of consensus: certain things, certain types of statement, certain types of work have seemed for the Orientalist correct.'[11] Orientalists, then, for all their original contributions to texts and even interpretation, have still to write within the discursive tradition in order to belong to it and in order to be understood by the European audience to which they are speaking. So, even for Said, the author seems at least partially dead.

For others, the author cannot be dead, and postmodernists stand accused of saying that 'the author has no relevance to the content of a text at all'. Richard Evans has stated: 'An awareness of the multiple meanings of texts, and their relative autonomy from the intentions of the author, has long been part of the stock-in-trade of the historian.' But he asserts that 'we cannot impose any meaning we wish to on such a text either. We are limited by the words it contains, words which are not, contrary to what the postmodernists suggest, capable of an infinity of meaning.' It is unlikely that any postmodernist suggests 'an infinity', but few could accept Evans's next point: 'And the limits which the language of the text imposes in the possibilities of interpretation are set to a large extent by the original author.'[12] They may be set 'to a large extent', but the postmodernist position is that this still leaves limits *not* set by the author and not capable of being set by the author – especially if the context of the reader is different from that of the author's intended or primary audience. A text written in the seventeenth century will be read differently in the twentieth century. A classic example is the Bible, which has been reinterpreted very many times in different ways by different cultures and ages – not least the present, when large parts of its position on sexuality (on homosexuality, sex before marriage, and birth control) are subject to enormous interpretational variation. So, the significance of a text historically is not confined to meanings stated, implied, or delimited by the author. Ways of interpreting words, silences and metaphors within a text may change very substantially from culture to culture.

For some radical feminist scholars in literary criticism, there is another problem with the case for 'the death of the author'. Liz Stanley reacted with disdain, speaking in ironic tones: '... these authoritative authors, French intellectuals, speak the death of the author: how marvellous'. Stanley is herself working in areas of theory dealing with many of the ideas of postmodernism, but as a feminist she argues that a woman author is a woman (just as a white, middle-class, first-world, elite, self-styled intellectual is such). It *matters* in feminist theory who the author is or was.[13] This is an argument with considerable force. But it may not have to displace the other. The 'death of the author' can be used as a temporary methodological concept that encourages examination of discourse and the pre-circulation of its contents, then permitting recourse to authorial consideration and content analysis in a combined study. Indeed, most postmodernist research does exactly this. The modes of research should not be limited by postmodernism. On the contrary, they should be multiplied to help prevent a single authoritative position from being established.

Poststructuralism

Poststructuralism has been more influential and better received than any other aspect of postmodernism. Yet, it comes in for both generalised and specific criticism from other historians.

Amongst generalised criticism is the belief that poststructuralism is the tool of literary theorists. By using a language-based arts approach to attack scientific method, it is asserted, poststructuralists could raise literary criticism to an equal footing with science. Certainly, the literary issue is one that some see as uppermost in what makes the postmodernist, and discern in it an undermining of the integrity, utility and intrinsically necessary quality of empiricism of History.

In some British Marxist criticism of poststructuralism, there is a preoccupation with what is seen as the perfidy of the French intellectual left in the 1960s. There is an air of bitterness over damage done by their supposed intellectual eccentricities (which went by the names of Maoism, Situationism, poststructuralism) during and after the student and worker revolt in Paris in May 1968 – events which reportedly dismayed the structuralist Lévi-Strauss, but which some on the barricades recognised immediately: 'Here we are in mid-Foucault,' said one Sorbonne professor on the first night of the barricades on 10 May. Poststructuralism was the name then given to the emerging modern cultural theory that was perceived as diverting the radical movement from its Marxist roots. It still attracts peculiar opprobrium from the left for being a foundational ideological error. The bitterness of some of the heirs to Marxism is palpable. They invariably use a decayed structuralist (class) analysis to explain the appearance of postmodernism. Callinicos attributed 'the proliferating talk of postmodernism' and the acceptance of its ideas to the prosperity of the western new middle class and the political disillusionment of its most articulate members.[14]

Criticism of Baudrillard's hyper-reality has brought postmodernity itself into critical view. Marxist theorists attack postmodernism extensively by attacking postmodernity – both Lyotard's conception of it as the period, and Baudrillard's vision of hyper-reality dominated by simulacra (or copies) in place of 'originals'. To mount a semblance of a theoretical challenge, cultural Marxists like Fredric Jameson reclaim postmodernity as really 'late capitalism', characterised by postindustrialism and cultural production, multi-national capital and globalisation. Meanwhile, Norris dismisses Lyotard for allying theory to a 'condition', saying that it is unacceptable for theory and theoretical inquiry to be denied an existence separate from social and cultural context. Callinicos regards Baudrillard as likely 'to license a kind of intellectual dandyism' that abandons critical inquiry for banal media study.[15] Such critics come up with differing gauges of whether modernity has ended or not. These are political and philosophical issues of some moment, but they do not materially disturb most poststructuralist historical study (though they may need to be raised in historical study of post-1950 European culture).

Amongst specific criticism is a belief in the efficacy and commonsense benefit of dividing up the social world into the structures that are 'evidently' out there – structures of class, religion, race and so on. British History has for more than 20 years been a battleground over language and social class, and the work of Stedman Jones and Joyce has been the target for sustained scrutiny and attack from left-wing historians – even if there were concessions to re-imagining the nature of class. Yet other critics dole out unrelenting vitriol. One historian of the left signalled the accomplishments of British empiricist Marxist historiography as 'a standing rebuke to the theory and practice of postmodernism', a philosophy he labelled as 'mindless'. Another, more considered, response was to see Joyce's work as implying passivity rather than agency in the common people. Yet, whatever distance historians of the left travel to acknowledge the methodical and even empirical value of postmodernist work (in all its great variety), Marxist historians at root cannot admit that the language power resident in discourse is equal to, let alone greater than, what they regard as the 'larger and more potent structures of oppression'.[16] For their part, postmodernists *can* explain the inclusion of materialism, agency and politics in their theory and method, but, notwithstanding this, for many on the left, poststructuralism may always remain the unacceptable prioritisation of discourse over class, linguistic over social oppression, and words over economics.

Scott and Riley's works on poststructuralist approaches to women's history led in the 1990s to scholars adopting a series of different positions on feminism and poststructuralism. Laura Downs, for instance, accepted the de-centring, anti-totalising objective of Derridean poststructuralist **deconstruction**, but claimed that in practice it 'conflates truth and history, textual relations with social relations' in which the historian becomes more concerned with 'gender as a metaphor for power than with gender as a lived and labile [US: unstable] social relation'. Downs criticised 'binary extremism' in which she felt analysts were commanded to see things as real or socially constructed. Joan Hoff considered poststructuralism to be using 'gender as a category of analysis to reduce the experiences of women, struggling to define themselves and better their lives in particular historical contexts, to mere subjective stories', thereby being anti-historical, making a compromise with postmodernism's misogynist French origins, and undermining the political women's movement (especially in countries like Ireland and Poland where writing the history of women's subjugation was then in its infancy). For some feminist historians, what was emerging was 'a male-defined postmodern version of gender'[17] – a view that led to vehement protest from poststructuralist feminist historians. Since the 1990s, the ferocity of these debates has diminished greatly as poststructuralist method has become more assimilated into the research agenda.

The problem with poststructuralism for many critics is that it downgrades the experience of peoples in the past who suffered under the real economic or oppressive weight of structures. The peasantry suffered real economic hardship under feudalism and neo-feudalism, the industrial working classes experienced real suffering under class struggle, and women have for millennia been face to face with subordination under patriarchy. The realness of the suffering becomes a totem of the realness of the structure. The postmodernist will argue that the structure was still not real but was *really imagined* by the oppressors and imposed on the oppressed. The discursive quality of the structure emanates from the past, not from the present. For this reason, all structures are socially constructed, vary by period and place, become hybridised and variable, and need to be studied by the historian in those terms.

Text

The text is a major venue for debate between the postmodernist historian and his/her critic. Derrida's statement: 'There is nothing outside of the text', and how to interpret it, has been a pretty constant source of dispute. Critics object to the historian's task being drawn too close to that of the literary critic, suggesting an undermining of the distinctive role of the historian to discover and interpret the 'reality' or truth of the past. Additionally, some regard many forms of historical source as incapable of being looked upon as texts. Evans cites tables of statistics of criminal offences or graffiti on a Roman wall as bearing no resemblance to texts.

He says of these: 'The conventional tools of literary analysis are of little use in dealing with such materials.'[18] A third level of criticism is that the notion of the text equates the historical source with the historian's narrative (primary with secondary source) and that this is not valid. A fourth is that there is a new metanarrative – the one in which postmodernists claim a privileged and irrefutable understanding of texts, meanings and History itself. A fifth is that textual awareness is nothing new – Karl Marx having 'precociously' experimented with 'postmodern narrative techniques' in proto-deconstruction.[19]

The postmodernist response is on various levels. Firstly, postmodernists are not calling the past a text – they are calling all *representations of the past* texts. Derrida's talk of the inability of the human to represent anything outside of the text, was an attack on representationalism, not a

denial of the existence of reality. This misunderstanding has continued for
some years, in part because of some poor expression by postmodernists.
But it has now been widely established in clear language; as Jenkins
reports, what postmodernists say 'is not to doubt for a moment that the
past actually existed'.[20] But critics continue to raise this issue. Evans
accuses Derrida of arguing: 'Everything was a mere arrangement of words,
everything was "discourse" or "text". Nothing existed outside language.
Because we apprehended the world through language and nothing else,
everything was a text.'[21] This is no longer a credible criticism, even if once
it was, but it leaves some intellectual debate stubbornly stalled at a 'he said
– no he didn't' position.[22] To repeat, the postmodernist (including Derrida)
argues that the past existed, but reconstruction of the past is not possible,
leaving only the *representation* of it in texts for the historian to study.

As regards the question of whether all historical sources can be
regarded as having the quality of textuality (as postmodernists aver), very
many historians – postmodernists and non-postmodernists – have shown
how textual analysis of statistics, for instance, is not only possible but
absolutely necessary. Many historians regard a table of statistics as highly
revealing in textual terms – of the way a subject has been conceived, categorised and structured in a given society, and how discourses have
determined tabular inclusions, exclusions, column heads and uses of the
data. Three obvious examples are criminal, religious and educational statistics, each of which show by their mere collection (mostly after c.1800)
that a society narratises the place of criminality, religion and education
very differently from societies (most often before 1800) that have not sta-
tistised them, and that 'moral statistics' can reveal the structures of
Victorian social reform debate. A fourth example is government occupational censuses that have been famously and widely criticised by feminist
scholarship for marginalising or ignoring female forms of labour. This is
discourse in action in statistics. It needs to be analysed.

The analytical divisions of narrative into emplotments and modes have
been welcomed by most of the critics of postmodernist History. Some
regard it as introducing into the History profession a healthy awareness of
the nature of the text – both in historical sources and in historical writing.
But metanarratives are more controversial. Some anti-postmodernists
agree with Lyotard on the existence of master- or **metanarratives** in historiography, though not with his limitation of their promulgation to
oppressive or state power. Yet, even the fiercest critic seems to acknowledge that there is a new awareness of metanarratives amongst historians,
even if Foucault *et al.* are seen as merely creating a new one.

In truth, deconstruction as such seems less an object of the critic's ire than the position of being 'a deconstructionist', and the interpretation that such an historian excludes 'facts' and abjures the empirical study of them. In Callinicos' words, it 'denies theoretical texts their apparent cognitive content'.[23] This would indeed be true of deconstruction if it were employed in isolation. But it is not. The postmodernist historian does not suggest using deconstruction *without* reading a text cognitively – for what may be learned about events, processes, names, places, people, contemporary understanding and so on. That is a pre-requisite, and no postmodernist would suggest that there is no cognitive gain from most historical sources. Empirical study precedes and then never leaves the deconstructionist inquiry – as the Chartier case above reveals (see pages 49–50 and 108–9). In relation to reading the primary source in the same way as the secondary source, one critic regards this as a fair method, noting that each task will 'use the same procedures', but then suggests that the historical source differs from the literary text because the source is not 'usually' the description of an event, state of mind, or a story, but is more likely to be lists, statistics, buildings and other sources 'that do not directly tell a story themselves'.[24] This statement can be challenged on two levels. First, very many sources are telling stories: most criminal and civil court records, the records of ecclesiastical justice, newspaper and journal articles, and even compilations of statistics are 'usually' in narrative form (certainly pre-1800). These constitute a main body of the evidence historians use in social, gender, cultural and religious history. Second, all sources are telling embedded narratives – including architecture (concerning national, religious or party emblems, grandeur, or the opulence of the owner). This is where the empiricist argument that an historical source can be 'story-free' breaks down. Certainly, the postmodernist counsels the historian to read every source to see *if* there are stories present that need textual deconstruction. And, as Barthes said, it is the subtlety of the deconstructionist to make apparent that which appears normal.

In a sense, critics seem more concerned that talk of 'text' sullies the History discipline than that ways of reading stories are a methodological problem. 'Reading against the grain', often used to describe the deconstructionist task, is even acknowledged by some critics as perfectly fine, defining what historians have been doing all along. But 'the text' also incurs wrath for apparently rendering what happened in history as mere fiction – as unknowable. The quality of textuality pushes the 'real' to somewhere else, and anything that suggests loss of a historian's domain over facts may never be acceptable to some. The irony is, of course, that the postmodernist does not deny the existence of 'truth'. Truth for the historian is based on fine judgements concerning the likelihood of things having happened, on balance, this way rather than that way. The judgement involves *in part* assessing the ways in which the past has been written by the historians, and it is absolutely valid to scrutinise this past as a text as well as empirically and cognitively. But the critics' argument that tends to follow from this is that deconstruction (even when properly defined) leaves no real difference between writing History and writing fiction. This again results from issues concerning words and their meanings. Postmodernists argue that historiography is discourse-laden, and needs to be treated in the same way as a literary specialist treats fiction. A favoured term is that historiography is 'fictive' in its nature. But deconstruction is only one part of the historian's task (the other parts include non-literary empirical tasks, as we have seen), and, anyway, this is not suggesting that fiction equals non-History. Postmodernists say that historiography should be treated *like* fiction (that it is fictive), not that it is untrue. A historian may deploy references to historical events in his/her narrative that are verifiably true, but her/his discourse is about selecting and bundling references to events of his/her choice into a periodised and boundaried-off interpretative narrative defined by her/ him, that *as a whole* is invariably empirically untestable. It is this narrative that is the real end-product of the History profession, and if its constituent 'small' facts may be verifiable, the thing as a whole is fictive in form and needs to be treated as such.

Some critics accuse postmodernists of denying that the past existed. The criticism first surfaced in relation to Roland Barthes' 1967 essay 'The discourse of history', in which he was accused of denying the existence of history as anything but a text. But this was not what Barthes said, and he said so. In 1971 he told an interviewer: 'The teaching problem of today is to upset the notion of literary text and to manage to make adolescents understand that there is text everywhere, but also that everything is text.' Barthes' concern was to challenge the positivistic and deterministic aim of history-writing that in France, for instance, saw everything that happened pre-1789 as leading to 1789; as he said, 'all history with an end-point is a myth'.[25]

I have left the most disputed to last. Facts, discourses and texts became moulded together in the 1990s by many critics in their use of the Jewish Holocaust of the Second World War to attack postmodernist historians. 'Auschwitz was not a discourse,' wrote Richard Evans in 1997. 'It trivialises mass murder to see it as a text.'[26] This is powerful and emotive ground, and it proves very difficult for the postmodernist to make headway, especially when s/he may not be an expert in this field. But a postmodernist position would go something like this. Postmodernists, like all other historians of repute, assert the fact of the mass extermination of Jews and other groups. They are not Holocaust deniers (despite the occasional critic who sails close to the wind in trying, even tangentially, to associate the two groups). But the mass murders at Auschwitz and elsewhere have been developed since 1945 in the popular histories of a number of nations (Israel, the United States and post-war Germany to name three) in complex discourses on evil, human and national culpability, remembrance, genocide, how to prevent it recurring, religious prophecy, and current Middle East policy. Such discourses are manifest in a wide variety of symbols, rhetoric, rituals, testimonies, religious literature, architecture of remembrance, and political movements. To describe and discuss this discursivity is not to deny that the events have occurred. It is to look at how the events have been narrated, structured, authenticated, deployed and interpreted in various ways for various purposes of our present world. And it seems possible to agree that the way this is undertaken by the historian is by a process of interaction between the world of the present and the authenticated world of the past. Postmodernist and empiricist should be able to agree on this, and move on.

The problem with the self

Some critics level the allegation that postmodernism constitutes a denial of the agency of the individual. The Enlightenment empiricist pronounces postmodernism wrong because it declares the self is all discourse, it denies human agency and it proclaims that the individual is irrelevant anyway because, of course, the author is dead. Here is historian Roy Porter's critique of 'the anti-humanist Foucault':

Conventional understandings of subjectivity – individual writers and readers, having minds of their own and exercising free will through thought and action – all were deluded. Rather Foucault argued for the primacy of semantic sign systems, cognitive structures and texts. We don't think our thoughts, they think us; we are but the bearers of discourses, our selves are discursively constructed.[27]

The free will of the self has become a classic focus for the empiricist historian concerned with intellectual individualism. Postmodernism is accused, even in cultural studies, of ignoring human experience and constituting the ultimate in condescension upon the people of the past.

Foucault's work certainly urged the historian to turn his/her attention from the author to the culture within which discourse circulated. But the use made of Foucauldian theory in History is much more aware than Foucault's own writings of the agency of the individual. As with the similar criticisms we have noted already in relation to discourse and text, this critical position fails to include the rest of what postmodernist theory has evolved – the necessity for each individual to negotiate through discourse within the context of their body and their material environment. Lacanian psychology sees no such submissive, manipulated and passive self.

The critique of postmodernist philosophy and psychology of self is replicated within the History profession. The historian Patrick Joyce was once considered as an outstanding practitioner of Gramscist social history, but has come to be seen since the early 1990s as occupying an extreme position. One left-wing historian regarded Joyce as recanting his earlier Gramscist work (in which 'subjects (people) are seen as constructing meanings') to adopt a new position in which 'meanings construct subjects'. This new position was criticised for relating people to discourse with keywords like 'emplotment' or 'narrativisation' of their lives, suggesting the passivity of the individual in the face of cultural processes.[28] In other cases, similar criticisms come from Marxist historians who have studied how proletarian revolution was prevented by the people's 'false consciousness' – which may be a bit like the kettle calling the pot black.

A second level of criticism against the postmodernist history of the self is that a focus on discourse deflects attention from historical change. This is unfair on two counts. First, there is a wealth of material being collected on discourse change. Foucault himself was preoccupied with the massive discourse differences between epistemes, and historians since then have focused on major discourse changes. Second, historical change is central to the postmodernist agenda, and indeed Foucault's work developed precisely in response to the apparent denial of change by the French *Annales* school. More vitally, changes to the self within history are equally a concern of Enlightenment empiricist history, and indeed as a research topic this provides a very important meeting of empiricist and postmodernist historians' minds. For the postmodernist, changes to the self mean changes to human action. Understanding actions in the past becomes better informed through a knowledge of the self.

Is History really moral?

The postmodern historian's engagement with morality raises three major issues amongst critics. The first is the question: 'Is this History?' The second is the allegation that postmodernist history is immoral, amoral or ethically relativist. And the third is that postmodernism is endangering History as an academic subject.

Is this History? Some academic historians have problems with studies on sexualities, disability, and the survival of the flea market in contemporary society. They see some of the topics as marginal, uninteresting in terms of 'real' history (of the powerful and governments), and some of them declare studies that use history in conjunction with other disciplines (sociology, economics or cultural studies) to deconstruct contemporary society as 'not history at all'. Such attitudes have far from disappeared from the History profession.

However, postmodernism provides some of the most innovative techniques, the most exciting agendas, and some of the most electric conclusions concerning past and present. It is not just the agenda, but also the way History is 'done', that has changed. As Keith Jenkins puts it, citing Rorty, the discourse of history once described by White and Barthes is now being replaced by a discourse of history as 'an ironic, anti-foundational, freedom-orientated, conversational style of discourse'.[29] The way the historian speaks becomes less dogmatic and less privileged. What Jenkins calls 'the sublime nature of the past' – its unknowable confusion and infinity of events, uncompressible to narrative form – means that we should not falsely discipline the past to some single, centrist form that we thrust forward as the answer to the future of History and our present condition. Where modernist History sought closure, postmodernist History seeks none.

Is postmodernist History immoral or amoral, and does its ethical relativism allow intolerance and prejudice to thrive? The moral implications of postmodernism are probably the most conspicuously controversial area of debate with its opponents. Some of the early debates surrounding postmodernist history were morally charged *ad hominem* attacks. Geoffrey Elton described postmodernism in 1991 as 'the intellectual equivalent of crack' promoted by 'devilish tempters' of 'innocent young people'. He launched vitriolic criticisms of theorists, speaking of the 'cancerous radiation that comes from the foreheads of Derrida and Foucault', and described Hayden White's ideas as 'altogether meaningless verbiage'.[30] This surely cannot count in anybody's estimation as meaningful criticism.

Yet empiricists (from the conservative to liberal to Marxist) alike revel in levelling the charge of amorality at postmodernist method and thought. We noted earlier how a common term used to denigrate the postmodernist historian is 'relativist' or, worse, 'hyper-relativist' in relation to the factuality of the events recorded in historiography. But it is also alleged that a 'postmodern climate' is leading to absence of certainty over morality. Critics directly equate relativism over facts to relativism over ethics.

The problem, a postmodernist position might say, is the other way around. It is modernist and empiricist History that, in its training through college, school and popular culture, spawns generations who claim spurious superiority over other peoples, races or religions. It is the *absence of relativism* that is dangerous. It is that absence that allows hegemonies of illiberal culture to blossom, and encourages the training in a History discipline that permits the principle of incontestable Historical certainty. A certainty that establishes 'correct' facts (the Holocaust happened) amongst the moral majority also permits the establishment of a certainty of incorrect facts (the Holocaust did not happen) amongst the immoral minority. Certainty produces error as well as accuracy. Essentialism is the child of unchallenged History narratives, and relativism is its enemy. Endless contest over 'facts' in History debates wins some short-term gains against immoral contemporary ideologies. And they should be fought. But it is not enough. It is not enough because the gains are only short term, and only affect a tiny part of the whole of essentialist History. A bigoted History is rarely bigoted because it gets its facts wrong. It is almost always bigoted because it has a narrative that is erected upon a deliberate selection of verifiable facts, and smeared in essentialist overtones. Empiricism will never defeat bigoted and immoral history. Only by challenging the principle of uncontestable History narratives can vile claims to historical superiority be removed from defacing the contemporary world.

Some critics construct the moral relativity issue as one about ideology. Marxist Terry Eagleton has been battling against both post-Marxists and postmodernists since the 1980s. He reasserts the primary significance of ideology over discourse. Ideology is the product of an unjust society, he claims, whilst the postmodernist ignores it (and materiality) in favour of the endless rhetoric of a discourse falsely observed as veined through with 'the play of power and desire'. Discourse is the category that has, for him, sadly undermined 'erstwhile revolutionary political positions'.[31] Yet of course, ideology in itself is not the object of attack for all postmodernists, many of whom regard themselves as radical and even 'left wing' in their politics. Regrettably, this assertion is unfathomable to those with entrenched positions concerning what postmodernism is. Postmodernists are just as likely to sustain their radicalism as those who retain traditional left-wing or Marxist positions. It is a particular concern of the Marxist and former Marxist that, in a world in which Marxism has apparently succumbed to almost abject failure in government and social justice, something is to blame. Postmodernism (or poststructuralism, or some other element of it) may seem to fit the bill.

 Finally, the death of History (the subject) through postmodernism 'killing' the place of history (the idea of the past) is cited by most critics. The way this 'killing' is perceived varies. One fear is that its multiculturalism is politicising history through denying 'the common humanity of all people', fragmenting it to incoherence and discontinuity, and rendering it void of all meaning.[32] Others (especially on the left), as we have seen, fear it for the opposite reason – for depoliticising the past of class struggle. Some critics fear postmodernism more for its method than its philosophy – largely because they perceive History as dependent for its identity upon the craft and its empiricist skills rather than upon the sense of the past that it conveys. History (the subject) is still needed, still loved and will not wither for want of interest. Student numbers boom, historical scholarship of both modernist and postmodernist mode proceeds apace. Consequently, history (the past) will not wither in our postmodern world. But there is now a constant critical rejection in play, in which the postmodern condition constitutes a new moral affirmation. Respect for the body (our own and others) and for the planet (in the environmental and anti-globalisation movements) constitutes a new proto-metanarrative that rejects so much of the exaggerated humanity of the eighteenth century. In its place, there is a fresher and (literally) unproven morality of our own making. In this, history (as the lessons of the past) has very little part to play, but hopefully History (as the study of discourse, experience and morality) will have to play an enormous part.

Guide to further reading

Theory

Accessible critiques of postmodernism include A. Callinicos, *Against Postmodernism: A Marxist Critique* (London, Polity Press, 1989); C. Norris, *What's Wrong with Postmodernism: Critical Theory and the Ends of Philosophy* (Baltimore, Johns Hopkins University Press, 1990) and see also T. Eagleton, *Ideology: An Introduction* (London, Verso, 1991), pp. 206–8. On Jameson's influence, see P. Anderson, *The Origins of Postmodernity* (London, Verso, 1998).

History

The most influential and widely read critique of postmodernism in History is Richard Evans, *In Defence of History* (London, Granta, 1997 and later editions). See also Arthur Marwick, *The New Nature of History: Knowledge, Evidence, Language* (Basingstoke, Palgrave, 2001). There are many websites dealing in material relating to postmodernism and historical theory, including *www.history.ac.uk/ihr/Focus/Whatishistory*.

Critiques from Labour and left-wing History include Bryan Palmer, *Descent into Discourse: The Reification of Language and the Writing of Social History* (Philadelphia, Temple University Press, 1990); Willie Thompson, *What Happened to History?* (London, Pluto, 2000); M. Savage and A. Miles, *The Remaking of the British Working Class 1840–1940* (London, Routledge, 1994) and R. Price, 'Postmodernism as theory and history', and E. Yeo, 'Language and contestation: the case of "the people", 1832 to the present', both in J. Belchem and N. Kirk (eds), *Languages of Labour* (Aldershot, Ashgate, 1997).

On postmodernism and feminist history see K. Canning, 'Feminist history after the linguistic turn: historicizing discourse and experience', *Signs: Journal of Women in Culture and Society*, vol. 19 (1994), pp. 368–73; L.L. Downs, 'If "woman" is just an empty category, then why am I afraid to walk alone at night? Identity politics meets the postmodern subject', *Comparative Studies in Society and History*, vol. 35 (1993), pp. 414–37; L.L. Downs, 'Reply to Joan Scott', *Comparative Studies in Society and History*, vol. 35 (1993), pp. 444–51; J. Hoff, 'Gender as a postmodern category of paralysis', *Women's History Review*, vol. 3 (1994), pp. 149–68; S.K. Kent, 'Mistrials and diatribulations: a reply to Joan Hoff', *Women's History Review*, vol. 5 (1996), pp. 9–18.

On the holocaust and historical theory, see Evans *In Defence of History*, pp. 125–6, plus R. Chartier, *On the Edge of the Cliff: History, Language and Practices* (Baltimore, Johns Hopkins University Press, 1997), pp. 35-8 and H. White, *Figural Realism: Studies in the Mimesis Effect* (Baltimore, Johns Hopkins University Press, 1999), pp. 27–42.

For two other critiques of aspects of postmodernism in History, see R. Porter, 'Introduction', in R. Porter (ed.), *Rewriting the Self: Histories from the Renaissance to the Present* (London, Routledge, 1997) and

M. Pickering, *History, Experience and Cultural Studies* (Basingstoke, Macmillan, 1997), esp. pp. 82–3, 108, 131, 164, 244.

Books which seek some middle ground between postmodernism and its opponents, with distinctive descriptions of the nature of History, include Mary Fulbrook, *Historical Theory* (London, Routledge, 2002); Ludmilla Jordanova, *History in Practice* (London, Arnold, 2000) and Beverley Southgate, *Why Bother with History?* (Harlow, Longman, 2000).

Notes

1 Arthur Marwick, author's response to review of *The New Nature of History: Knowledge, Evidence, Language*, at *www.history.ac.uk/ihr/*

2 W. Thompson, *What Happened to History?* (London, Pluto, 2000), p. 123.

3 *The Guardian*, 6 September 2003.

4 Richard J. Evans, *In Defence of History* (London, Granta, 1997), pp. 115, 126, 128.

5 Thompson, *What Happened?*, p. 103.

6 Quoted in B. Palmer, *Descent into Discourse: The Reification of Language and the Writing of Social History* (Philadelphia, Temple University Press, 1990), p. 55.

7 Ibid., p. xiv.

8 Evans, *In Defence*, p. 94.

9 T. Eagleton, *Ideology: An Introduction* (London, Verso, 1991), pp. 206–8.

10 L. Roper, *Oedipus and the Devil: Women, Sexuality and Religion in early Modern Europe* (London, Routledge, 1994), pp. 15, 17.

11 E. Said, *Orientalism* (orig. 1978, Harmondsworth, Penguin, 1985), pp. 23, 94, 202.

12 Evans, *In Defence*, pp. 103–4, 106.

13 L. Stanley, *The Auto/biographical I* (Manchester, Manchester University Press, 1992), pp. 16–17.

14 K.A. Reader, *The May 1968 Events in France: Reproductions and Interpretations* (New York, St Martin's Press, 1993); A. Callinicos, *Against Postmodernism: A Marxist Critique* (London, Polity Press, 1989), pp. 71–2, 85, 167–8.

15 C. Norris, *What's Wrong with Postmodernism: Critical Theory and the Ends of Philosophy* (Baltimore, Johns Hopkins University Press, 1990), pp. 26–30; Callinicos, *Against Postmodernism*, pp. 94, 147.

16 R. Price, 'Postmodernism as theory and history', in J. Belchem and N. Kirk (eds), *Languages of Labour* (Aldershot, Ashgate, 1997), pp. 11, 17; Palmer, *Descent into Discourse*, p. 183.

17 L. Downs, 'If "woman" is just an empty category, then why am I afraid to walk alone at night? Identity politics meets the postmodern subject', *Comparative Studies in Society and History*, vol. 35 (1993), pp. 414–37 at p. 424; L. Downs, 'Reply to Joan Scott', *Comparative Studies in Society and History*, vol. 35 (1993), pp. 444–51 at p. 448; J. Hoff, 'Gender as a postmodern category of paralysis', *Women's History Review*, vol. 3 (1994), pp. 149–68 at pp. 150, 157.

18 Evans, *In Defence*, p. 111.

19 Norris, *What's Wrong*, pp. 30–8.

20 K. Jenkins, On *'What is History?' From Carr and Elton to Rorty and White* (London, Routledge, 1995), p. 18.

21 Evans, *In Defence*, p. 95.

22 R. Evans, '*In Defence of History*: Reply to Critics', on 'History in Focus' website, *www.history.ac.uk/ihr/Focus/Whatishistory/evans.html* accessed 10 September 2003.

23 Callinicos, *Against Postmodernism*, p. 68.

24 Evans, *In Defence*, p. 110.

25 Quoted in A Stafford, *Roland Barthes, Phenomenon and Myth* (Edinburgh, Edinburgh U.P., 1998), pp. 137, 67.

26 Evans, *In Defence*, p. 124.

27 R. Porter, 'Introduction', in R. Porter (ed.) *Rewriting the Self: Histories from the Renaissance to the Present* (London, Routledge, 1997), p. 11.

28 E. Yeo, 'Language and contestation: the case of "the people", 1832 to the present', in Belchem and Kirk (eds), *Languages of Labour*, p. 45.

29 Jenkins, On *'What is History?'*, p. 98.

30 Quoted in ibid., pp. 68, 93.

31 Eagleton, *Ideology*, pp. 28, 201–3.

32 Gertrude Himmelfarb, quoted in J. Tosh (ed.) *Historians on History* (London, Longman, 2000), p. 294.

Conclusion

 Postmodernism has changed the way History as an academic subject is conducted. These changes are not uniformly felt across every topic, every university, every individual historian nor every published book and article. But the changes are still significant.

First, postmodernism has changed the methods of historical research. It has brought a new sensitivity to language, to the role of the historian's subjectivity, and to the way we write History. It has repositioned History for many researchers away from social science method and towards arts and humanities method. For many, this means a combination of methods. The historian no longer applies purely social science techniques (using statistics and other evidence to uncover rules of society), but looks at the past with an eye to textual issues, to aesthetic ones, and to the multiplicity of paradigms now at the disposal of the professional historian.

Second, postmodern theory has helped to change the agenda of History. It has introduced and intensified study of new fields – popular culture, the study of personal testimony, the reconstruction of testimony from second-hand accounts, and the deconstruction of texts. It has helped to theorise women's history, gender history, gay history and postcolonial history. This process is by no means ended and new fields may emerge.

Third, postmodernism has changed the ways in which History is taught. Students are increasingly exposed to issues of historical theory when previously, certainly in Britain, this had been confined to the social science end of history (economic and social history). Now, postmodernism has forced the profession to engage with the breadth and diversity of theories and the resulting broadening of agenda and method.

Fourth, postmodernism has brought to History a widening of the discipline. It has made us more interdisciplinary, more receptive to looking at the work in subjects like social anthropology, ethnology, English studies and literature, linguistics, and even philosophy. There is a greater engagement with new ideas and theory. This still does not make the profession as a whole especially informed on theory. But it is much better than it was in the 1980s.

Fifth, postmodernism has divided History as a subject into more segments, interest groups and opponent camps. Ironically, this has happened at the very same time as the subject divisions in History – notably those between Economic History, Social History and History – have been eroding markedly. Historians now believe that there is one discipline that benefits from teaching and researching in one subject area, as witnessed by the formation of large 'Schools of History' at the major universities of the UK. Where formerly History leant only in the direction of social science, it now leans towards the literary humanities at the same time. Indeed, many of those involved in this 'leaning' lean in both directions. Those with an interest and training in social science are very often those who have developed since the 1980s a leaning towards language issues (in signs, discourse and textual deconstruction). Cultural history is now the centre of adventurousness. Social science of the old school struggles to keep up.

Sixth, postmodernism has disturbed the acceptance of the big stories of yesteryear's History books. The **metanarrative** is now something to which historians are – or at least should be – sensitised. We need to think about what those big stories might be, because they may not be always obvious. But we are constantly seeking them and problematising them.

And seventh, postmodernism has tremendously stimulated the History profession. It has caused excitement, thoughtfulness, the search for works of theory to engage with or to refute new ideas. As a proponent of its many virtues, I would, of course, argue that the greatest excitement is to be had as a practising historian who engages with theory and infuses it into study. Whatever, I suspect that the discipline has been changed with no going back.

Glossary

This contains brief explanations of major key words employed in relation to postmodernist History.

agency   In History-writing, agency is the power to change and affect History. Who possesses agency is always a problem for the historian. The historian is essentially deciding this as the History is written. Is it the elites (whether political elites or those with new ideas), the common people, the individual, or impersonal forces – such as economic forces – that change history?

bio-power   A term coined by Foucault to describe the power of the Enlightenment over the human body, exerted by doctors, churches and the state through circulation of **discourses** on male and female bodies, that fostered puritan internalised discipline in every individual for modern capitalism.

category of analysis   Frame of reference (often a **structure**) for an historian's investigation. A Marxist historian most often uses social class as the category of analysis, a women's historian uses gender, a **postcolonial** historian race. There is no one correct category of analysis, and every one needs to be de-centred at some time to allow use of different categories.

cognitive   Containing knowledge or data. A cognitive analysis of an historical source is an exploration of the information it presents. Contrast this with **discourse** analysis.

culture   Contents and means of human intercourse within a group (from small to national). Culture covers the things said and the ways of saying them. Usually, culture is used by historians to provide the means to identify and distinguish groups. Indeed, postmodernism argues that groups are defined by things said and the ways of saying them, and not by **essential** attributes (like gender, race or nationality defining human intelligence, capability or level of 'civilisation').

de-centre   To question the origins and fixed value of concepts in scholarly analysis. For instance, the term 'social class' will be questioned by postmodernists and others in case it should be taken as a concrete reality when, in fact, it is a social construction with specific origins as a term, and changing meanings over time. To de-centre concepts and words is to stand back and question them.

deconstruction   Postmodernist analytical technique for scrutinising texts by reading against the grain of the surface content, and invoking awareness of the assumptions between author and reader.

discourse   A non-material entity, expressed in a language system (words or images or another medium) that conveys a meaning, in the form of a duality (the thing and its Other) – for instance, the discourse of the dour Scot (and its opposite, the happy English person). Discourse conveys the construction of knowledge in a given period (or **episteme**), and is the most readily accessible item of culture for study.

empiricism   see Box 1.1, page 13.

episteme   see Box 2.4, page 44.

epistemology   Theory of knowledge. So an 'epistemological problem' is one concerning the nature or construction of knowledge.

essentialism   Attributing social qualities to a group, nation or people by virtue of an alleged shared innate physical, religious, mental or racial trait. Essentialism covers racism, sexism, religious bigotry, and discriminatory attributes to people on grounds of dis/ability.

hagiography   History written in uncritical praise of a subject, usually a person.

historian   A person who studies history (the past) and is usually a member of the academic discipline of History.

history   The past, the background.

History   The study of the past which, in the last 200 years, has been an academic subject.

historiography   Written History, often taken to refer to the debates on a given subject (as in the historiography on the French Revolution). Confusingly, some university classes teach historical method under this title.

ideology   Any policy-based, power-seeking form of thought, reducible to a manifesto and determined by the policy. Distinguished from a **knowledge** that lacks the policy-determination.

intersubjectivity   The impact of two subjectivities upon each other, as when the age, gender, race and social background of an oral history interviewer sensitise an interviewee to respond to questions in certain ways.

intertextuality   see **text**

knowledge(s)   Way(s) in which the world is understood in language, in reference to a given structure of understanding. Different **epistemes** have different knowledges based on different language systems, and thus the way **power** is exercised varies from culture to culture.

linguistic turn   Analytical turn upon, or problematisation of, the words used in a field of study. Sometimes used to refer to the 'turn' made to scholarship in the late twentieth century.

metanarratives   Grand, ideological, generalised stories by which societies understand themselves, and which are so normative and all-consuming that individuals in a society are not aware of them as constantly recirculated. Metanarratives only work when they become invisible by having no acceptable opposites. The Enlightenment generated many metanarratives – of progress, science, reason, 'normal' sexualities, the superiority of white races over others, Christianity over non-Christian religions, men over women, European over non-European cultures. This is not an exhaustive list.

moralities   Postmodernists argue that morality is something founded on decision and proclamation and not, as modernists have argued, on empirical historical example. This makes postmodernist historians **reflexive** in their study, and able to acknowledge that morality is **socially** and **culturally constructed**. This draws the criticism of moral relativity upon postmodernists. In reply, each postmodernist is likely to argue that they are morally certain in their own person, but that the absence of moral certainty makes morality unavoidably relativist. Thus it does not legitimate all moralities, but rather motivates the heightened proclamation of immorality.

modernity   The episteme introduced by the Enlightenment, and stretching roughly from 1800 to 1960.

myth   The first (empiricist) meaning is that of a fictional (untrue) belief. The second (ethnographic) meaning is that of a belief that defines a culture. The third (postmodernist) meaning is that of a language system, constituting a discourse, and composed of many signs whose meanings support each other and bolster that myth.

peer review   The system developed for checking the value of an academic's research. In History, a book or article is read by other experts in the field before publication, reviewed by others after publication, and then subjected to critical appraisal as new research comes out. In this way, the value of research is monitored, and tendencies to factual or interpretational error are traced and contradicted.

periodisation   The art of the historian dividing up the past into periods that seem coherent eras. Traditionally, these are eras such as the 'early-modern period (c.1450–c.1750)', and 'the long nineteenth century (1789–1914)' which generally conform to changes at major historical events (such as the French Revoltuion and the end of the First World War). By contrast, postmodernism proposes radically different periodisations, called **epistemes**, which conform to eras of distinctive knowledge systems (**modernity** and **postmodernity**). This reflects the agenda shift of postmodernist research from events to knowledge as the important milestones of human history.

postcolonialism   The growth, mostly since c. 1950, of the awareness of colonialist and racist attitudes (labelled by Edward Said as 'Orientalism') that have been deeply embedded in western culture, politics and knowledge (especially since the eighteenth century). It is also the project in all branches of learning, politics and culture to combat such attitudes as former colonies and people of colour everywhere seek full empowerment. Some theorists regard this project as including non-white peoples in their combat with the psychological impact of colonialism upon themselves.

postmodernism   the intellectual system associated with the condition of **postmodernity**, which is characterised by specific attributes intended to subvert **modernity**. These attributes include (1) a denial of the ability to represent **reality** in any form; (2) a denial of the empirical foundations of **moral** judgement; (3) a denial of the existence of universal rules governing, or the **reality** of, abstract social, racial, religious or gender systems; (4) a conviction as to the strength of language as the source of all power, and as to the vulnerability of all **power** to language; (5) self-awareness of (or **reflexivity** to) subjective issues brought to intellectual, social and moral endeavour; (6) an awareness and repudiation of **metanarratives** by reference to which all forms of rhetoric may be related.

postmodernity/the postmodern condition   see Box 0.4, page 8.

poststructuralism   see Box 4.3, page 80.

power   Power is seen by postmodernism to be predominantly the result of how **knowledge** is constructed and operates through language. Through language comes **discourse**, which seeks to induce a "normative" behaviour in people. That behaviour is an internalised exhibition of power. The exercise of external power (by the state, by the church and so on) in coercive forms is the result of discursive power amongst the oppressive elites. Modernity in western society was characterised more by discursive than coercive power, with the opposite being true in pre-modernity.

pre-modernity   This is usually taken to be the period before about 1800, though sometimes pre-1650. Usage can be quite loose, especially by late-modern historians or sociologists. **Periodisation** is a key issue in postmodernism.

primary source   Evidence used by an historian about a period and theme of study. It is often a document (letters, court records, census returns, newspaper, etc.), but can include paintings, drawings, music, oral testimony, film and video.

problematise   (A term that is often seen in cultural history books especially) To turn an accepted word, concept or idea that appears in History analysis into a problem, to question its origins and value, and what issues of personal bias might exist with it. Problematise has a similar meaning meaning to **de-centre**.

rationality   see Box 1.1, page 13.

reality   see Box 0.3, page 7.

referent   see **sign**.

reflexivity   The act of an historian thinking about what presuppositions, pre-figuring and personal issues are being brought to the subject of scholarly inquiry. Being reflexive is considered central to the act of de-centring **knowledge** from the **modernist** pursuit of an illusory 'reality'.

relativity   In the context of History-writing, this is a pejorative term aimed by critics at postmodernists, but which the latter argue is an attribute. Postmodernists acknowledge the inability of the historian to judge the past according to fixed moral positions. As a result, critics see them as 'moral relativists' who would 'let anything go'. For their part, postmodernists see such relativism as a defence against totalising (and totalitarian) History-writing that imposes one judgement upon all people, and which tends to pass moral responsibility from the present-day to the past. See **moralities**.

representation   The act of writing History makes a representation of the past, and nothing more. Postmodernists agree that, in historical narrative, there is never any ability to reconstruct the past 'as it actually was'.

secondary source   A book, article or item of other media written by scholars and supposedly distinguished from the **primary source**, thereby indicating the alienation and neutrality of the observer from the thing being observed. The postmodernist historian will not acknowledge any difference in principle between the two types of source, arguing that both require to be handled as **texts**. In practice, the postmodernist historian is likely to distinguish the two sources for practical **cognitive** purposes (i.e. a primary source is likely to give evidential information, whereas a secondary source merely replicates it).

self   The self is the individual. Most historians have only tended to see the elite person (the politician or military general) as interesting for study, whilst regarding the ordinary person as the victim of impersonal historical forces (class struggle, for instance). By contrast, postmodernists see the self as **socially constructed** by his/her own culture, but developed and projected in the processes of everyday life. As a result, the self is a mediation between the discourses of culture and its bodily and material experience. The extent of the individual's **agency**, or power to change history, is controversial.

semiology, semiotics   The study of signs.

sign, signifier, signified   These three come as a trilogy in semiology. The sign is constituted by the relationship of a signifier (a medium, such as a road sign, a word, a gesture) to a signified (also known as the referent, the 'thing' being signed). The signified is not the thing itself, only a concept of it. Anything is a sign that stands for something other than itself.

social construction   The condition attributed by postmodernists (and many others) to things that were traditionally regarded as having innate or inbuilt qualities. Socially constructed things include language, discourses, and the self. Social construction means the acquiring of attributes through the interaction between circulating discourses and the psychological, bodily and material experience of the self. For example, a woman is socially constructed (in sexist modern culture) as a poorer car driver than a man, and is not innately so.

social science   Social science was the advancement of empiricist method and philosophy of knowledge to the realms of society, especially in the 1950s and 1960s, positing the existence or rules governing the history, structure and future of society. Poststructuralism and postmodernism were strong reactions against social science from the late 1960s.

structure, structuralism   see Box 4.1, page 76.

subjectivity   The qualities of the individual that both constitute the self and that are exhibited by a person in society. These qualities are not fixed and immutable, but are multilayered and interchangeable, often altering with context. They alter especially in meeting the subjectivity of another person (for instance in an oral history interviewee) in what is called **intersubjectivity,** and thereby can change personal narratives and the self according to context.

text   Any item in any medium that tells a story. It can be a book, a play, a drawing, a court record and so on. Every text has qualities of textuality (it excludes the real) and intertextuality (it borrows narrative characteristics from other types of text). For the postmodernist historian the point of identifying texts is textual analysis in which the past is only available for scholarly study by taking the form of a text. Every representation is a text, and every attempt to get outside of that representation creates another text.

truth   A quality in postmodernism approached at different levels of existence. An historical event (e.g. the Battle of Hastings, 1066) is a truth, but in itself is not that interesting. When it is inserted in a statement (e.g. The Battle of Hastings marked the transformation of England into a Norman kingdom) it acquires a sign quality within an interpretational context, and the truth-quality starts to be de-centred. When that statement becomes part of a larger text (e.g. The Battle of Hastings led to the creation of a superior mediaeval government), the qualities of 'truth' become more distant, fluid, contingent, and lacking central agreement.

unreflexive (of an historian) Lacking, or failing to express, self-awareness of 'where they are coming from' in terms of ideology and personal politics. See **reflexivity**.

whig History The whig approach to History-writing is the notion of the upward movement of humankind, that of constant, often heroic, progress – a progress that may experience snares and set-backs, but which leads from a poorer past to a better present. Its optimism tended to be pro-western and see Europe as leading the world.

Further reading

Items asterisked are highly recommended as the first stop for further information under each heading. The divisions below between the groups of books are far from absolute, and there are some items that transcend these categories. Some authors may indeed balk at my pigeon-holing of them, but I read their work as contributing overall to the category in which I place them.

Postmodernist historical theory

Chartier, Roger, *On the Edge of the Cliff: History, Languages, and Practices* (Baltimore, Johns Hopkins University Press, 1997)

Currie, Mark, *Postmodern Narrative Theory* (Basingstoke, Macmillan, 1998)

de Certeau, Michel, *The Writing of History* (orig. 1975, New York, Columbia University Press, 1988)

Jenkins, Keith, *Re-Thinking History* (London, Routledge, 1991)

Jenkins, Keith, *On "What is History?": From Carr and Elton to Rorty and White* (London, Routledge, 1995)

*Jenkins, Keith, *Why History? Ethics and Postmodernity* (London, Routledge, 1999)

Jenkins, Keith, *Refiguring History: New Thoughts on an Old Discipline* (London, Routledge, 2003)

*Munslow, Alun, *Deconstructing History* (London, Routledge, 1997)

Munslow, Alun, *The Routledge Companion to Historical Studies* (London, Routledge, 2000)

Southgate, Beverley, *Why Bother with History?* (London, Longman, 2000)

White, H., *Metahistory: The Historical Imagination in Nineteenth-century Europe* (Baltimore, Johns Hopkins University Press, 1975)

White, H., *Tropics of Discourse: Essays in Cultural Criticism* (Baltimore, Johns Hopkins University Press, 1978)

White, H., *The Content of the Form: Narrative Discourse and Historical Representation* (Baltimore, Johns Hopkins University Press, 1987)

White, H., *Figural Realism: Studies in the Mimesis Effect* (Baltimore, Johns Hopkins University Press, 1999)

Also worth consulting is *Rethinking History: The Journal of Theory and Practice.*

Postmodernist theory and semiology

*Appignanesi, Richard and Chris Garratt, *Postmodernism for Beginners* (Cambridge, Icon, 1995)

Barry, Peter, *Beginning Theory: An Introduction to Literary and Cultural Theory* (Manchester, Manchester University Press, 1995)

*Barthes, Roland, *Mythologies* (orig. 1957, London, Vintage, 1993)

Barthes, Roland, *The Eiffel Tower and Other Mythologies* (orig. 1979, Berkeley, University of California Press, 1997)

Baudrillard, Jean, *Simulacra and Simulation* (orig. 1981, Ann Arbor, University of Michigan Press, 1994)

*Chandler, Daniel, *Semiotics: The Basics* (London, Routledge, 2002)

de Certeau, Michel, *The Practice of Everyday Life* (orig. 1984, Berkeley, University of California Press, 1988)

Derrida, Jacques, *Writing and Difference* (orig. 1967, London, Routledge, 1997)

Foucault, M., *The Order of Things* (orig. 1966, reprinted English edn, Routledge 2002)

Foucault, M.,*The Archaeology of Knowledge* (orig. 1969, English edn, Routledge, 1997)

Lyotard, Jean-François, *The Postmodern Condition: A Report on Knowledge* (orig. 1979, Manchester, Manchester University Press, 1984)

Anti-postmodernist historical theory

Appleby, Joyce, Lynn Hunt and Margaret Jacob, *Telling the Truth About History* (New York, Norton, 1994)

*Evans, Richard J., *In Defence of History* (London, Granta, 1997)

Marwick, Arthur, *The New Nature of History: Knowledge, Evidence, Language* (Basingstoke, Palgrave, 2001)

*Palmer, Bryan, *Descent into Discourse* (Philadelphia, Temple University Press, 1990)

Thompson, Willie, *What Happened to History?* (London, Pluto, 2000)

Anti-postmodernist theory

Callinicos, Alex, *Against Postmodernism: A Marxist Critique* (Cambridge, Polity, 1989)

*Eagleton, T., *Ideology: An Introduction* (London, Verso, 1991)

Norris, Christopher, *What's Wrong with Postmodernism? Critical Theory and the Ends of Philosophy* (Baltimore, Johns Hopkins University, 1990)

O'Neill, John, *The Poverty of Postmodernism* (London, Routledge, 1995)

Theory reference

Barnard, A. and J. Spencer (eds), *Encyclopædia of Social and Cultural Anthropology* (London, Routledge, 1996)

*Hughes-Warrington, Marnie, *Fifty Key Thinkers on History* (London, Routledge, 2000)

*Leitch, V.B., (gen. ed.), *The Norton Anthology of Theory and Criticism* (New York, Norton, 2001)

Readings

Green, A. and K. Troup (eds), *The Houses of History: A Critical Reader in Twentieth-century History and Theory* (Manchester, Manchester University Press, 1999)

*Jenkins, Keith (ed.) *The Postmodern History Reader* (London, Routledge, 1997)

Perks, R. and Thomson, A. (eds), *The Oral History Reader* (London, Routledge, 1998)

Rabinow, P. (ed.) *The Foucault Reader* (Harmondsworth, Penguin, 1984)

Roberts, G. (ed.) *The History and Narrative Reader* (London, Routledge, 2001)

*Tosh, J. (ed.) *Historians on History* (London, Longman, 2000)

General guides to doing history

*Burke, Peter (ed.) *New Perspectives in Historical Writing* (2nd edn, Cambridge, Polity, 2001)

Fulbrook, Mary, *Historical Theory* (London, Routledge, 2002)

Jordanova, Ludmilla, *History in Practice* (London, Arnold, 2000)

Southgate, Beverley, *History: What and Why? Ancient, Modern and Postmodern Perspectives* (2nd edn, London, Routledge, 2001)

Tosh, John, *The Pursuit of History: Aims, Methods and New Directions in the Study of Modern History* (3rd edn, London, Longman, 2000)

Web links

Websites are constantly in flux, and there are hundreds dealing with post-modernism. A search engine entry of 'postmodernism' and 'history' will show the choices. The sites below are my favourites. They have lasted some years and hopefully will be sustained. I have only listed sites that were free-to-view when I accessed them.

Contemporary Philosophy, Critical Theory and Postmodern Thought: This site at the Denver School of Education, University of Colorado contains extremely good extended intellectual biographies of virtually all of the leading and minor theorists, together with links to etext copies of key essays by the theorists (including Barthes' 'World of Wrestling'). This is comprehensive, and highly recommended.
http://carbon.cudenver.edu/~mryder/itc_data/postmodern.html

PopCultures.com (described as Sarah Zupko's Cultural Studies Center) also has intellectual biographies of the theorists which, though briefer than those at the Denver site, are very useful. The site also contains a lot of information and links.
www.popcultures.com

The eJournal Website: Critical Thinkers' Resources. This personalised site provides a classic individualised reading of the meaning and deployment of postmodernism. It is based in Canada, and has material on all the leading theorists, especially Foucault, together with topical texts on current affairs.
www.synaptic.bc.ca/homepage.htm

Baudrillard on the Web provides an excellent portal to essays by and about Jean Baudrillard.
www.uta.edu/english/apt/collab/baudweb.html

Derrida-Online is devoted to this theorist, providing a reference resource and bibliography hub.
www.hydra.umn.edu/derrida/

Untimelypast.org is a Maryland, USA-based bibliography site on post-modernism and History, very up-to-date, together with discussion pages. It describes itself: 'For those interested in the intersection of historiography with postmodernism, poststructuralism, and related varieties of theory/practice.'
www.untimelypast.org

History.ac.uk is the site maintained by the Institute of Historical Research London, as a general resource for the profession. It contains ongoing reviews, short essays and debates on postmodernism, as well as on many other topics.
www.history.ac.uk

British Academy Portal is a site devoted to the study of the humanities and social sciences and, though it is less useful on theory, it contains excellent pages of links to history resources.
www.britac.ac.uk/portal/

Index